SAWTOOTH TALES

Front cover:
Mount Regan and Sawtooth Lake

SAWTOOTH TALES

by
Dick d'Easum

Drawings by John Collias

Photos by Ernie Day

CAXTON PRESS
Caldwell, Idaho
2002

First printing October, 1977
Second printing March, 1980
Third printing March, 1990
Fourth printing July, 2002

Library of Congress Cataloging in Publication Data

D'Easum, Dick.
  Sawtooth tales.

    1. Sawtooth Valley, Idaho—History—Addresses, essays,
lectures,   I.   Title.
F752.B65D4   979.6'32   76-24379
ISBN 0-87004-259-9

Printed and bound in the United States of America by
CAXTON PRESS
Caldwell, Idaho 83605
168692

For
Mary
Jim Brown
Al Walther

CONTENTS

ILLUSTRATIONS

ACKNOWLEDGMENTS

BOOKS, maps, and periodicals used in writing this book include:
All Along the River by Nellie Ireton Mills, published by B. C. Payette, Montreal, Canada; *Fragments of Villainy* by Dick d'Easum, The Idaho Statesman by Caxton Printers, Ltd., Caldwell; *Hearings of House and Senate Subcommittees on Parks and Recreation*, U.S. Government Printing Office, Washington, D.C.; *History of Alturas and Blaine Counties, Idaho* by George L. McLeod, Hailey Times; *History of Idaho* by John Hailey, Syms-York Company, Boise; *History of Idaho* by James Hawley, S. J. Clarke Publishing Company, Chicago; *History of Idaho* by Merrill D. Beal and Merle W. Wells, Lewis Historical Publishing Company, New York; *High on the Wild with Hemingway* by Lloyd Arnold, Caxton Printers, Ltd., Caldwell; *Land of the Yankee Fork* by Esther Yarber, Sage Books, Denver; *The Pacific Northwesterner*, Spokane, Washington; *Idaho Treasure Tales and Treasure Trails* by T. R. Glenn, Boise; *Maps of Early Idaho*, Western Guide Publishers, Corvallis, Oregon; *Memories of Old Alturas County, Idaho* by Lucille Hathaway Hall, Big Mountain Press, Denver, Colorado; *Middle Fork History* by Joe Midmore and Ken Adams, Harrah's Club, Reno, Nevada; *Sawtooth Mountain Area Study – History*, U.S. Forest Service and National Park Service; *Sawtooth National Recreation Area*, U.S. Forest Service; *Sawtooth Saga* by Hank Senger, Bob Sessions, and Nick Villeneuve, Caxton Printers, Ltd., Caldwell; *Six Decades Back* by Charles Walgamott, Caxton Printers, Ltd., Caldwell; and *The Idaho Almanac – Territorial Centennial Edition*, Idaho Department of Commerce and Development by Syms-York Company, Boise.
Files of *The Idaho Statesman, Boise Capital News, Ketchum*

Keystone, Hailey Times, Belleuve Sun, Challis Messenger, The Idaho World, Yankee Fork Herald, Salmon Recorder-Herald, Owyhee Avalanche, Mackay Miner, Elmore Bulletin, and *Salt Lake Tribune* were useful.

I appreciate the generous assistance of the Idaho Historical Society and the Idaho Department of Tourism and Industrial Development.

SAWTOOTH TALES

Chapter 1

THE SAWTOOTH CRAGS

The Sawtooth crags are mighty snags.
Their crests rise up like spires.
The air is thin where goats have been,
And their beauty never tires.

SOMETIMES the last clause comes out "and their peaks are full of liars." That is not true. There may be lies about things that happened or didn't happen in the Sawtooths, but it is no lie that the mountain range is one of the most magnificent in the world. People who have lived there and people who have visited there do not stretch the truth when they describe the towering parapets in glowing terms.

The Sawtooth range and its neighbors, all in west-central Idaho, are inspiring because of their scenic grandeur and their vigorous history. The mountains are rugged. So were the trappers, miners, and ranchers who clawed at their treasures long before the values of raw wilderness were translated into assets of tourism.

Although none of the Sawtooths ranks in altitude among the most lofty peaks of the world, or even of the United States, there are other attributes that set this chunk of admirable landscape in a class by itself. The geography is high, wild, and handsome. It has long been known for its grandeur, its picturesque pastoral meadows, and a variety of land forms which, according to a Forest Service summary, go together to make a highly scenic setting.

The area commonly regarded as the Sawtooths takes in far more than the Sawtooth range. Technically speaking, the Sawtooths are specific mountains. Their neighbors such as White Cloud Peaks, Boulder Mountains, and Pioneer Mountains are all part of the region. The empire of peaks, lakes, historic mining camps, and towns — steeped in the sauce of western vigor and still rich in recreational opportunity — extends over parts of several counties, numerous watersheds, and a network of administrative agencies. For example, Atlanta on the southwest and the Pioneer Mountains on the southeast are within the domain in general reference. Mount Hyndman at the head of Wild Horse Creek in the Pioneers is the fifth tallest peak in Idaho at 12,078 feet. It isn't technically a Sawtooth, although it is within the family of giant spires in that magnificent district.

The four highest mountains in the state are not in the area. They are Mount Borah, 12,655 feet; Mount Leatherman, 12,230 feet; Hawley Mountain, 12,130 feet, all in the Lost River Range; and Bell Mountain, 12,125 feet, in the Lemhi Range. They are not far from the Sawtooths, however, and are within comfortable travel range of Sawtooth visitors. The tallest sure-enough Sawtooth is Thompson Peak, 10,766 feet. Mount Heyburn, the most conspicuous battlement above Redfish Lake, is 10,229 feet.

Jagged peaks of the Sawtooth country pierce the clear, blue sky, offering the visitor a scenic panorama that is difficult to surpass, to use the words of a report to the Congress. The statement says forty-two peaks jut more than 10,000 feet. Scattered throughout these mountains, often called the Alps of America, are some 180 gemlike lakes ranging from glacial swimming holes to 2,000 acres. Traversing this setting are several hundred miles of rushing streams that form the tributaries of five important sources of the Columbia River Basin — the Salmon River and its East Fork, the South Fork of the Payette River, and the North and Middle Forks of the Boise River.

"Over the centuries," the report says, "the surface has been gouged by glaciers and eroded by waters and winds to form the soils typically found in the area. The type of animal life is closely associated with the food supply available in the ecological chain. Man's activities are largely controlled by these same features. They make the area attractive for outdoor recreation, and because of their rugged physical characteristics they remain largely unchanged." Below the mountaintops are green pastures on which cattle, sheep, and horses graze "and on which an occasional rustic ranch house can be seen beyond the log fences."

Photo by Ernie Day

Sawtooth Mountains from the air

Sawtooth Valley is bounded on the west by the rugged peaks of the Sawtooth Mountains. Stanley Basin lies at the northern end of that range. High peaks of the White Clouds and the Boulders provide the backdrop on the east. These include some of the region's loveliest uplands and have attracted skiers, hikers, horsemen, hunters, and photographers.

The higher elevations are mostly bare rock, taking on various colors depending on season and weather. Purple and pink predominate. The White Clouds are distinguished by glistening crests that seem to be sand dunes translocated from the Sahara. The heights in all directions support meager vegetation, except for verdant Alpine meadows. In contrast, the lower slopes are timbered and the valleys are mottled carpets of grass, sage, and willow. "It is this spacious, peaceful setting," a government report says, "which most visitors come to enjoy. The view across the broad, open ranchlands, a mountain meadow, or an emerald lake with a rugged crest of mountains in the background gives the Sawtooths their grandeur."

Many people of prominence have expressed awe for the country. Looking at the Sawtooths from Galena Summit, Ernest Hemingway said: "You'd have to come from a test tube and think like a machine to not engrave all this in your head so that you'd never lose it."

Senator William E. Borah was also impressed. In 1915 when a bill was in Congress to create a park and he was taken on a tour of the district he said: "Whether man ever frames the record to read 'National Park,' God has made and placed it there."

Senator James H. Brady, for whom a similar visit was arranged the same year, said: "I am enraptured by the panorama of peaks, lakes, and forest primeval."

Alexander Ross, a fur trader, beat them all to it with an observation in 1824 from Mount Simpson (probably Galena Peak). "No elevated height in this country," he said, "can present a more interesting prospect than that viewed from the top, the west in particular." He was somewhat dismayed by the forbidding wilderness. He wondered how his party could get through. "The doubt remained," he wrote, "until I turned to view the quarter we had come from, and seeing it nearly as rugged and wild as country could be, it struck me that since we had passed through the one we might attempt the other."

The challenge and the charm of the Sawtooths have ever been thus. One towering ridge blends into another; one breath-taking spire is dwarfed by its neighbor. One eye-bugging delight is topped by the vista around the corner. The Sawtooths have been there a long time. Their career is just beginning in terms of human enchantment.

Chapter 2

MOUNTAIN MEN

THE SAWTOOTHS were discovered by white men about 1800. Records are vague as to the first explorer to see the peaks. It may have been a trapper who wandered down from Canada. It may have been a Spaniard checking out stories of gold told in Mexico. Fables abound. Facts are few, and none of them establishes firm credentials about the original visitors. It is generally accepted, however, that the early arrivals didn't think much of the place. The mountains were monstrous — jagged, snowy barriers to beaver country and unfit for travel, let alone settlement.

Indians didn't think much of the area, either. The high wilderness was avoided by all but a few small bands of Bannocks, Shoshoni, Lemhi, Sheepeaters, or whatever tribes they may have been associated with. Clear-cut identification of the Indians has been a matter of debate among researchers since serious study of human history began. Leaders of trapping expeditions called the Indians various names, according to what the trappers thought they were on the basis of sketchy reports or because of food the Indians ate at a certain time, such as mountain sheep. Indians of the Sawtooth area probably enjoyed a wide variety of game and fish, but it happened that trappers who wrote diaries usually ran into them when they were roasting sheep. Therefore the Indians were known as Sheepeaters. Other bands a few miles away were drying salmon or making baskets. The Salmon Eaters and the Basket Makers may have been members of one big family with the sheep-eating fraternity.

Whatever tribe or tribes the native inhabitants belonged to, they shared a common idea that the peaks were no place to be. The cliffs were tall, tough, and treacherous. Except for a few sheep and goats that might be found among the glaciers, there was nothing upstairs for the red man. He sensibly did his hunting, camping, and homework in the meadows. Purple peaks were okay for admiration on a clear morning but not to be invaded. Perhaps because they were practical and perhaps because of superstition, the Indians did as little mountain climbing as possible. Stories that Indians revered the mountains and feared to tread them because of tribal religion have been passed along, usually by white people creating traditions for Indians. There is more substance to the theory that Indians were afraid of the lava plains to the east, where fire demons puffed up smoke and ashes on what are known today as Craters of the Moon. Even at that, some skeptics feel that the Indians may have shunned the lava beds because they were mean to walk on, just as the Sawtooth ramparts were miserable spots to pitch a tepee.

Available evidence suggests that Indians did live in lower reaches of the mountains during summer. They had fairly good pickings of game, fish, and berries. When winter came they dropped back to more comfortable quarters such as Lemhi Valley, Camas Prairie, and Snake River. They were, therefore, the first people to enjoy the Sawtooths as a summer resort.

The first white men to approach the region didn't want any part of it. They caught glimpses of the peaks from a distance and decided they were out of bounds for a rational citizen. That was the case when Lewis and Clark went through Idaho in 1804. The expedition had dabs of data, mostly rumors. The frustrating experience of trying to go down the canyon of the Salmon below the Lemhi forced Lewis and Clark to take the Lolo route some distance north. A map published in London in 1814 from notes of William Clark reinforced the belief that the Sawtooth region was too rugged to enter. It shows a vast chunk of Idaho as unexplored geography labeled: "These Mountains are Covered with Snow." It locates some hot springs, lakes, and the South Fork of Lewis's River, roughly resembling what became the Snake — and all imagination as far as subsequent surveys determined. None of the mountains is named or pinpointed. As is understandable, the great nowhere was drawn as a forbidding jumble.

John Colter may have been among the first mountain men to see the Sawtooths. He was a member of the Lewis and Clark expedition. After that adventure he rammed around alone in the boondocks of Idaho, Wyoming, and Montana, trapping beaver and saving his own pelt from Indians. He discovered Yellowstone Park, particularly the geyser basins which were known as "Colter's Hell," and made his way through the Tetons. He was also on the Idaho side, where he left the Colter stone inscribed with his name and the date, 1808. It seems likely that he had at least a distant look at the Sawtooths, although there is nothing in written accounts to support the idea. Colter was a man who looked about him a great deal. He could scarcely have missed the towering sentinels while he was on points of vantage along the Wyoming border.

Actual travel in the Sawtooths was left for fur-trading companies led by such stalwarts as Donald McKenzie, Alexander Ross, Finan McDonald, John Work, and B. L. E. Bonneville. These gents in buckskin breeches spent many days testing the flinty environment of the Sawtooths. They came out with a few beaver and profound respect for the terrain. They found it rough as a cob.

Reliable paragraphs on the fur traders versus the Sawtooths are given in "Sawtooth Mountain Area Study," prepared by the U.S. Forest Service and the National Park Service in 1965. Much of the history of the trapping period was written by Merle Wells, director of the Idaho Historical Society. Considerable history of later periods was also assembled by Wells for other chapters in the 130-page document.

Each of several beaver expeditions contributed something to public knowledge of the Sawtooths during early years of the nineteenth century. Alexander Ross was one of the first to appreciate the scenery and to name a peak. Most of the time the robust gents were more concerned with finding a way through the gosh-awful canyons and beating rivals to disappointing supplies of beaver than with admiring beautiful sunsets on purple parapets.

"Ascending the summit at the head of the 'south branch' on June 24, 1824," the Sawtooth Study relates, "the party descended westward to Big Wood River, at the present Ketchum where they at last found an abundance of beaver." (The Ross party had reached Ketchum by way of Lost River after going up the Salmon to the Pahsimeroi and thence to the Little Lost. The descent to Wood River appears to have been over what later became known as Trail Creek.)

"From here Ross went south and then, by way of Camas Creek,

to the drainage of the South Fork of Boise River. Then, after a wide swing westward to the Payette and Weiser rivers and a trip south of the Snake River, he again returned to Big Wood River. Ascending this stream to its source, the company on September 18, 1824 stood on a height of land 'between the sources of the River Malade (Wood River) on the west and Salmon River on the north.' They were at or near the present Galena Summit.

"While the main party rested, Ross and one man climbed a nearby peak of the Boulder Mountains, on top of which was a small circular pond of water about twenty feet in diameter. 'The view we had enjoyed repaid us well for our troubles,' said Ross. He named the peak Mount Simpson after the governor of the Hudson's Bay Company's northern department. And he called the little lake 'the Governor's Punch Bowl.'

"Certainly Ross or his men looked down into the present Sawtooth Valley and to the mountains beyond. 'No elevated height in this country can present a more interesting prospect than that viewed from the top of Mount Simpson, the west in particular,' he wrote a number of years later. Ross was thus the first visitor on record to express an appreciation for the spectacular grandeur of the Sawtooth range.

"Looking northward from Mount Simpson — perhaps the present Galena Peak — Ross was dismayed by the jumble of peaks and canyons that lay ahead. He wondered how he was to find his way in that direction.

"From the summit, Ross and his men plunged northward 'into the narrow and unknown strands of Salmon River' with their old camp at Canoe Point (either Salmon City or Ellis) as their objective. The route may have been down the East Fork of Salmon River. The first portion of their travel was through deep canyons in a country so rough that the trappers believed it probable 'that no human being had ever trod in that path before.' But they found this supposition to be in error when they came across a wounded pheasant (grouse) pierced by a freshly shot arrow. The Sheepeaters had the invaders under observation.

"After descending what he considered to be the main Salmon River for an estimated forty-seven miles from Mount Simpson, Ross reached a place he called 'the Forks,' where a fine stream 'nearly as large as the main reach,' entered from the west. This branch, which was thirty to forty yards wide with deep water and a strong current, the trappers named 'Bear River' because of a bear hunt they had at its mouth. The Forks might have been the junction of Valley Creek and the main Salmon River at present Upper Stanley or, more likely, it was at the confluence of the East Fork and the Salmon about thirty miles to the east of Stanley.

"Ross now turned down the main Salmon once more toward Canoe Point. About ten miles below the Forks he entered a 'narrow and gloomy defile, where mountains on each side closed in on the river, between which the river became confined like the water out of a millrace and shot through the channel in a white foaming cascade with the noise of thunder.' Passing this perilous point, which perhaps was the gorge above the present Challis, by climbing along the riverbank cliffs and by crossing the stream, the company scrambled along through the canyon of the Salmon River until Canoe Point was reached on October 16, 1824. Here Ross noted in his diary: 'Length of Salmon River covered this year 100 miles.' Regardless of the difficulty in determining Ross's exact route at times, it is obvious that he quite thoroughly explored the upper reaches of Salmon River. While his trapping returns were not by any means uniformly disappointing, it had also been established that the Sawtooth area was not a beaver paradise."

On his return to headquarters, Ross was fired by Governor Simpson, the man for whom he had named a peak. Hudson's Bay Company was believed to be unhappy with Ross because he had not kept American competition from the area and had, rather, shown rival companies the way through the mountains. To replace Ross, the British group selected Peter Skene Ogden. That gentleman steered clear of the Salmon River for several years after making a trip up Little Lost River. Beaver were so scarce that Ogden didn't go back until 1827-28. On that expedition he went up Wood River to about the site of Ketchum and then crossed to Big Lost River up "a steep ascent, most dangerous to man and beast."

On that leg of his trip Ogden was following in reverse the journey of Alexander Ross in 1824. Ross went down Trail Creek from the Lost River country; Ogden climbed up. From Big Lost he went to Little Lost, probably through a pass near Mount Borah, and then on to the Portneuf. He went down the Snake and back to Walla Walla, arriving in June 1828.

In the summer of 1831 a party of American Fur Company trappers covered much of the Sawtooth district and its suburbs. This expedition, which included several Indians, found buffalo on Big Lost River. Notes of Warren Ferris, a member of the party, say buffalo were abundant. The fact was worth recording because buffalo were getting scarce. Common reports of the day said there were hardly any left in that neck of the woods.

Refreshed by buffalo feasts, the American trappers plodded on to the headwaters of Salmon River. What route they traveled is not clear. The notes tell of deep ravines and rocky pitches down which horses frequently fell. The description suggests Trail Creek, but the theory doesn't fit because the Trail Creek pass was familiar to mountain men by that time and previous traffic would have been mentioned. The route to the upper Salmon may have been around the White Clouds. Then again, it may not. Speculation on matters for which there are no answers in the back of the book is a fascinating hot-stove sport. Anybody can take a map, a given expedition, and a pinch of imagination and come up with a blueprint that may be fantastic or accurate. Further research into points that now seem trivial may establish routes of this and other expeditions. At present the matter is open to guesswork.

In any event, the Ferris company reached on July 13, 1831 a prairie "forming the central portion of a large valley half grown up with lofty pines, which is watered by one of the largest and most westerly sources of Salmon River."

"Almost certainly this prairie was in the present Sawtooth Valley," says the Sawtooth Mountain Area Study, "and evidently these American Fur Company trappers were the first persons, not Indians, to enter the upper portion of this beautiful basin."

This distinction for American fur traders is apparently based on the idea that the Ross party of 1824 found its way down the Salmon without going through Sawtooth Valley. Could be, historians say. Reconciling modern geography with the field notes of old-timers is frequently difficult. Whether they were first or not, it is reasonable to believe that the party of 1831 did reach Sawtooth Valley. The trappers met Indians without horses. The company hunted beaver, caught salmon, and rested their stock. Beaver business was a flop, so they went on down the river and over the Continental Divide to Montana.

A Salmon River trapper about whom a great deal was written for popular consumption was Captain Bonneville. He came along as a sort of pigtail and clean-up man for the big beaver excitement, not getting into the act until 1832-33. Washington Irving made him famous in a diary of adventures. Bonneville's trips through remote stretches of the Northwest were proclaimed as fur hunts. Bonneville was an officer of the U.S. Army on leave. Therefore there was whispering — and occasional shouting — that he was sniffing out the spoor of the British, or the French or the Spanish, or any other foreigners who might be mixing medicine out yonder.

Bonneville and his lads knocked around on the headwaters of the Salmon. They were well acquainted with Wood River. They followed old trails on Big and Little Lost rivers and added to the growing bundle of Sawtooth facts.

Some historians believe Bonneville spent the Christmas of 1832 near Stanley. If so, he was the first in that category. The Stanley-for-Christmas theory is based on a Washington Irving passage about a trip and a holiday. The trip was through a narrow gorge made by the "North Fork of the Salmon River."

The account says: "Captain Bonneville soon found that the Indians had not exaggerated the advantages of the region. Besides numerous gangs of elk, large flocks of the ahsahta or bighorn, the mountain sheep, were to be seen bounding among the precipices. These simple animals were easily circumvented and destroyed. A few hunters may surround a flock and kill as many as they please. Numbers were daily brought into camp, and the flesh of those that were young and fat was extolled as superior to the finest mutton.

"Here, then, was a cessation from toil, from hunger, and alarm. Past ills and dangers were forgotten. The hunt, the game, the song, the story, the rough though good-humored joke made time pass joyously away, and plenty and security reigned throughout the camp."

After reading the chapter carefully, comparing notes on progress up the river from previous camps, and linking this narrative to modern maps, Dr. Wells believes the place Bonneville had reached was near Stanley. The conclusion seems reasonable on the basis of Irving's account, which is understandably vague as to metes and bounds. There is a good deal of feeling that Irving concocted some of Bonneville's diary. Bonneville himself was not noted for accuracy. He was not above invention now and then to make his exploits exciting. The nature of his mission gave him an excuse for spinning yarns.

Be that as it may, there is substantial evidence that Bonneville's party celebrated a festive Christmas near Stanley. Trappers and Indians feasted, saluted the holiday with firearms, ran races, and drank an extra ration of rum. References elsewhere in Bonneville's diary suggest that toasting was part of the ceremony. Bonneville broke out his own concoction of rum and honey for special occasions. Christmas in a pleasant valley with plenty to eat would certainly have been one of them.

Next day the company went on toward Lost River and eventually to a rendezvous in Wyoming. Some of his freemen, however, had barged off over the mountains, perhaps from Sawtooth Valley to the vicinity of Atlanta. They were frightened off by Indians on Boise River and retreated to the Sawtooths, where Bonneville took them back under his wing. Whether they were actually attacked by Indians, or just afraid they might be, is not known. Hostilities or not, the total company thought it wise to get out of the country. Fur business was mediocre, canyons were tough, and accommodations — except for the valley around Stanley — as miserable as the trappers had endured anywhere on the expedition.

Other scouting parties of major fur brigades went to the head of Salmon River during and after the Bonneville period, but they added little to their bank accounts or to public knowledge of the Sawtooths. Such men as Thomas McKay and François Payette, both notables of Fort Boise, may have ventured as far as Stanley. Independent mountain men, of whom there were many during early days of the Oregon Trail, undoubtedly caught a little fur and scratched out an existence in the high country. But the curtain was rung down on the big show by Bonneville, who, incidentally, is not remembered as much for his Salmon River explorations as for his naming of Boise. He is credited with shouting, "Les bois, voyez les bois" ("The woods, see the woods") from a hill east of Boise in 1833. It seems ironic to some people these days that a man who had seen the splendors of Sawtooth Valley under a Christmas moon reserved his outburst of delight for a clump of cottonwoods surrounded by sagebrush. Probably it is charitable to assume that Bonneville was stricken speechless by the view from Stanley. Thousands have been thus afflicted since.

Chapter 3

ALTURAS COUNTY

ALTURAS COUNTY was the original Sawtooth empire. The term "original" in this sense refers to political history. Before developments of the last century the area was, of course, the realm of Indians, fur brigades, and occasional miners. They found it tall, tough, and terrible. For many years after explorers penetrated the region it was a vast unknown as far as maps were concerned. Early travelers with a bearing on the Tetons gazed at the Sawtooths as another distant landmark but generally steered clear because the terrain was harsh and uncharted. Maps drawn in the nineteenth century show a gaping void. Hardly anybody knew what was out there. Those who professed to know were put down as windbags. Most of the area has since been surveyed, but there are sections where official transits have never been planted.

The Alturas County empire was created by the Idaho Territorial Legislature in 1864. The area was huge. It covered 19,000 square miles, sprawling from Snake River on the south to what is now the Montana border on the north. The dividing line was a ridge of the Rockies. Montana was part of Idaho at the time. Old Alturas was larger than the states of Vermont and New Hampshire combined. Some wags insist it would have been bigger than Texas if it had been ironed out; much of Alturas stands on end. The name is said to mean "Heavenly Heights." Lofty it certainly was and still is. The heavenly qualities that are appreciated in modern times were not so evident at the outset. Practically all that was known in 1864 was that Alturas was about 200 miles long, 70 to 130 miles wide, and unfriendly to human beings.

Population was so scarce, in fact, that the county founders had to take a couple of stabs before they could get a community to accept the county seat. Esmeralda, a clutch of five or six cabins on Feather River, turned it down for lack of money and men. Rocky Bar assumed the responsibility, at first with some reluctance and later with vigor when another part of the county wanted the plum. Rocky Bar was a bustling gold town located in 1863-64, allegedly by Harry Comstock of Nevada fame. Its only serious rival in Alturas at that time was Atlanta, about twenty miles north on the fringe of the Sawtooths. Atlanta was too small and too remote to be considered for the county seat, so Rocky Bar filled the bill to general satisfaction.

The camp produced millions in minerals before it faded to a ghost. Some properties are still more or less alive, but the bloom has long gone. Several memorable events occurred there. Clinton DeWitt Smith, secretary of the territory and acting governor, died August 19, 1865 at the Franco-American Hotel. His death was reported at the time as sudden. He was a young man, and although he had been playing chess — an oddity for Rocky Bar — he was considered sound in mind and body. Later investigation suggested he was suffering from a "dismal and melancholy disease." His departure was regretted throughout the territory, except at Lewiston, from which place he had recently removed seal and archives to Boise in what Lewiston termed a diabolical plot by Governor Caleb Lyon to steal the capital.

A second event that shook Rocky Bar was a fire in July 1892 that destroyed most of the town, including the courthouse. By that time, however, loss of the courthouse was not a severe blow because Rocky Bar was no longer the county seat.

The change came about because Hailey sprouted from nothing to top banana. In one sense, it was the Bannock Indian War of 1878 and the Sheepeater Indian War of 1879 that created Hailey and left Rocky Bar in the ash can. It is argued with logic that the mines that made Hailey, Ketchum, Vienna, and the other towns would have been discovered even if there had been no Indian outbreaks. But it did happen that a mining boom followed promptly when the Indians were subdued.

Union Pacific Railroad photo

Sawtooth Valley from Galena Summit

Both campaigns involving the Sawtooths were related to the Chief Joseph War of 1877. Bannock scouts serving with U.S. troops against Joseph expressed disgust with the merciful policies of the army. They fumed because General O. O. Howard took so long to corral the Nez Perce. Buffalo Horn, a firebrand Bannock, was particularly outraged. Stimulated by whisky and by the notion he could whip the United States, he launched an attack on settlers of Camas Prairie in the spring of 1878. The war jumped to Owyhee County where Buffalo Horn was killed, crept across a chunk of Oregon, and back into Idaho. It was a hit-and-run war in which the military absorbed almost as much punishment from critics as from the enemy. Every pool hall spawned experts who knew more about running the war than the field commanders.

In spite of second-guessers and headline strategists, the troops did run the Indians out of Lost River and portions of the Sawtooths which were still sparsely settled. Indians pulled off some ambushes, such as the killing of Jason McCaleb near Mackay and several men on Salmon River, but the last of the hostiles called it quits in Yellowstone Park. They returned to Fort Hall, where most of their buddies had already gathered to receive government rations. Books have been written about the war. There is no intent or need to go into detail here, except to connect the episode to development of Wood River and the upper Salmon River.

Bold miners had been swinging picks in the district long before the Indian uproar. They had anchored camps in the '60s at such way-out points as Leesburg, Stanley, Atlanta, and Rocky Bar. A few years later they were at Orogrande, Loon Creek, Capehorn, and Bonanza City, to name a few promising hamlets. But they kept their rifles handy and had an eye out for Indians. Most of the Indians they did meet were peaceful. Nevertheless, the threat was real. When the Bannock War ended, or recessed, in the fall of 1878, mining took a shot in the arm. Men who had been hesitant before plunged into the mountains. Things were humming quite merrily at Bonanza City and neighboring strikes when the second half of the war broke out.

Several miners were killed and buildings burned at Orogrande. Most of the victims were Chinese. Blame fell on Sheepeater Indians, variously identified as nomadic offshoots of Bannocks, Shoshone, or Nez Perce. Whoever they were and whether they were responsible for the tragedy or not, they brought down the wrath of outraged citizens. Troops from Boise and Lapwai went after them. The war, like its predecessor, was a frustrating mess, with more snafus than successes. The terrain was frightful. Supply lines were long. Maps were guesswork. Weather was miserable. Orders were confusing. And, again, the public back home was impatient.

It turned out there were few Indians to be conquered. Some of them didn't know they were on the warpath until they were obliged to surrender. A tattered band of bucks and squaws threw in the towel when winter came. The end of that sorry uproar paved the way for another upsurge of mining. Civilians already in the hills explored new areas in comparative safety. Their ranks were

swelled by soldiers who had drawn a bead on likely ore while looking for Indians. They returned to stake claims, influencing a rush to
Sawtooth Valley and Wood River. Mining camps mushroomed
where none had been before.

The district was ripe for pick and shovel. No doubt it would
have been developed soon, even if there had been no Indian hubbub. However, the ruction and the peace that followed contributed
to development. Galena, Ketchum, Bellevue, and Hailey sprouted
on Wood River. Sawtooth City and Vienna boomed on headwaters
of Salmon River. All of them put a fresh charge in the battery of
far-flung Alturas. Ketchum was born in 1879 and named for David
Ketchum, formerly of Idaho City. The original name, Leadville,
was rejected by postal authorities because there were too many
Leadvilles. Bellevue was located in 1880 by Owen Riley, merchant
and first postmaster. Hailey came along in 1881 on land patented
by John Hailey, a stage-line operator and territorial delegate to the
U.S. Congress. Galena was laid out during the same period.

Hailey cut the widest swath. It flexed its muscles promptly in
seeking transfer of the county seat from Rocky Bar. In a hot election in 1881 it wrestled Bellevue, Ketchum, and Rocky Bar. The
first count showed Bellevue the winner by one vote, 1071 to 1070,
but there were two missing precincts. A recount turned the tide to
Hailey by about twenty votes. Political power of the northern end
of the county was overwhelming. Rocky Bar withered.

Hailey's role as top dog was threatened, however, by neighboring towns, mainly Bellevue. The fight led to mayhem on old Alturas, once so powerful that it dominated the territorial legislature.
Various precincts wanted a larger part of the action; creation of
more counties was their method. The operation was long, painful,
and successful from the standpoint of the political surgeons, but the
patient died.

Elmore and Logan counties were created in 1889, with Rocky
Bar the seat of Elmore and Shoshone the seat of Logan. In 1891
another bit of legislative surgery hacked up Alturas again by creating Alta and Lincoln. Alta was abolished before it got off the
ground by a ruling of the Idaho Supreme Court. Meanwhile Custer
County lopped off a chunk of Alturas in the Stanley Basin area, a
division that still remains a bone of contention.

In another round of the prolonged battle, Blaine County was
established in 1895 with Hailey as the seat. Blaine was named for
James G. Blaine, the "plumed knight from Maine," secretary of
state in the Garfield and Harrison administrations and Republican

candidate for president in 1884. Blaine County rose from the ashes of Alturas, which was abolished along with Logan — a county that, along with Alta, was not long for this world. During this involved process, Lincoln County was re-created with its seat at Shoshone, first designated as the hub of Logan.

Politicians were by no means through with their dismemberment of old Alturas. The empire it had once occupied was further hacked into Butte, Gooding, Jerome, Camas, and Clark counties and parts of Fremont, Bingham, Bonneville, Power, Jefferson, Madison, and Minidoka counties. The division was still going on as recently as 1919. The heartland, Blaine, was reduced to a patch of Alturas. It retains little but the heavenly heights, but they are a considerable asset in this age of increasing appreciation for inspiring mountains.

One of the first developments after creation of Elmore County was removal of the county seat from Rocky Bar to Mountain Home. Rocky Bar liked the county seat business, having served Alturas in that capacity and feeling that its efforts to split Elmore from Hailey should be rewarded. But Rocky Bar was up the creek a far piece from the center of population at Mountain Home, which was on a railroad and had a thriving livestock industry. So Mountain Home got the county seat. Rocky Bar surrendered its papers and prerogatives under court order. As far as current use of the Sawtooths is concerned, that is a minor matter. Rocky Bar is way down south in a corner of the wonderland and still far from the beaten path to the peaks. There is a road to Rocky Bar and a road of sorts from Rocky Bar to Atlanta, but there is only a pack trail over the mountains from Atlanta to the Sawtooth valhalla.

Chapter 4

STANLEY

STANLEY is named for Captain John Stanley, leader of a group of miners who made the first discovery of gold in the valley in 1863. Captain Stanley was not a military officer, and the strike was not made at the present town of Stanley. The title of captain was given to "old man Stanley" because he was leader of a prospecting party from Florence exploring the Sawtooths. At the age of about 55 he was regarded as a senior citizen. He was an experienced miner, having sunk his pick in several western camps, including the bonanza of Baboon Gulch at Florence in northern Idaho.

Other members of the party that reached the upper region of the Salmon River with Stanley included Frank Coffin, Dick Douglass, Matthew Zapp, and A. P. Challis, the latter a miner who developed claims in the area for many years and for whom the town of Challis was named.

The Stanley strike was in Kelly Gulch, about fifteen miles from the mouth of Valley Creek, according to Jesse R. Black's *History of Custer County*. The site, developed to little more than a scratch by the original work, later became the Summit Mine. The scene was some distance from what later became Stanley.

Stanley's platoon of ten men did not linger long. For one thing, the group was running short of supplies and was uncertain how far it was to the nearest settlement. For another, there was uneasiness about Indians. Hanging onto scalps was more important than finding gold. There might be profitable nuggets; on the other hand, the find might be a flash in the pan. Therefore the party set out for the headwaters of Boise River, expecting to come out somewhere around Atlanta.

About fifteen miles from Stanley the miners ran into Indians. Apparently the Indians were not expecting company. The two parties ducked into the forest, suspicious of each other but not taking positive action. Although Stanley was unable to detect hostility he was worried because his group was heavily outnumbered by the sixty Indians. He decided to turn back. Several miners joined him in his withdrawal to Florence. Frank Coffin took charge of the main company.

The Indians presently came out of the brush, making signals of cordial relations. By signs and a few words understood by both sides it was made clear they were as anxious as the white men. They didn't want trouble. They were on a hunting trip and had no intention of starting a fight. The white men were the first the Indians had seen. They had heard rumors of whites from their grandfathers, but none had been seen in the Sawtooths since the fur-trapping era. The Indians said they had plenty of mountain sheep. Hence, they were called Sheepeaters. In all probability they were a band of Bannocks or Shoshoni spending the summer in the mountains before returning to the plains.

In the spring of 1864 a party of twenty-five men left Boise for Stanley by way of Boise River. Travel over the summit between Atlanta and Sawtooth Valley was difficult because of deep snow. The miners floundered along an Indian trail. They met Indians at a place they called Warm Springs, about forty miles above Stanley by their reckoning. The Indians were surly, not at all in the frame of mind they had exhibited the previous summer. There was no peace pipe, no exchange of gifts, no welcome.

Taking the hint, the visitors went on to the mouth of Valley Creek to set up camp for the season. Tents were pitched at the present site of Stanley. Within a short time the place was crowded. Nearly 200 men arrived, lured by reports of gold. Most of the likely ground was staked quickly. Few of the new arrivals could find anything worth the trouble of locating and the agony of development. Pickings were slim even for those who had first choice.

Something the prospectors did find was a mysterious ruin. Comments in later articles about the trip stated:

"A few miles above Stanley on the side of a hill one or two hundred yards from Valley Creek are three forts in a row and a few feet distant from each other. They are built of unknown granite boulders and have an ancient look, being almost filled with earth. When the first white men visited them in 1863 and built a cabin which still stands in a gulch north of the Duffy place between the intersection of Valley and Stanley creeks, they appeared as old as they do at the present time. By whom they were constructed or what their purpose was will remain, as the massacre, unknown."

What "the massacre" refers to is as puzzling as the location of the ruin. One interpretation of the report is that the observer assumed there had been a fight in which the builders of the fortification had been wiped out. No record of such a disaster has been found. Could the fight have been between Indians? Not likely, say some researchers. Indians were not inclined to build with boulders; they made shelters of skins and brush. Another point discounting the Indian theory is that Indians seldom, if ever, remained in the valley all winter. They did not need permanent housing. Okay, it must have been white men. But who and when? There is nothing in the reports of fur brigades to suggest that they built a rock fort. They didn't have time or necessity. Bonneville and others camped a few days and went their way. Furthermore, they enjoyed friendly relations with the Indians they encountered.

Was it possible the structures were built by the freemen who cut loose from Bonneville, were frightened by Indians on headwaters of Boise River, and turned back? That theory is shot down by the fact that Bonneville found the wanderers. There is no mention of a fortification. It remains possible that they may have holed up on Valley Creek — but they were not massacred; they went back to Bonneville's trapline.

If there was an expedition to the Sawtooths between the 1830s and the discovery of gold near Stanley in 1863, it is not recorded. The area was practically untouched for thirty years. Advocates of a Spanish theory argue — somewhat tongue in cheek — that the Stanley Stonehenge was built by Conquistadores ranging far from Mexico about 1800. They say there is evidence of Spanish mining near Rocky Bar about that time and they reason that those Spaniards could have gone as far as Stanley. The speculation is interesting but remains pure speculation, resting as it does on "old letters" of doubtful origin. Fur trappers made no mention of such rockworks. Of course it is possible they did not notice them because they were intent on beaver and game. However, it is also logical to believe they would have taken note of such evidences of civilization.

Whatever the ruins may have been, if they did exist, they have disappeared. The vestiges have succumbed to time, road construction, and other revamping of the landscape.

Indians left a record of their meeting with the Stanley party in 1863. They carved essential information on a tree. The pictograph was found several years later about fifteen miles from Stanley. It showed clasped hands of friendship, the number of Indians and whites involved, and the directions each party went after the brief encounter. The message tree, like many of its kind on ancient trails in Idaho mountains, is no longer there. It was burned by campers.

The census of 1870 lists twenty-nine people in the Stanley Basin Mining District. All were men. Most were young. They had to be to get their mail from the nearest post office at Leesburg, about 150 miles away. Population of the area was increased in 1871 by a mining strike on Yankee Fork, about six miles above Robinson Bar. Twenty men moved in to earn an estimated $8 per day.

The camps were still going, although not vigorously, when Bonanza City surged in 1879 with the double boom of mine development and the Sheepeater War. Moses A. Kempner of Idaho City provided stage and saddle service to Yankee Fork. His stage ran from Idaho City to Banner twice a week and the saddle trip from Banner to Bonanza — a two-day ride — once a week. The fare was $45. Kempner carried mail and express, giving Stanley Basin much quicker service from Idaho City than from Leesburg.

Activity near Stanley later shifted to Joe's Gulch, a short distance below what is now Lower Stanley and named for Joe Garadina, an early miner. Several claims were worked there. Homes were built, and women for the first time brought their influence and talents to the remote outpost. Women were on the scene as early as 1880, as witnessed by correspondence from Joe's Gulch in the *Yankee Fork Herald* of January 1, 1881. The article signed "Cy." said:

"Isolated as we are from the outside world, shut out by snow-clad mountains, we have our amusements and take much comfort.

"Sometime before Christmas it was announced that a dinner would be given by the ladies of Joe's Gulch, Mrs. Wells and Mrs. Cooper. Everybody in our little mining camp was invited and we all waited patiently for the merry day to come. It came with a cloudy sky and a light snowfall. It seemed nothing would break the

Photo by Ernie Day

Ranch near Lower Stanley

gloom, but when dinner was announced our isolated homes and gloomy weather were forgotten.

"The table was spread with all the delicacies our mountain valley affords, from ripe fruit to the most delicious pastry prepared by tasteful hands. Well might our Bonanza friends envy us. None sat down to a finer repast than we. Space will not allow me to give the names of the numerous dishes but suffice it to say that the table was so heavily laden with good things it groaned beneath them.

"As we looked along the table it brought our minds back to years gone by when we sat down to frugal meals. We could not but think what mighty changes time has brought. We talked of early days when there were none to make merry with or to answer our call but the whirling drift or the thunder of the avalanche. But now the fair sex have come to our mountain home to cheer the gold hunter and to make cheerful our way, though it may seem hard.

"Our toil and care are forgotten when we think we see a brighter future for our rising country as time moves on. Our long hopes will be rewarded.

"The table being cleared at an early hour in the evening, the Joe's Gulch String Band gave the signal for the dance. We forgot our ages and all joined in dancing which was occasionally suspended for a song or a mince at the sweetmeats. Then on with the dance until the clock tolled the hour of the Sabbath. Then came the time for parting with dear friends. As we looked at each other the question was asked: 'Will we all meet again next Christmas?' None can answer, knowing full well the great change time brings but hoping for the best. We shall never forget that Christmas spent in Stanley. We all went home happy over our merry time, none being slighted, with well wishes to all returning to our homes to spend the rest of the night in slumber."

At that time and for several years, Stanley was second fiddle to Bonanza City, a thriving camp on Yankee Fork of Salmon River. Gold was found on Yankee Fork in 1866 by the Jack Richardson party from Montana. Most of the men were Yankees. They named the location for that fact and as a counterpunch to Secesh Creek in the Warren vicinity, named earlier by Confederates. The first quartz strike on Yankee Fork was made by W. A. Norton in 1875, about nine years after the first placer claims were worked. Norton's mine became the Charles Dickens, a famous property. The town of Custer was founded in 1876, the year of General George A. Custer's defeat. The General Custer Mine, its richest asset, produced millions. Several other mines of the vicinity were prosperous for a decade or so. Some are still active on a small scale. Bonanza and Custer are ghost towns. Most of the buildings are gone. Those that remain are weathered witnesses to boom and bust.

Yankee Fork came through the Bannock War of 1879 unscathed, although the incident that started hostilities occurred on Loon Creek at Orogrande, a mining camp supplied and largely manned by Bonanza. Troops moved through Bonanza. Indians blamed for an attack on Loon Creek mines steered clear. Several Sheepeaters who did approach the town were friendly. Miners, merchants, and freighters had more trouble with bear attracted to the river by migrating salmon.

By the time the war scare had worn off, the prospects for financial rewards were so bright they played an important role in creation of Custer County in 1881. The county was carved out of chunks of Alturas and Lemhi. Bonanza made a bid for the county seat, but it went to Challis. Custer contains many of the Sawtooth Mountains and the headwaters of the Salmon and Lost rivers.

During the boom on Yankee Fork, mining at Stanley was in the doldrums. A new industry for Sawtooth Valley developed in the form of beef for Bonanza. Abundant grass grew fat cattle. The operation was small but afforded a livelihood. It was the forerunner of livestock production that later became, and still is, a major enterprise.

With Indians out of the way and some of the mines fading, there was a migration to Wood River by way of Galena Summit, with stops for mining excitement at Sawtooth City and Vienna. The scene of major action shifted to Ketchum, Hailey, and Bellevue.

Chapter 5

BEAVER DICK'S MOUNTAIN
OF SILVER

THE NAMES of Matt Graham, G. W. Stilts, and Sumner Pinkham rank high in Idaho history for various reasons. Graham was a mining magnate of Atlanta, Silver Mountain, and Wood River. Stilts, a blacksmith, earned a reputation as the prime practical joker of Boise and other places. Pinkham, a territorial police officer of Boise Basin, was shot by Ferd Patterson in a celebrated row near Idaho City. One of the most dramatic adventures in the West linked them in a joint endeavor long before they went their separate ways to find individual status.

They rode the Salmon River in scows. Their trip down the canyon on a fantastic mission occurred in 1862. The date established them among the first navigators of the river over whose falls an armada moves every summer in current times. Today people float down in metal boats, rubber boats, and skin boats. Others come upstream with outboard motors, inboard motors, airplane propellers, and eggbeaters. Records are claimed by the first left-handed man with freckles to survive the Blue Hole. There are stout assertions of first up or down by citizens named Reginald who live in towns west of the Mississippi without one-way streets. Gamblers run it to win bets. Kids ride it for marbles, chalk, and kicks.

The Graham-Stilts-Pinkham expedition did not make much impression on the river. It didn't exactly get anywhere, but it did make a big splash. If effort counts in these matters, the men deserve credit for pioneering the rapids. The trip started rather far downstream; by some standards it is not within bounds at all. The Graham party was not in the canyon between North Fork and Meadow Creek, the most isolated and forbidding stretch. Authority for the account of the drama of '62 is the *Hailey News-Miner*. The paper told the story in 1884, after some of the participants had died. The account was reprinted in the *Idaho World* of Idaho City. According to available measures it appears authentic. A word for support of its veracity is required because Stilts was a member of the crew, and it was from his lips as well as those of Matt Graham that the morsels of recollection fell. Stilts enjoyed such a reputation for leg-pulling that only a greenhorn would believe his notarized statement that Monday came after Sunday.

It was Stilts who barbered and painted Jim Agnew's dog, then took the pooch on a leash and joined Agnew in a hunt for the perpetrator. It was Stilts who wrapped metal wires around Fourth of July torches so that all who picked them up put them down in a hurry. He jobbed gullible drummers. He kept Boise in hilarious uproar. Even when he was the fall guy for one of his own jokes, he was the soul of merriment. When the mining boom hit Wood River he joined it, transferring his wit and wisdom to a new audience. This bit of background is tossed in for benefit of doubting Thomases. There is no reason, however, to doubt essentials of the river adventure.

The Salmon River voyage was planned at Florence. A rough-cut mountaineer named Beaver Dick uncorked a tale of a mountain of silver. It was down the river, he said, somewhere between Sheep Creek and Snake River. He was so impressive that a party of miners started from Lewiston. They rode to Florence on horses and built boats of whipsawed lumber on Meadow Creek, a short distance below the old mining camp.

"After being out three weeks," the story says, "Jeff Standifer broke up the party by letting a boat take a sheer on him. It got away and went down the river with all the provisions and arms. Lots were drawn to select men to go after the boat. It fell to George Stilts and four others. They ran past the boat without seeing it, on account of its being in an eddy."

That was a pretty pickle. It was certainly not in Stilts' style. There was no joke; it was find the boat or else.

Other miners in the gang stumbled onto the scow, half sunk, battered to bits and quite soggy. Wet as they were, grub and guns were secure, having been lashed down in case there was a bump in the road. While Stilts was scrambling along the rocks looking for the ship half a mile downstream, the salvage crew attempted to pack everything out on one portage. A man named Rice (another blacksmith, this time from Scott's Bar, California) tried to stagger off with a load that would squash a mule. First harnessing himself with an assortment of plunder, he hoisted a bale of wet blankets on his back, along with a long-handled shovel. He plodded from the beach to a rocky ledge, missed his footing and fell. As he attempted to save himself the shovel struck the ground, pushing him over a seventy-five-foot cliff. He fell in a pile of boulders. Companions buried him, the account says, "as well as circumstances would allow." They threw blankets over him, heaped stones on the blankets to keep animals away, and left him there. A monument of rocks marked the spot. The location is unknown. In '62 not enough people went down the Salmon to require signposts.

Stilts and his boat hunters made contact with the rest of the party a short time later. The shock of Rice's accident had lost its tragic edge. Perked up by a supply of rations and the knowledge that they were reasonably safe, although still way off in the dead end of nowhere, the boys gave Stilts a shot of the medicine he later dished out with gusto.

"Find the boat, George?" asked one.

"No," said Stilts. "Thought it might be back up the river someplace."

"Didn't see it," said the miner. "You better go along back down the canyon and catch up with it. We'll all starve."

Stilts was too tired to argue or explain his failure. He flopped on a rock to rest. While he was lying on his back with his eyes half closed a man walked by with a rifle. Stilts jumped up and grabbed it.

"Hey," he shouted, "that's mine. It was on the boat. Where did you get it?"

"Bought it in Lewiston," the man insisted. "You're having a sick spell in the head, George. Seeing things. Lie down and eat a chunk of beef."

The grinning tormentor shoved a plate of vittles under his nose.

"Guess you're right," groaned Stilts. "I must be delirious. That's food from the boat."

"Yeah, we found her," said the miner. "You bumblefooted right over it."

"Where?" asked Stilts.

"Up a tree."

After a day or two exploring the canyon and figuring out what best to do, the party abandoned the idea of building another boat. "The men returned to the haunts of civilization," the report said, "nearly famished and destitute of clothing." The expedition was a flop. It didn't find the mountain of silver. It didn't find a dime's worth.

The full revelation of what a wild goose chase it had been broke some months later. Beaver Dick learned the news. "It seems," the newspaper said, "that he had been prospecting up the river and had come to Walla Walla with some very fine specimens which were secretly changed on him for Virginia City rock. In having an assay made he concluded he had struck it rich. In order to make the most of his discovery he had told a windy tale about the location."

The mountain of silver Stilts and company looked for on Salmon River was actually about a thousand miles away in Nevada.

Several members of the expedition survived the voyage only to meet violent death elsewhere. William Bostick was shot by Sioux a short time after he left Salmon in '62. Knowing he was fatally injured, he took his partner's pistol and shot himself. John Keenan was shot in Oneida County. Beaver Dick, the cause of it all, disappeared into the limbo of mountain men. Pinkham was the victim of an assassin's bullet at Idaho City. Only Stilts and Graham lived long enough to look back on the episode from the viewpoint of two decades. It was of small importance to them that they had dipped paddles and sweeps into a river of no return. They never went back. Once was enough. They left modern navigation to Captain Henry Guleke, Monroe Hancock, and John Cunningham.

Chapter 6

MINING

LEVI SMILEY opened the door to mining at the headwaters of Salmon River. He was responsible for discoveries that led to establishment of Sawtooth City and Vienna, a pair of camps that boomed in the 1880s, sputtered occasionally in later years, and then became ghosts. Smiley's name is perpetuated by a creek. There is nothing left of the Emma, his first mine, or of many other mines that followed.

Exploration of the upper Salmon came at the same time Bonanza City and Custer were coming into prominence on Yankee Fork. Smiley, a former Montana resident and a mine superintendent in Utah, led a small group from Challis. They followed an Indian trail — possibly one used by fur traders more than thirty years earlier — up a tributary of the Salmon to the divide between the Salmon and Boise River drainages. The tributary became known as Smiley Creek. Near the summit, high in the Sawtooths, Smiley found good ore. He was unable to develop the claim, according to Forest Service and Park Service analysis, because a messenger warned him the Bannock War had started. Although there may have been no immediate danger, prudent parties pulled back from the hills. Smiley returned to Challis and stayed there until the war cooled.

In the fall of 1878, after the Bannocks called it quits, Smiley returned to his spring claim. He and T. B. Mulkey filed on a batch of mines. The following spring a full-scale rush began. Scores of prospects were staked. Among them was the Vienna, discovered in June 1879 by E. M. Wilson. Glowing reports of that vein and of such claims as the Silver King, Columbia, and Nellie attracted a stampede. A mining district was formed, construction of a wagon road was begun to link the area with Galena and Ketchum, and Sawtooth City was organized in Beaver Canyon. (Little is left of the original town. Another hamlet called Sawtooth City has been created along the highway. It is several miles from the genuine pioneer site.)

It is appropriate to note that Indians, either present or absent, had a part in the time schedule of mining. John Stanley's party played hide-and-seek with Indians in 1863. The Indians proved friendly, but Stanley took no chances; he withdrew. Then, fifteen years later, the Smiley company postponed its activities because of Indians that weren't there at all, but might have been.

The district grew rapidly. Items in newspapers such as *Yankee Fork Herald, Wood River Times, Idaho City World,* and *The Statesman* show Sawtooth City to have been a town of about twenty-five homes in 1881 with the usual assortment of saloons, restaurants, stores, and laundries. By June of 1882 Sawtooth had at least 250 people. There was also a hotel, as evidenced by the note: "Mrs. Ida Huffman furnishes excellent lodging accommodations." At the same time, rival Vienna reported 150 men about town and forty employed in mines. Payrolls that fed both communities were provided by numerous mines. Sawtooth City relied mainly on claims in Beaver Canyon, where the Columbia and Beaver Company was most prominent. The Pilgrim was another leader. Silver was the main product of most of the claims. Gold cut little figure at Sawtooth City or Vienna.

Mines in Smiley Canyon supported Vienna. Among the biggest and brightest was the Vienna, operated by the Vienna Consolidated Mining Company, an outfit that enjoyed periods of prosperity, felt the blight of depression, and finally blew up in a dramatic meeting of stockholders in Chicago. The major troubles, however, did not come until World War I. While Vienna was young and vigorous the Vienna Mine was its pride and joy. Under the management of Chris Johnston in the 1880s tunnels were drilled considerable distance to tap valuable veins that pleased the management and brought joy to stockholders.

Success of the mines stimulated the town of Vienna until it equalled or passed Sawtooth City. By the summer of 1882 there were six cafes, fourteen saloons, three general stores, and two meat markets, as well as livery stables and blacksmith shops to serve the transportation business. Among the saloons was one run by George

Pierson, "Johnny-Behind-the-Rocks" Hall, and "Banjo Nell," of whom there is more information in another part of this book. There was also the billiard hall of Castro and Cooper where a man was shot for sitting on the table. There is additional data on that incident, too.

Vienna reached such giddy heights that a newspaper was started. Messrs. Stevens and Jones printed their first edition July 4, 1882 for 200 subscribers. The paper died in infancy, lasting only until November when it was absorbed by the *Ketchum Keystone*. The name of Vienna was changed to Redwing in the fall of 1893 and right back again the next year, to nobody's surprise.

Main points in history of the mining district are given in the publication *Sawtooth Mountain Area Study* by Victor O. Goodwin of the Forest Service and John A. Hussey of the Park Service, published in 1965. Some paragraphs:

"In May 1885 the Vienna Company struck a rich ore vein, but the strike was quickly contested by managers of the neighboring Lion Mine. The vein had been discovered on Vienna property but was followed into Lion ground. The settlement depended upon the location of the apex of the ore ledge. Attorneys were retained by both sides, and in June the Lion management filed suit for an injunction to prohibit further exploration of the contested ore body and for $70,000 damages already incurred. Pending settlement, the Vienna mill shut down, but only for as long as it took to prepare for the new ore strike. The suit was apparently settled out of court following an amicable meeting of the parties in Hailey in July. At any rate, no further mention is made in the Hailey papers of a court suit.

"A new flurry of activity overtook the Sawtooth City camp in the summer of 1885. The Columbia and Beaver mill, which had been idle most of the time since its completion, had been renovated by the Sawtooth Mining and Milling Company. New foundations were laid and machinery was overhauled. . . . The company superintendent, W. S. Vernam, seemed confident that he could start the mill early the next spring. In the meantime, ores from the Chloride, Summit Numbers One and Two, Cambria, Mammoth, Pilgrim, Siver King, Real Estate Ruth, Sunbeam, and Atlanta mines were sent to the Philadelphia smelter in Ketchum.

"One of the most significant improvements in Beaver Canyon during 1885 was the erection of a concentrator near the Silver King Mine. From old dumps of the Silver King and other mines, concentrates were produced which smelted at Ketchum for $500 to $800 per ton. Further improvements were planned for 1886 which would enable 70 to 80 percent of the ores heretofore considered of no value to be recovered. Access to the area was enhanced by widening of the packtrain road from Sawtooth to Atlanta, making the trip to Atlanta a one-day journey.

"In 1886 the Columbia and Beaver mill started up and had a successful run all season. A mail route was established between Sawtooth and Atlanta, and the camp seemed to be gaining a firm foothold for the first time. Two hundred men were employed in and around Sawtooth, and there were forecasts for as many as 500 employees in the area for the next season. The principal mines operating in 1886 were the Silver King, with Major William Hyndman as its manager; the Pilgrim, operating under lease; the Columbia; and the Beaver. All processed their ores at the Columbia and Beaver mill.

"The 1887 season failed to materialize on the grandiose scale predicted the previous fall. The Columbia and Beaver mill was idle all summer because the Sawtooth Company did not return Mr. Vernam, the manager who had pushed the new development of the mill. There was some speculation that the mill would be leased during the next season by the owner of the Summit Mine, T. F. Shaw. Working all through the winter of 1886, the employees of the Summit were driving a tunnel at the 450-foot level, cutting from Beaver Canyon to Lake Canyon, with six openings into the mine. The only active mine in the area during the season of 1887 was the Silver King, which was working eight to ten men. The mine laid in enough supplies to continue work through the winter. The Vienna company had closed both its mine and mill. . . . By November only one man was left in the town, the company watchman. Superintendent Johnston of the Vienna had moved to Hailey and then to Custer County for a job with the Buckskin Mining Company.

"By 1888 Sawtooth City was nearly dormant but seemingly unable to give up completely. The Silver King continued to run after a temporary shutdown caused by a mine flood. Major Hyndman assumed active management of the property, purchasing in June the leasing interests of one Wallingford who had run up sizable debts on the mine. By June the mine had shipped twelve tons of ore to Portland, netting $2,738.

"The most surprising development of 1888 was the renewal of activity in Vienna. No ore was extracted, but men worked in the mine driving a tunnel through the hill in the Boise side, 800 feet deeper than the previous workings, at a cost of $60,000.

"The situation in the Sawtooth City region changed very little from 1888 to 1891. The Silver King remained the only actively producing mine, but such others as the Bluebird, Lucky Boy, Pilgrim, and Summit shipped small quantities of ore. By 1891 Major Hyndman had assumed a three-year lease on the Silver King which had been producing as much as a carload per day. In the summer of 1891 he installed a new pump and pipes, spending more than $20,000 on improvements. Through the winter the mine was worked to a point where there was enough rich ore in sight to work ten men a full year, and by the summer of 1892 it was prepared to operate at full steam. But on August 2, 1892, came the disaster that ended large-scale mining in the Sawtooth region for many years. Fire swept through the Silver King shaft, destroying the entire hoisting, pumping, and air works. Hyndman was unable to obtain the cooperation of his company to rebuild the workings. The Sawtooth region collapsed as a mining area."

Vienna withered along with its rival camp. The Vienna group of mines was sold for taxes in 1906. Several of the claims have been worked off and on since then, and as recently as modern times there has been some picking about. By 1914, according to one observer, nothing remained of the more than 200 buildings in prime Vienna but piles of cordwood. The settlement was razed. Only a few remnants can be seen by summer visitors. The ghostly situation is similar at Sawtooth City.

While it was dying, but not quite ready to give up, Vienna gave several vigorous kicks. About 1914 Vienna Consolidated Mining and Smelting again took control of the Vienna and Solace groups, built a new mill, and tried to breathe life into the deserted town. The revival didn't quite come off. Miners protested nonpayment of wages. Stockholders protested lack of returns. Matters came to a head in Chicago where about sixty stockholders, representing 99 percent of the shares amounting to $5 million, raked management over the coals. The encounter took place in May 1918.

Signs that all was not well had been visible for several seasons. For instance, there was the action in 1916 by miners to attach the company because they had not been paid for several months. Some stayed in Vienna where there was adequate food and a supply of phonograph records, cards, and magazines. There was work, too, but the men didn't do it because they doubted they would ever be paid.

Other miners snowshoed to Ketchum and Hailey, a trip of about three days. A dozen or so came out in January and February. Two

Upper Bench Lakes and Mount Heyburn

women also made the trip. They had a hard time but finally made it after spending an extra night at Pierson, a camp between Stanley and Sawtooth Valley. One of them, Anna Sullivan, rode down Galena summit on skis without a pole. It was something few men tried in those days. The lady piled into a drift and sprained an ankle but gamely went on to Ketchum under her own power.

Five of the miners who had hiked out to sue the Vienna company nearly eliminated themselves on the way. They were walking along the railway tracks in a snowstorm and didn't see a freight engine until it was fifty yards away. They scrambled up walls of snow, all escaping with only a few bruises.

Zephaniah V. T. Cherry, mail carrier, joined the miners in their suit. He said the company owed him about $185. He estimated total debts for wages and supplies at $5,000. Cherry was a small, wiry man accustomed to deep snow and low temperatures. He harnessed himself to a hickory sled loaded with as much as 250 pounds of mail and merchandise. While the Vienna failed to pay him, he said, he would take a vacation from his mail job. It was simple to ease off without making Uncle Sam angry, he said, because there were hardly any trains from Shoshone, therefore no outside mail for his area. And if authorities got huffy, he would quit. He had a small mining claim, a farm near Vienna, and a string of packhorses. By spring he was over his peeve. He collected at least some of the money due him from the mine. He continued to carry mail, and by the middle of April was spreading dirt on the snow of Galena Summit so autos could get traction. By that time a few cars were making it to Stanley Basin.

The miners made enough noise to shake partial payments from the Vienna nabobs. The company shelled out some back wages and promised to do better. The chairman of the board said a new manager would take charge. He said the old manager had gone insane; that was the excuse for the embarrassing mess.

However that may have been, the stockholders who met at Chicago in 1918 were not convinced that Vienna Consolidated was a sound investment. After the company secretary read a glowing report of fabulous bodies of ore about to be tapped and of grand things to be accomplished by the mill, he was hissed and booed.

Particular target of criticism was R. T. Tustin, general manager. He was a kingpin in several mining ventures of the area. Some of them were quite successful. He was a man of respected reputation in mining circles. The Vienna was not one of his brightest jewels.

One of the executives at Vienna was Bismarck von Wedelstadt, son-in-law of Tustin. What he did was not clear. Certain associates said he was incompetent. D. B. Higgins, mining engineer and former superintendent (not the one who was alleged to be off his rocker), said Bismarck couldn't drive a nail without pounding his fingers. He said he "drew a fat salary under an assumed name."

Other stockholders chipped in comments to the effect that reports of officers were hogwash. Whether Bismarck was a good worker or not, they said, something was wrong with the company. For instance, accounts of rich ore were a myth.

That paved the way for Bismarck von Wedelstadt to read a prepared speech refuting the charges. He said a study by engineers showed a great deal of good ore remained. He said the directors, except papa-in-law, were dishonest. A. W. Worsley, one of the directors present, took exception to such language. He called Bismarck a liar. Bismarck replied: "If you don't shut up you will need a doctor."

Stockholders jumped up and parted the antagonists before blood was shed. Von Wedelstadt was so upset he abandoned his speech. Stockholders unhappy with Tustin and Bismarck introduced letters purporting to show that Wesley B. George, an officer of the company, had conspired with Tustin in a fraudulent scheme for organizing the company in 1912. "Let's promote," said a letter from George to Tustin. "Make our commissions out of payments and let those who take up the deals run the properties to suit themselves. Let them put their friends or relatives or whomever they care in charge. . . . Now let us be honest with each other and with ourselves. Let us be satisfied with good commissions and let the dividends come or not. Float a property. Then take up another and float that."

Somewhere in the floating, the stockholders alleged, $115,000 had floated away; the money had disappeared. "The letters showed Tustin and George were out to get their money and let the suckers look out for themselves," said T. E. Picotte, editor of the *Wood River Times*.

That comment caused Tustin and George to threaten libel charges against the paper. Picotte responded with further correspondence between George and Tustin and with statements from persons who believed the Vienna Consolidated had done them wrong. The suit was dropped.

By that time Tustin was no longer president. Stockholders booted him out and installed a fresh slate which made a stab at running the mine. The odds were too great, however. The venture dried up. One of the big troubles with mining in the Sawtooth-Vienna area was that the silver ore could not be reduced by common methods and special treatment was too expensive. There was a little profit in operating a top producer, but the costs were high. Transportation was no bargain either, in spite of road construction. Vienna and Sawtooth City were way off yonder. it took about as many dollars to sustain them as they produced.

One of the most interesting claims was that of a hermit — name unknown — who holed up near Sawtooth with two snakes and a bear dog. He discouraged visitors and came out only twice a year to buy groceries. He needed only a few store things as he lived largely on game and fish. Persons who got a fleeting glimpse of his hangout said the place was littered with corncob pipes and whisky bottles. Rumor had it he made a modest fortune from a silver mine behind his shack and then went to California. Whatever he got out of the ground, he didn't leave any ore. Persons who investigated after he had been missing for several months found only snakes.

Among Tustin's properties was the Senate group near Galena, a famous combination because of historic importance and output. It was in 1914 that Tustin took over the Senates, according to the *Wood River Times*. The paper said the mines were opened by prospectors from Yankee Fork in 1880, making them among the first, if not the very first, on the Wood River drainage. The Senates were sold to Colonel Green — an Idaho Indian fighter — for $30,000. He sold to the Moore Brothers of California. They built the first smelter in the district at the junction of Cherry Creek and Wood River two miles below Galena. The Moores spent an estimated $250,000 at the mine and smelter. But the ore didn't smelt. They closed the operation in 1885.

Any enthusiasm the Moores had for Idaho waned rapidly. One brother died after his wife divorced him. Another spent a fortune defending himself against a charge of killing a Chinese on one of Moore's ships. Arthur Moore was reputed to be the owner of Catalina Island — the whole thing, not just a home there. He was freed of the murder charge on grounds that the United States didn't have jurisdiction on the high seas where the Chinese was killed. In any case, Moore contended, the Chinese was attacking him and the deed was self-defense.

The Senate group was abandoned for several years. Eventually it was sold by the county for taxes in 1912 to Wesley B. George. A short time later Tustin took an option from George. The venture was one of several in their association as guiding spirits of the Vienna Consolidated.

Sawtooth City was the site of a culinary affair unique in the annals of cooking and the law. Facts of the case were first related to the outside world by the Reverend G. W. Grannis, a man of truth. He told the *Bellevue Sun* that Harry Giese, proprietor of the Sawtooth restaurant, had a dispute with a customer. It seems the diner on a summer day in 1882 ordered the house special that included codfish balls. He ate his dinner and asked for his bill. Giese noted that the codfish balls were still on the plate. "Eat them," he said. "They are good food. Food isn't easy to get in these parts." The customer declined. So the boss shot him in the leg.

The probate judge tried Giese immediately. The jury decided the proprietor was innocent. The verdict said a man has a right to force a customer to eat codfish balls if he knows they are on the menu and asks for them.

A bunch of the boys were whooping it up in a Vienna saloon in the summer of 1883. W. Kennedy, a carpenter, was doing his best to play pool. One way and another he had trouble. For one thing, several men were sitting on the table. He brushed off a few, but one obstinate miner insisted on staying where he was. Kennedy drew a pistol and fired. He missed the sitter but potted Pete Worth, and innocent bystander, in a fleshy portion of the lower anatomy. That broke up the party. Kennedy had plenty of room to play pool, but he didn't take another shot. He left the community in a hurry. Worth recovered.

Recreation took over as a major industry long before the auto made the Sawtooth Mountains a tourist attraction of the first magnitude. Miners found the fishing fantastic. They caught and speared salmon and trout by the barrel. They let the word get out, and before they could bar the door hundreds of outsiders swarmed to their streams. One fellow did a thriving business at Hailey in fresh and smoked fish from Sawtooth Valley. He sold tons. There was a roar about it, but by the time the lid was clamped down the damage was done. The "good old days" lasted only a few summers.

Scenery of an uncommon sort shared billing with eye-popping vistas of real mountains. In the fall of 1883, Captain T. R. Wills, superintendent of the Pocahontas Mine on East Fork of Wood River, rode over Galena and looked at a ridge of peaks. He said he watched a row of mountains rise up and fall back as though the tops had been blown off by a volcano. But there was no lava ash. He said the cataclysm seemed more like a gas explosion. He got away

from there as fast as possible. Names of the peaks that blew their
tops were not given. Their location was said to be between Galena
and Atlanta, or maybe a little to the north of the trail. That would
put them in the vicinity of the White Clouds. These mountains
have been reasonably quiet for geological eons, but they have been
the scene of ecological-industrial eruptions. The peaks are still
serene as ever, but a great deal of skin has been taken off miners
and environmentalists in their noisy brawling.

Economic conditions, plus the whims of mining men, were fatal
to Sawtooth City and Vienna, as they have been fatal to scores of
mining camps. While the crowds went howling on to bigger and
better fancies of the moment, the twin cities of the upper Salmon
quietly died.

There is a hush in the area now. It is considerably quieter than
it was July 4, 1884, at Vienna. Mike Rose fired a salute with dynamite. All six sticks went off prematurely, demolishing his cabin and
knocking him out for six hours.

Chapter 7

TRIPS TO YANKEE FORK

IN THE SPRING their fancy turned to notions of getting back to the mines. From Idaho City to Yankee Fork (where things were booming after the Indian scare of 1879) the lads with itchy feet and great expectations could hardly hold off until April.

They watched the snow fade from the peaks as they digested every weather report from occasional travelers in the sticks. As soon as the trail looked reasonable they hit for Bonanza City — more than 110 miles on foot.

These days of oiled roads and fancy cars there's nothing to it. You can go from Idaho City to Stanley in a couple of hours and on to Bonanza in another thirty minutes.

There was something to it in 1880. That was the year of the big stampede to Yankee Fork, a year of treacherous drifts in Deadman's Canyon, and the year a group of Idaho City businessmen made an epic trip through a cold and cruel country. A trip from Boise Basin to the promised land out yonder was an undertaking of high caliber. You couljn't just gas up a car and grab a shoebox of sandwiches. You had to be in good physical shape, have the right supplies, and be able to stand hardship.

You had to have time, too. A month or more. Maybe all summer, if things panned out.

The story of a party of six who took the plunge is preserved in the diary of E. W. ("Bert") Jones, editor of the *Idaho World*. He kept a log of the adventures of S. T. Davis, J. C. Fox, James McGee,

Frank McGee, Augustus Beck, and himself. They started as early as
they could in 1880. They had to hold back until May 4 when winter
let up a little, then they took off on foot. Eight miles above Idaho
City they put on snowshoes. Rain fell; going was slow. They
camped the first night at the Tatro cabin and made Banner next day
about 2 o'clock. From Banner they dropped down the Payette, hitting the river at Jordan Bridge and going upstream about nine
miles to camp. (There is still a dim trail from Banner to Jordan,
used for years by miners taking Saturday baths at Kirkham Hot
Springs.)

On the way up the Payette the party found Eight-Mile Creek
too high to cross. They felled a pine for a footlog. While they were
getting the hang of that, a bear came out of hibernation to investigate the racket. Sam Davis grabbed his rifle. He shot the bear in
the foot and went up a hill. The bear charged. Davis shot again,
and the dead bear fell over a cliff. They dragged it to camp and
feasted on bear for dinner and breakfast.

The narrative continues:

"Ran into snow again at Warm Springs Creek. Considerable difficulty. Took upper trail around cliffs hundreds of feet from the
river. Few inches of fresh snow over crust. Many slips. James
McGee fell fifteen feet, caught on a rock. Saturday went from camp
three miles above Warm Springs to Rock Creek, seven miles above
Cape Horn. Dinner at the mouth of Deadman's Canyon and started
up at 1 P.M. Snow soft. All felt uneasy ascending it. Several times
we could feel the snow settle and see cracks in it, but the only
thing to do was keep going.

"Once, the snow settled for hundreds of feet above us, and we
could hear snapping all the way up. As Mark Twain would say, we
were not scared but made for the summit as fast as possible. We
made the top, a distance of three miles, in two hours and fifteen
minutes.

"Sunday we took dinner at the Cape Horn House and went to
the foot of the summit. Monday we came into Bonanza, twenty
miles, arriving at 6:30 o'clock. The trip was pretty rough, yet all
stood it first rate. Sam Davis broke trail all the way and arrived
fully as well as the rest of us, if not better.

"We did not have one good day for traveling on the whole trip
of six days. It either snowed or rained every day. As dark as the
weather was, we all arrived snow-blind and going around blinking
like owls, although we used goggles and black cloth to protect our
optical organs.

"The crowd was a jolly one. All agreed, however, that should they ever return to Idaho City in the winter they would go via railroad and the Kelton stage."

James McGee and Sam Davis went back to Boise Basin in June after spending less than a month in Bonanza. Return travel was faster; they made it in four days. They saw many deer and mountain sheep on the Payette.

J. C. Fox stayed at Bonanza to start a sawmill. Bert Jones bought the *Yankee Fork Herald* from Mark Musgrove and published the weekly during its most thriving period.

The spring trip to Yankee Fork was fairly routine. It was nothing spectacular; many people did it. The particular journey stands out because it was recorded by an editor.

The Jones party was important to one Andy Guiness, a stranger on the trail from Yankee Fork to Banner in the middle of May. He got lost, ran out of food, and nearly lost his life. He finally stumbled onto the remains of the bear shot by the Jones gang. That saved him. He eventually staggered back to Banner. He said he was glad there was some traffic that spring but was disturbed that the back country was getting full of people.

Chapter 8

HUMBOLDT JOE

HUMBOLDT JOE was an early-day tourist in the Sawtooths. His role was not that of a gee-whiz-look-at-the-mountains visitor. he was a prospector, and he was killed by Indians at Cape Horn, a way station on the trail from Boise Basin to Yankee Fork. His death in the summer of 1878 attracted public attention to the area.

The most shocking thing about his finish, as far as miners and freighters were concerned, was that it happened almost under the noses of United States troops combing the back country in frustrated attempts to punish scattered remnants of Indian bands that started the Bannock War.

The woods on the periphery of the Sawtooths bristled with hostiles. Men obliged by their business to travel the wilderness from Idaho City to Bonanza did so in the chilling knowledge that odds were against safe arrival.

That frightful summer for what is today one of Idaho's most scenic sections began with the massacre on Payette River near modern Cascade of William Munday, Jacob Groseclose, and Tom Healey. They were ambushed while trying to recover some stolen horses. The Indians, retreating from a fight that fizzled in the Blue Mountains, sneaked east to the Middle Fork of the Payette, the fringes of Garden Valley, the Middle Fork of the Salmon, and the edge of the Sawtooths. Their destination was Fort Hall — and rations from the government they had lately fought. On the way they indulged in a blood-letting vacation.

Cavalry beat the brush to head them off. Troops rode here and there, following tips from mountaineers and ranchers. The army swooped on an occasional redskin. Frequently the troops arrived just in time to bury prospectors and follow a cold trail of Indian tracks up a blind alley.

Humboldt Joe was an innocent victim of circumstances. Out of touch with the world since coming to Idaho from Nevada, he and a partner chipped away at ledges, prospecting one gulch and another on the outskirts of the big strike that sent thousands of men to Loon Creek and Yankee Fork. He probably had no knowledge of the Bannock War. If he did know there was a fuss, he quite likely assumed it was far from his haunts. He went about his business as usual. Being part Indian himself, he had more to fear from troops than renegades.

The *Idaho World* at Idaho City relates that Joe and an associate were fired upon by eight or ten Indians. Joe was killed. His white associate escaped and spread the alarm at Bonanza City, where volunteers promptly organized under Amos Franklin. The posse buried Joe. A platoon of nineteen soldiers presently reached the scene. They scouted, found fresh Indian sign, and marched to Idaho City for supplies and further orders.

Meanwhile, W. A. Norton of Bonanza led another party on an independent tour of Indian suppression. Norton was a leading citizen. He had discovered and developed the Charles Dickens Mine, one of the famous properties of Yankee Fork. He brought back word that his small party had jumped seventy or eighty Indians in the Cape Horn district. The volunteers did not attack because they were hopelessly outnumbered. It was a job for the troops. And anyway, the volunteers said, how was it the army couldn't find the enemy? Could it be because the soldiers were down in Idaho City hunting beer?

The case of Humboldt Joe grew into a hot issue, not because Joe was such a much but because he was a symbol of what one very vocal faction seized upon as the fumbling futility of the army. Supporters of General O. O. Howard, campaign commander, shot back rebuttal to the effect that it was a big country, troops had to drop back to points of civilization for groceries while the Indians lived off the land, and things were really going as well as could be expected.

Miners at Atlanta did not wait for a decision on the debate. Ten

volunteers from the Bonaparte Mine and Riley's mill undertook to
end the menace. They rode to the headwaters of Boise River,
climbed the pass near Spangle Lake, and dropped a short distance
down to a lake in the Sawtooths on the Salmon drainage. They met
the enemy at dawn in traditional Indian-fighting style. All was calm
at the Indian camp. No bucks were on guard. No dog barked. The
miners crept over a ledge under cover of scrub timber. Then a
trigger-happy miner fired by accident. Indians popped up all over
the place.

It quickly turned out that the accidental shot saved the miners.
There were more than forty hostiles. If the volunteers had been
obliged to stand their ground they would have been whipped.
They fired a blast or two in retreat and withdrew to Atlanta with
considerably more respect for the actions of the army.

One unit of troops — a battalion by modern standards —
scoured the upper reaches of Lost River in the hope of meeting
Indians when they came out of the mountains. The force was up
the wrong fork when Jesse McCaleb's freight train toiled to the
canyon between Mackay and Challis. McCaleb was a Challis merchant, a native of Tennessee, and a member of the legislative as-
sembly from Lemhi County. A wagon train of goods in which he
was interested with Colonel George L. Shoup of Salmon was long
overdue from Blackfoot.

With six men, including Joe Rainey, a scout, McCaleb rode from
Challis to see what had happened. They met the train near the
present site of Mackay and camped for the night. Next morning
Indians attacked. The wagons were in an exposed position in a narrow canyon. In the first volley McCaleb was shot in the head. He
lived for a short time. The remaining thirteen men wheeled the
wagons into a formation that gave the most protection. The wagons
contained, among other things, 40,000 pounds of flour that afforded
some protection against bullets. The little group held off the Indians all day. There were no further casualties.

At midnight Rainey and William Trebour saddled their horses.
Leading the animals, they sneaked out of the ambush. Finding the
coast clear, they rode to Challis for help. Twenty-six men answered
their appeal. The relief party found no Indians. They had moved
on toward sanctuary at Fort Hall.

Citizens of Challis wrote a resolution of respect and regret in
which McCaleb was described as "highly honorable, a worthy and
useful citizen." A mountain near the scene of his death bears his
name.

Indian depredations continued through the summer and fall. A Chinese tottered into Placerville with a report that 200 had attacked Bonanza. Volunteers investigated. They discovered Bonanza unaware of its disaster. A few braves had been seen in isolated areas but there had been no violence.

George Washington Stilts, the former Boise blacksmith, had later moved to Hailey and, at the time of the Indian depredations of 1878, was a resident of Salmon. He brought in evidence of two Indians who had taken part in the McCaleb incident. He said they had been caught and made "good Indians." He had their scalps.

Back among the troops there was embarrassment. J. B. Foster, a correspondent for *The Statesman*, was the goat. While galloping in the vicinity of Copper Basin near headwaters of Lost River he spotted Indians. He reported to the commander and dashed back with the cavalry to what he expected to be a decisive battle. Before shooting began, a sergeant with field glasses put a cork in proceedings. "That's not Indians," he said. "It's Captain Wagner butchering beef." It subsequently developed there were no Indians within many miles.

The war in the Sawtooths and neighboring terrain sort of wore out. When cold weather came the Indians drifted back to Fort Hall. Troops pulled out of the mountains before snow added to their misery. The stalemate was no comfort to Humboldt Joe. That innocent bystander was in his grave at Cape Horn.

Chapter 9

BEAUTIFUL LAKE TAHOMA

ONE OF THE first persons to glorify the Sawtooths in print was Mrs. W. H. Broadhead, wife of Colonel Broadhead, a lawyer and mining executive. She lived for a time at Sawtooth City and later at Hailey. Her cultural background and enthusiasm for the remote country are evident in articles her observations inspired. The following essay was published by the *Salt Lake Tribune* in the spring of 1883 and reprinted in several Idaho papers:

"Nestled among the lofty peaks of the Rocky Mountains, away up in the Sawtooth range in Idaho, at an elevation of 8,000 feet above the sea level, lies beautiful Lake Tahoma. Beautiful lakes are no rare thing in these mountains, but amid them all it would be hard to find one presenting a more perfect picture of quiet beauty than this. Idaho means 'Gem of the Mountains,' and surely Lake Tahoma deserves to be called the Gem of Idaho. It is not large, being only about three miles long and one wide. On either side the mountains rise abruptly; on one to the height of 1,000 feet, thickly wooded from its summit down to the very edge of the water, with stately pine, spruce, and fir trees.

"On the other side is a narrow, level space as though nature had provided it expressly for the road that gives access to this fair spot. Beyond the road the mountain rises steep, rugged, and rough, 1,500 feet higher than the surface of the lake, a mass of bare granite crags, with only a few scattering clumps of trees here and there, presenting a wide contrast to the evergreeness of the woods on the opposite side. The woods extend around the lower end of the lake, and the slope there is more gradual. But one standing at the upper end and looking down the lake seems enclosed in a deep basin, the narrow outlet which carries its water to the Salmon River being invisible, while beyond rise the more distant peaks of Sawtooth, their sharp pinnacles softened and made indistinct by a purple

Baron Lake

haze, and still beyond rise two peaks of a loftier and more distant range, looking like towers of some gigantic castle.

"Dazzling white, they glisten in the sunlight like polished marble, and at sunset assume all the changing colors of an opal. They seem too beautiful and ethereal for this work-a-day world, and one fancies they belong to fairyland or is reminded of that city, 'the foundations of whose walls were garnished with all manner of precious stones.' No doubt a nearer view of these lovely peaks would look prosaic enough, but seen in the distance their sole purpose in the world seems to be to add the perfecting touch to the beautiful picture of the lake.

"At the upper end the ground is level and stretches away into a lovely valley, with its groves of trees and open, meadowlike spaces where grass grows luxuriantly and wild flowers in almost infinite variety live out their brief day, and through which runs a creek of clear, sparkling water, which feeds the lake. At this end, too, there is a beach of fine, white sand which extends into the lake in a gradual slope a few yards to where the water is eighteen to twenty feet deep and so clear you can see the pebbles on the bottom and the fish darting about as plainly as if they were in a glass globe.

"Then the bottom of the lake descends almost perpendicularly several hundred feet, from which point the water grows gradually deeper toward the middle of the lake. It is said that it has been sounded to the depth of 2,700 feet, but that story is not well authenticated. It has, however, been measured with a wire line 1,000 feet without finding bottom, and it has been estimated by surveyors that its greatest depth may correspond to the height of the highest peak in the vicinity, which is about 1,500 feet, though no accurate measurement has yet been attempted.

"A visit to this charming spot and two days' experience of camp life there are among the most pleasant recollections of a summer spent in the Rocky Mountains. At the time of our visit there were two rude bateaulike boats on the lake, which could be rigged with clumsy sails. But when we went out in one we preferred trusting to arm power rather than risk an upset which might prove not only unpleasant but dangerous, for the water, besides being very cold, possessed some peculiarity which makes it very difficult to keep afloat in it, or, as a man who has spent some time at the lake, and spoke from experience, expresses it: 'There is no substance to the water and a man can't swim easily.' The water, though so beautiful to the eye, is unpleasant to the taste, being very brackish as it contains 18 percent chloride. Within a few yards of it, however, is a large spring of pure, sweet water, so pleasant and refreshing that after drinking of it one longs to be thirsty again so as to enjoy another draught.

"The lake is full of fish of different kinds. It is often called Redfish Lake on account of the brilliant red fish that swarm in its waters. These red fish are one of the chief attractions of the lake and prove a source of unfailing delight to the numerous visitors who have already found their way to the delightful place. Their remarkable beauty charms the eye, their peculiar habits will repay close study and observation. Served hot for breakfast, no daintier fish could be desired.

"They are quite large, weighing from two and a half to four pounds. Their bodies are a bright red and the heads and fins a light brown. They look in the water like scarlet satin. The male has a decided hump on his back and a turned-up nose, while the female is perfectly straight. In the spawning season they run up the creeks that feed the lakes in vast numbers to the gravel beds in shallow water. An hour or two spent watching them is by no means lost time. They dart hither and thither in such a multitude that the water seems at times an almost solid mass of color. Sometimes two fish will take a fancy to the same spot of gravel, and then it is amusing to watch their maneuvers to get each other away; often it ends in a fierce fight.

"They must live on animalcule, for no food is ever found in their stomachs, nor are their digestive organs fitted for solid food. They will not take bait of any kind, and are speared and taken like salmon, to whom I suppose they must be some family relation. Soon after spawning the male and female both die. When the young fish are hatched they soon seek the deeper waters of the lake and there disappear, probably going to the deepest part, where they remain until nearly full grown, or about three years. At the end of that time they are seen early in the spring going down Lake Creek into the fresh water of Salmon River. After remaining there for about three months they return to the lake and make their way up to the spawning beds. It is then that they are seen in their perfection, and only then that they are fit for the table.

"This, one of nature's loveliest retreats, has been almost inaccessible until within a year or two, but now a good wagon road connects it with the towns of Sawtooth mining district and those of Wood River. The Oregon Short Line is now completed to Hailey on Wood River, only fifty miles from Lake Tahoma, bringing it within easy reach. Last summer large parties from different Wood

River towns visited the lake, taking tents and provisions and camping out. The owner of the land at the head of the lake has spent his summers for the past six years in his little cabin there, doing what he could to improve the place by cutting down the dead trees and clearing the underbrush, until now the lake is like a park.

"He loves the place and appreciates its beauties as only one can who has lived close to nature and studied her every phase. But lack of means has prevented him from improving it as he knows it needs to be. Some day there will no doubt be an ample hotel erected and accommodations provided for summer visitors. Already it is a favorite resort for those who know of its attractions, although they have to camp out while there, and that is not always pleasant or convenient.

"When the system of railways is completed that is bringing the mountain scenery of the Northwest within an easy journey, tourists and pleasure seekers will be surprised at the wealth of grand and glorious scenery still unexplored in our own land."

Chapter 10

LOST MINES

IS AAC SWIM lost a mine and his life on Salmon River. The mine has been sought for years in the vicinity of Robinson Bar. His body is also missing, although he was presumed drowned in the spring of 1882 when the skeleton of his mule was found in the river. Swim had staked a claim in the Bonanza District and recorded it at Challis.

Swim, a miner at Sawtooth City, returned to his home in Owyhee County with glowing reports of a rich strike. He went back to the Salmon the following spring, gave the slip to people following him, and disappeared. Many expeditions which geared their hunt to the point the drowned mule was discovered have looked in vain for the mine.

Lew Clawson, a watchman at Sunbeam Dam many years later, said a skeleton was found below Clayton at a bend called Dead Man's Hole. Some believe it was Swim. Ground in that vicinity has been combed thoroughly. The search has also extended up Warm Springs Creek. One theory is that the mine was beneath a waterfall. Men have tried to find it by following ouzels — water robins — as they dip and dart to nests under cataracts. Men who put some faith in this yarn have to swim as they look for the lost Swim Mine.

The lost Cleveland Mine takes its name from T. J. Cleveland, a tenderfoot cook with a party from Montana. He played pranks, such as putting rocks in the socks of his associates. Curious about a few of the rocks, experienced miners had them assayed. They proved to be worth about $40,000 a ton. But poor Cleveland couldn't remember where he had picked them up. He spent years hunting.

Another version of the discovery is that Cleveland was rounding up horses and picked up a lot of ore. When he got to camp the boss made him throw it away to lighten packs. He kept a few pieces in his pocket, had them tested at Boise, and went back to investigate a territory north of Clayton. He hired Tom Horton to pack him. They discovered dutch ovens and other utensils the party had buried at the mouth of Camas Creek. But the lost vein remained lost.

An unidentified prospector who went crazy in the mountains after finding and losing a bonanza is responsible for the name of the Lost Packer Mine in the Loon Creek area. Clarence Eddy, Idaho's prospector-poet, promoted claims of the district in glowing prose and verse. After an expedition in 1902, Eddy's party proclaimed a new Eldorado on Loon Creek. He said the ore was fabulous — gold in grains like wheat in "white quartz mingled with hematite of iron." Veins were ten feet wide. Eddy described it as the "greatest strike in Idaho." He said it was probably the Lost Packer. He named another of his claims the "Silver Messenger" for the Challis newspaper and gave the editor part of it. That didn't do his publicity any harm. However, he over-egged his pudding and was arrested at Salt Lake City on a charge of obtaining money under false pretenses. He was accused of selling 27,000 shares of the Cash Box Mining Company for $1,650. The stock was said to be worthless. Eddy argued that there was a misunderstanding. He made amends and continued his mining development.

He had an impact on the region, not only as a mine discoverer and exploiter but as a literary figure. Born on an Oregon farm and graduated from the University of Idaho, he became the Robert Service of the Sawtooths. His book of poems, *Pinnacle of Parnassas,* contains verses about Lizzie King, the star-crossed lady of Bonanza City, and other characters of old times.

Between mining expeditions he ran for probate judge at Challis. He was defeated. The campaign, however, spread an aura of honesty because of the office involved (and which there is no substantial evidence to doubt) and helped him sell the Lost Packer for $20,000, a sum Eddy said was only a fraction of its worth. The buyers were Jay Czizek and Ravenal McBeth of Idaho, and Joe Barnett and C. A. Mordson of Salt Lake City.

Photo by Ernie Day

Arrowhead, upper left, near Cramer Lake

Eddy sang praises of the Sawtooths in many newspapers and magazines. A portion of his article on Stanley Basin in *New West Magazine* for July 1916 says:

"Sublimely terrible mass of titanic crags and peaks — a solemn memorial of one of the earth's most awful cataclysms. Calm now and robed beneath with mighty forests they are solemnly beautiful — the Alps of Idaho, the Switzerland of the New World. Gold of the dusk and dawn makes glorious their summits. When the light of day has vanished from the valley and the robin chirps from the tree tops his last goodnight, a heavy crimson still hoods the higher crags, fading softly to the silver of the moon and stars.

"Then the great owls flit from their daylight haunts and go hooting down the wooded dells. The coyote sounds his last ghoulish cry from some hillside copse; and save for these and the voice of winds or cataracts, the night and silence reign supreme.

"The tremendous towering mist-wreathed summits of the Sawtooth Mountains look over from the southeast like animate sentinels of the supernal. The summers wax and wane in solitude and the winters waft on silent ermine wings, for civilization has never come to build there its habitations."

There is a lost mine or a tale about one for nearly every township in the district. The roster of rumors would fill a library, as it has filled many a hot-stove session. For instance there is the story of John Lowden, reported to have struck a vein on Loon Creek worth $2,000 per ton — uncommonly poor for the type that usually starts at $10,000. He was killed in a snowslide, and the mine was lost. Then there was John Taylor, a Chinese (that's right), who found rich ore in the same vicinity and was chased out by Indians. He could not find his claim when he went back.

Robbers took substantial chunks of mine shipments. They are said to have snatched a fortune from Joe Langona's mine near Muldoon in the 1880s. During the same period a treasure is alleged to have been taken from a stage at Bayhorse. A wagon in a shipment over Trail Creek upset near the summit. By the time teamsters got help from Ketchum, six silver ingots were missing. One theory is they were buried near Phi Kappa Creek — a stream, incidentally, believed to have been named by a college person as Phi Beta Kappa but put on the map by a member of Phi Kappa, social fraternity. The original mine was purchased some years later by Ravenal McBeth, member of the Idaho State Senate. There was also a sawmill on Phi Kappa Creek which supplied mine and bridge timbers.

Thin rumors say there was a modest treasure in a dutch oven at Thousand Springs (Chilly). The story is that it was buried by Billy Dougherty in 1885 when he shot and killed Harry Melrose in an argument over who was to cook dinner. More tangible treasures than buried pots are found in the area by fishermen — in the form of large trout.

Whether or not the Star of Hope Mine on the headwaters of Lost River opposite Muldoon has its chapter of theft is not known, but it was a mine of consequence in the 1880s and later. The mine has also provided the name of a nearby peak in the Pioneer range, which by a twist of the root is known as "Standhope." By whatever name, it is 11,700 feet high and a worthy neighbor of Mount Hyndman.

An article in the *Hailey Times* in July 1886 says the Star of Hope was owned by James Pinkham, Charles Ross, and others. The manager was James Hickey. The account says a crew of ten would be employed during the summer. The water supply came from a lake. "The ore is chiefly high-grade galena," the story relates. "Twenty-three tons at the Philadelphia smelter netted $3,000."

Of all the remarkable mines in the Sawtooths, the most unusual was probably the Barnyard between Vienna and Sawtooth City. The story goes that a prospector filed on it, had little success, and hit on the idea of growing gold. He plastered the vein with chemical concoctions laced with livestock manure. He said the dressing would grow a crop of gold once every seven years. He explained his alchemy to many miners who thought he was off his rocker. But at the end of seven years he showed up in Ketchum with a cleanup that made eyes bug. Neighbors insisted he took the ore from another claim, but he said it was from the gold farm. Everybody had a good laugh. They poked fun at the old coot until he sold his fertilized mine for a reported $30,000.

Chapter 11

SAWTOOTH JACK

TWO OF THE largest grizzlies ever taken in Idaho were from the Sawtooths. Both went to the world's fair at New Orleans in 1885, one as a nine-foot rug and the other on the hoof. Sawtooth Jack, very much alive and kicking, drew considerably more attention than the pelt, although the mounted specimen was uncommonly big even for Idaho, which had a slather of king-size bear.

Sawtooth Jack, also known as Idaho Jack, weighed 900 pounds. They knew his heft because they weighed him several times. He was sound in wind and limb, and mean as sin. He went to the world's fair because he was caught in a trap and became a profitable article for the trapper. Sawtooth Jack found himself in that fix because several bear had ripped into a supply of fresh beef at Muldoon, a mining town on the ridge between Wood River and Lost River. Muldoon was a long jump from Jack's home near Sawtooth City. The geographical connection was made by an angry butcher.

Dutch Schwartz had a contract to provide meat for miners. From time to time he collected a few steers in a corral. He killed and quartered on the premises, hanging the carcasses from open frames. Bear got in and chewed a lot of fine roasts. Some people contend bear are vegetarians; Schwartz was a hard man to convince. Not only did he see evidence one morning that bear eat beef; he saw it several times. Just to make it definite, he surprised several bear hauling off a hind quarter while another belted a steer in the head, knocking it dead against the corral.

Schwartz and company declared war on bear. They thinned out the species in the immediate vicinity and made things tough on bear all over the area. Schwartz, in particular, regarded the only good bear a dead bear. Therefore, when reports spread that a huge grizzly bear was on the prowl near Sawtooth City, he hustled over to take a hand in the action.

Nervous residents showed him astonishing bear tracks. They were big as home plate, with claw marks like king crab. Nothing short of a monster could have made them. And nothing short of a giant bear could have mangled so thoroughly the remains of a horse presently found in a thicket. Schwartz and other hunters left pieces of the horse where they were, hoping the bear would return for another meal. They waited at a reasonable distance. The bear did come back. He sniffed, suspected something unfriendly, snorted, and turned away. Quick shots missed.

Schwartz told his boys to quit firing, as he had a scheme cooking. It might be smart, he said, to catch the critter alive. He was impressed by the size of the grizzly. He had been to circuses and had a notion a beast of such proportions would be worth a lot more intact than skinned. Nonsense, said his companions, a live bear could bring a nice price all right, but how would they go about it? Something might get killed, and it wouldn't be the bear. Schwartz said they could leave that to him. He would get the bear out of their hair one way or another with a little help. If the trapping idea flopped, they could shoot the animal. In the long run it didn't make much difference. Sawtooth City and the butcher agreed.

First, they set conventional steel traps of the largest size they could find. The bear sprung them and cuffed them around the forest. Then Schwartz built a cage of heavy timbers. He propped the gate open with a stick attached to a chunk of horsemeat. After several days when nothing but magpies visited the trap, the bear took the bait. The door slammed down and he was a prisoner. Whether or not he could have bulled his way out had he been in top shape is a moot question. He was not at full throttle because the falling door broke a front paw.

The injury reduced his activity but increased his protest. He roared. Schwartz and company heard him long before they got to the trap. Cautiously approaching the site of the bellowing and groaning, the men determined the bear was reasonably secure. The logs remained firm. The door was tight. Mister Bear wasn't going anywhere.

The next problem was how to remove him without putting a dent in the population of Sawtooth City. Ropes? Wonderful chance for somebody. Somebody else, not me. Schwartz, always resourceful, solved the matter by fetching chloroform. He tied rags to a pole, poured anesthetic on the rags, and waved the mop under the bear's nose. The bruin went out like a light. The men tied him down and kept him unconscious while they fashioned a set of wheels for the trap. It was a heavy, cumbersome load. Hauling it out of the forest was made more difficult because horses objected violently to the cargo. Half a dozen men had to pull it to town.

A crowd gathered. Everybody wanted a look at old what's-his-name. Schwartz came up with "Sawtooth Jack," in recognition of the location and perhaps in anticipation of the money he expected to get from his prize. While Sawtooth Jack was still languid they weighed him. He tipped the beam at 900 pounds — a real giant. He had a head like a barrel, and his paws were about a foot across.

Encouraged by the interest created in Sawtooth City, Schwartz hauled his grizzly to Ketchum and Hailey, where, for a nominal fee, people could observe at close range. Sawtooth Jack, again alert and snarling (but favoring the sore paw), was kept in condition on a varied diet of vegetables and meat.

After a time business fell off along Wood River because nearly the entire population had seen Jack once or twice and because those who hadn't visited him had bear of their own hanging on walls or chewing their livestock. Then fortune smiled on Dutch Schwartz.

The world's fair in New Orleans was about to open. George L. Shoup of Salmon, later governor and U.S. senator, was Idaho's commissioner for the fair, and he heard about Sawtooth Jack. He was fairly well versed about bears, having killed a few in his time and having survived a bear encounter in which he was treed and barely escaped with his life. The colonel thought Sawtooth Jack would fit in nicely as part of Idaho's exhibit. Before making arrangements with Schwartz, however, he made sure the Gem State would have at least one bear by obtaining the pelt of a huge grizzly killed in the Sawtooths.

Having arranged for the pelt and a couple of freight cars of other treasures, Colonel Shoup offered to pay expenses and a little something more for the appearance of Sawtooth Jack. It sounded good to

Schwartz; he took his bear to New Orleans. All was well until Sawtooth Jack crabbed the deal. He was so ornery in Cajun country he frightened people, particularly the exposition management. The powers frowned. The cantankerous brute might cuff somebody into the Mississippi. They wanted no part of him.

Schwartz didn't give up. Having hauled his grizzly all that way, he figured to make the trip pay, no matter what the fair said. So he placed Sawtooth Jack in a carnival near the exhibition grounds where he could rip and snort without official permission or welcome. The big bear drew thousands of customers. Schwartz made a piece of change, and Sawtooth Jack got used to grits and gravy.

About the time the fair closed, Schwartz decided he didn't want to tote the bear back to Idaho, so he sold him to a carnival man for several hundred dollars. Schwartz returned to Wood River, bought a few cows, and went into the dairy business. What became of Sawtooth Jack is not known, although there were reports that a gigantic grizzly called Idaho Jack was an attraction billed by road shows in various cities. A ton of man-eating grizzly, they advertised him. That was twice as big as Sawtooth Jack, and, to the knowledge of men who knew his history best, he had never killed anyone. But, carnival guff being what it is, the bear was probably the horse-eater of Sawtooth City.

Bear lore is abundant in Idaho's past. Nearly every mining camp and mountain ranch has its share of fact and fiction. The Sawtooths and their neighbors seem to have been hip-deep in bear.

H. A. ("Grizzly") Johnson, a resident of the Sawtooths more than seventy years ago, is undoubtedly the mostest bear fighter in Idaho history. He killed only one that got into the record, but he did it in uncommon fashion. On a ride from Atlanta to Wood River he met a grizzly. He shot it several times, but the bullets did little except make the bear mad. The grizzly rose up and smacked Johnson like John L. Sullivan busting a croquet player.

The blow broke several ribs and knocked Johnson under a dead tree. The bear plowed in to finish the job. As luck would have it, there wasn't room in the opening for more than the bear's head. Johnson grabbed the bear by the throat, got his own head free of the bear's mouth at a loss of considerable scalp, and choked the grizzly to death. Then he caught his horse and rode many miles to medical aid. His face and body were scarred the rest of his life.

Then there was the Swede in the Hailey country at the turn of the century who fought a bear over a love letter. In a happy mood after getting a note from his girl in the old country, he started hiking back to camp. On the way he saw a cub. The little bear was playful; so was the Swede. They were getting along famously when the mother bear joined the party. She wasn't amused. She cuffed the cub up a tree and growled at the Swede, who adjourned up another tree. As he scrambled for a higher branch, the bear tore off his hip pocket.

Safely perched, the miner saw the mother bear pounce on something flitting along the ground. Roaring a battle cry, the Swede jumped down and clouted the bear on the head with a sledgehammer fist. The bear blinked in astonishment. She bared her teeth and squared away to attack. The Swede bared his teeth right back, went into a crouch, spit on his hands, and dared her to have at it.

At that point two miners arrived. "Look out," one yelled. "She's mad."

"Let her look out," said the Swede. "I'm mad, too. I'll tear her apart."

He kicked the bear. Apparently dismayed at the odds of three against one, the she-bear turned tail. "Coward," shouted the Swede. He turned angrily to his companions.

"What did you want to butt in for?" he steamed. "It was a fair fight. Now I lose. She ate my letter."

Among the hairy stories without which no repertoire is complete, is the one about the grizzly in the bunkhouse. It takes various forms and is repeated from time to time as the personal experience of a wide assortment of men in numerous parts of the country. One version that may be the original and genuine (or at least it has a claim to authenticity because it was published as solemn truth in a newspaper) has its setting on Lost River. The account appeared in 1885 in the *Houston Press*, a weekly journal in a town that is so long gone it isn't even a shadow of a ghost.

There was a sawmill on Alder Creek. Near the sawmill was a bunkhouse into which the hands tumbled nightly, bone tired. They slept soundly, paying no heed to snores. They were accustomed, also, to the occasional late arrival of sports who were robust enough to walk to town for an evening in the bright lights. If the midnight crawlers raised a rumpus, it was the habit of the sleepers to stop the nonsense by heaving a boot or threatening to decapitate the offender with a double-bitted ax.

One night, said the *Houston Press*, an Irishman named Smiley heard his bunkmate come lurching through the door and pile into bed, grunting and groaning something horrible. Smiley rolled over and smote the grunter in the face. Reactions were instant and astonishing. The noisy fellow was a grizzly bear. Up to the time of being hit on the nose, it was merely curious. The unfriendly reception aroused primitive instincts.

The bear roared and rose on its hind legs to lunge at Smiley. Fortunately for the logger, a sleeper in the upper bunk had already taken action. He threw off his blankets. The covers fell on the bear, leaving the grizzly churning and cussing like a badger in a pup tent. All hands climbed rafters while the excitement lasted. The bear beat off the bedclothes and departed. The tracks, of course, were said to be as big as a nail keg. The Irishman did not measure the tracks. He was making his own. The account says he didn't stop to see what happened in the bunkhouse. As soon as he discovered he had hit a bear in the snoot, he ran all the way to Houston in his blue flannel shirt.

About a year later, turning to another bear story, Jack McCrory of Pioneerville heard a ruction in his chicken house at 5 A.M. on a winter day. He dashed out in his nightclothes to discover a brown bear. McCrory looked for a firearm, found none, and returned to the pen with an ax. The bear backed into a corner. McCrory took a swipe. The blow opened a gash in the bear's shoulder.

That would have been a good time to adjourn, and McCrory tried to. But the bear was between him and the door, and the bear didn't want to call it quits. The farmer swung his ax with courage and strength. When neighbors arrived, they found a gory sight. The bear was dead and the man was bathed in blood. They had to lift the bear off to see whether McCrory was alive. He was. He came out of the fight with hardly a scratch.

The few available files of the *Yankee Fork Herald*, published at Bonanza City, tell of numerous bears roaming those precincts in 1879. They were more of a nuisance then a menace. Few human injuries are recorded. But the arrival of Chinook salmon in August was responsible for intense rivalry between bear and men. The fish came up the river in numbers considered great even in those years of tremendous spawning migrations. Then came the bear to feed on the salmon. Residents said they saw bear running down the hills to be first at choice fishing places. Then came the human beings. They did not deliberately advance on the areas where bear were busy, but they chanced onto bear congregations. Finding the bear unwilling to spook from their fish, the humans retreated to town. Bear were not to be trifled with.

Several were shot. That didn't solve the problem. It thinned out and scared off the bear momentarily, but another difficulty remained. There were so many dead and dying salmon lying around that the area was offensive to nostrils and health. So the remaining bear enjoyed a sort of immunity. When a dude blundered in and shot one, he got raked over the coals by an outraged community. Sewage disposal was in greater demand than tourists.

Colonel Shoup's encounter with a bear, mentioned earlier, happened in 1881 while he was counting cattle on Salmon River. He heard stomping in a thicket, so he tied his horse to a sapling and went in, thinking it was a calf or heifer. A sow grizzly and two cubs came out. They were in no distress whatever and made it plain to the colonel that he was not welcome. The old girl rushed Shoup. He didn't have a gun or a knife, and there weren't any handy trees. All he could do was shinny up a sapling alder.

It was so thin it began to bend when he was about six feet off the ground. The bear reached for him. Colonel Shoup nudged up another inch. He looked down to see if he was in the clear. His hat fell off. It scared the bear. She backed into the brush. The colonel climbed down. Back came the grizzly. Up went the colonel, this time into another alder a little bigger. The bear stood on her hind legs and reached. One of the colonel's gloves dropped. Again the bear bolted. Shoup waited a few minutes. The coast was clear. He jumped down, recovered his horse, and rode back to the ranch.

An ironic bear hunt resulted in the death of Thomas Gray, justice of the peace in Indian Valley, near Council. The judge knew bear were killing his pigs. A neighbor volunteered to sit up with him all night and watch for marauders. Toward morning the friend heard squealing in the sty and thumping in the brush. In uncertain light he pulled the trigger and shot Judge Gray in the thigh. The poor gentleman lingered fifteen months, refusing amputation of a leg. When the doctor did amputate as a last resort, the patient died.

Another unusual bit of bear business took place in the Vienna country during the 1880s. The *Hailey Times* said hunters surprised a bear, and vice versa. A hurried shot went wild. One man hastened up a tree, dropping his rifle. The bear picked it up and broke stock from barrel. In so doing, it pulled the trigger and shot itself dead.

During the same season a reporter at Sawtooth City said bear were too numerous. He said they were bothering freight teams and making things risky for fishermen. "All along the lakes and Salmon River," he wrote, "bears are seen by the dozen. They are fishing and floating on logs. They drag out big fish with their claws. There

Photo by Ernie Day

Aspen, fir, and pine

are trails a foot deep beaten by bears along the banks." So many bear were killed, he said, that the meat was very unpopular. It was the practice to save only the liver. Hides were pulled if the fur was prime.

A bear got the blame for at least one stage accident. The mail coach to Ketchum was near the summit of the old Galena grade when the bear jumped out of a thicket, spooking the horses. They scrambled, the harness busted, and the stage lurched into a tree, breaking a wheel. The driver and two Chinese were injured. The bear departed unscathed.

There was a bear hunt on the school grounds of Quartzburg in 1875. The *Idaho World* relates that Dave Bunch had just returned from a deer expedition when children dashed up to him chattering about a bear on the playground. Bunch knew kids, and he knew black dogs, so he laughed it off. The grin faded when he investigated and found a bear practically on the school porch. He shot it dead and shooed the youngsters back to their classes.

A Mr. Dempsey, keeper of the Minnehaha station on the Boise-Idaho City toll road, gave stage passengers an unscheduled bit of excitement when a bear came in for lunch. It padded into the dining room. Dogs chased it up a tree, and the proprietor dropped it in the yard. It wasn't a very big bear. Dempsey apologized for the size. He said there had been some bald-faced grizzlies around. One track he had measured was sixteen inches across. The passengers didn't wait around to see that one.

Jacob Tate of Slater Creek had an adventure the like of which keeps eyes popping around campfires. He met a family of bears. He fired and missed, and the lady bear put him up a pine. From his perch he killed her and the two cubs. He went back for a horse and returned to the scene. The horse, objecting to bear dead or alive, bucked him off and left him in the brush. He had to walk home, without a bear hide and minus some of his own.

Fred Scoville of Ketchum found more hunting than he could handle. While looking for deer near Galena about 1890 he said he was followed by a tribe of cougar. He hit one in the face with his lantern, and by the glow of that uproar counted thirty-two catamounts, "with some allowance for stumps."

C. H. Moore of North Fork killed an immense grizzly ten miles above Leadore in January 1914. If the estimate of 1,000 pounds was accurate, it may have been the Idaho champion, outscaling Sawtooth Jack. Scales were not at hand, however, so the weight is in doubt. Circumstances of the shooting make the incident worthy of mention, record or no record. Moore and B. C. d'Easum (the author's father, then teaching at Lemhi) were prowling the boondocks for whatever turned up. Bear were not expected, as it was hibernating season. They heard something in a cave, and, thinking it was a little brown bear snoring peacefully, they entered. It turned out to be a tremendous grizzly, not at all pleased to be disturbed. Moore shot it in self-defense. The half-ton weight was guessed by Mr. d'Easum. His figure deserves consideration for two reasons: The bear fell on him, and he later became an Episcopal priest.

Charles Norton, a noted miner of Loon Creek and Bonanza, suffered grievously from an encounter with a grizzly in 1888. His experience is on a par with that of Grizzly Johnson, related before. But he didn't get the bear; the bear nearly wiped him out. The grizzly broke his jaw, mauled him severely, and left him for dead. Miners found Norton several hours later. They carried him on a litter thirty-five miles to Custer and called a doctor from Challis. Surgeons removed most of his jaw. He lived ten years by being fed through a tube.

Cougar stories chill the blood. Whether the big cats are more dangerous than bear is a subject for heated debate. Many natural scientists insist that cougar do not attack people. On the other hand there are numerous reports of the lions jumping on children and adults. Take, for instance, the matter of Charley Bannister and "Indian Jake" Woods. Their cougar fight is related in the *Emmett Index* in March 1897.

The two men and Frank Bannister were building a wagon road up Big Willow Creek. Frank knocked off early one morning to cook dinner. Jake and Charley followed at noon. As they rounded a bank, a cougar leaped on Indian Jake's shoulders. Charley picked up a rock and knocked the cougar to the ground, breaking one of its front legs. The lion was far from disabled. It attacked Charley while Jake assessed the damage to his back. He wasn't hurt badly, just scratched. Then it was Jake's turn to get in a lick. He bounced a boulder off the tangle of man and beast on the ground. Happily, he hit the cougar rather than Charley. The blow fractured the cat's skull.

Having conquered the enemy, they went to lunch, leaving the cougar until morning when they had time to skin it. Next day they found tracks of a larger cougar at the spot. The big cougar had eaten a good deal of his brother and had ripped the hide to shreds. The deed was contrary to common belief that cougar will stand guard over a fallen comrade. Scarcity of game may have been the reason. Whatever the circumstances, there was clear evidence that one cougar had dined on the other. Jake and Charley guessed that one or both of them would have been on the menu if the fight had not turned out as it did. They had no faith whatever in the theory that cougar don't stalk and attack men.

Similar views were expressed by such professional cougar hunters as "Cougar Dave" Lewis and George Lowe, who killed several hundred each. They had close calls several times and told of instances in which cougar jumped from ledges onto pedestrians. It was not a matter of mistaking men for deer. Cougar can smell and see better than that. They did concede, though, that given a way out the average cougar will evaporate into the forest rather than mix with men. The injured cougar is the dangerous type. Even so, a man in the mountains does not have much opportunity to determine the physical fitness of a catamount staring him in the face. He is thinking of other things than cougar arthritis.

Biggest kill of cougar — a shocking slaughter then and more deplorable now — was claimed by "Woodtick" Williams of Dixie, Idaho County. Without endangering himself he put the kibosh on fifty-three in one swoop. He did it in the spring of '93 and told the *Free Press* at Grangeville how it happened.

An avalanche near Dixie Diggings set the stage. Snow thundered down the slope, tearing out trees and leaving a naked scar. Woodtick heard the avalanche. He hurried over next day to see the wreckage. At the base of the slide he counted twenty-eight lions "walking around and grinning hideously." His revolver scattered them. Getting closer, Woodtick noticed holes in the snow where the cats had been digging. In one he found the hind leg of a moose. He scratched around and found whole carcasses. In all, he found seventeen dead moose.

Woodtick returned with a group of miners. They seasoned tons of moose meat with strychnine. Results were appalling, even to thick-skinned mountaineers. The harvest was fifty-three cougar, twenty-four lynx, thirteen black wolves, twenty-six wolverines, eighteen fishers, sixty-nine marten, nine gray wolves and smaller animals too numerous to count.

Woodtick said he figured the moose had congregated where they could browse. The avalanche hit them, and predators moved in. Men happened on the predators at the hour of concentration. It was a black day for animals and men.

Cougar are far less numerous than they used to be, not because of tragedies like the Dixie massacre but because their habitat has been reduced. As for bear, authorities say there are probably no grizzlies left in the Sawtooths, and very few, if any, elsewhere in Idaho. However, there are brown bear of several shades. They stay mostly in remote haunts far from highways and motorbikes. They eat berries, fish, frogs, and vegetation. Seldom do they pick fights with people. All the same, citizens who tread the path of common sense advise that it is wise to avoid them. If you do get in a bear fight, don't try to knock their teeth out with your head.

Luck might not be as good as it was for John ("Johnny Behind the Bear") Novak, a Bohemian with a grave marker near Atlanta. He disappeared on a prospecting trip. A year later a friend found his knife and a scattering of bones. He buried the remains and fashioned a rustic cross inscribed: "Sacred to the memory of Bohemian John, killed by a bear, 1893."

The following summer the friend was startled to see a familiar figure at Mountain Home. "You look like John Novak," he said.

"I am," the man replied.

"But you're dead. I buried you."

"News to me," said Novak.

"A bear got you," the friend insisted. "I could tell you had a fight with a bear."

"Right," said Novak. "I killed the bear."

The two men went to the grave where Novak happily read the marker, an experience few men are afforded. He explained the error. He had tackled a bear, he said. They went round and round. The bear bit his head, but he managed to kill it and take the hide. In the process he lost his knife. Then he rambled on, finally going to California without bothering to tell Idaho associates. Now he was back, quite surprised to find he was dead.

Chapter 12

SAMSON

SAMSON was undoubtedly the biggest animal shot in Idaho. He was an elephant. Idaho is not the natural habitat of such fauna but it was fitting that a creature of that stature should have been the star of an unscheduled rampage in the Sawtooths, a land of wonder and amazement.

Samson did his thing and people did things to Samson in early August 1884 at Hailey. It was a scorching day when the Cole Circus train arrived. Many spectators in the crowd had never seen a circus. Those who had were eager to repeat a rare experience. The town was crowded.

Lions, tigers, acrobats, clowns, monkeys, and dancing girls paraded the street. They performed well in the big tent. After the show the "most extraordinary collection of ferocious phenomena ever assembled on the face of the globe" adjourned to the railway siding for refreshment before the evening extravaganza.

The extravaganza broke out early. Samson was hot and thirsty. Chained in a clearing near his boxcar, he heard and smelled the cooling gurgle of Wood River. He trumpeted, lunged against his shackles, and was suddenly free. He rambled for the river.

Frightened citizens mistook his intentions; they thought he was on a mission of massacre. Their feeling can be understood. When several tons of hulking flesh lurches in your direction you do not wait for a bill of particulars. Men shouted. Women screamed. Kids hit for the brush. Chaos reigned.

Confused by the racket and cut off from the river by retreating hordes, Samson struck off for a grove of trees in Quigley Gulch. He had the right of way; nobody challenged his lane. Residents of Wood River were not about to tackle a loose elephant.

Circus employees rushed into action. They knew what to do. They went about it as fast as they could, having more trouble holding off a few daring civilians who volunteered as animal experts than they did with their job. They said Samson would be all right and to stay the hell away from him. In spite of that advice, certain gents grabbed guns and stalked the pachyderm.

Samson continued his ramble. Apparently upset by the uproar of strange voices, he paid little attention to his trainer. When he turned toward a clutch of horrified witnesses, somebody started shooting. Six or seven bullets thudded into his body. Samson retreated to the railway spur. He tried to climb a pile of ties. The pile collapsed and he sprawled in the cinders alongside the tracks. Circus people darted in with ropes and chains. A crowbar was shoved into his mouth, and he was soon secure once more. After a drink and a rest he was his usual jovial self. The bullets didn't seem to bother him. They were from light caliber rifles, mere beestings. The circus gave him several days off. He then resumed his routine.

The Sawtooth elephant hunt happily produced no trophy. It did leave a memorable mark in the big game accounts that flowed from the area. The survival of Samson left for Lewiston the distinction of bagging the only elephant known to have been killed in Idaho. That happened in the 1920s when a circus elephant went berserk. The mayor was obliged to dispatch it for public safety.

Regardless of how large or how terrifying Samson may have been at the time of his Hailey adventure, the ingredients were meager compared with stories that cropped up later. A magazine article published in 1920 said Samson was bigger than Jumbo, king elephant of Barnum's Circus. The article was purportedly from the pen of George Conklin, who was Samson's trainer during the Hailey episode. He said Samson upset the lion cage, knocked over four horses, and attacked Conklin, who jabbed him with a pitchfork. Then Samson tossed twelve cages all over the menagerie. Conklin recalled that he took off after Samson on a horse, firing a shotgun. He shot Samson in the trunk but the pellets "had no more effect than raindrops." Cowboys punctured him with rifle shots, inflicting minor flesh wounds.

The account goes on to say that Conklin, wearing shorts and a leopard skin, led Samson into a V-trap. Samson rammed an ore car, knocked himself groggy, and was tied up in a tent.

Conklin said he fed Samson by hand for a week. The trunk was very sore, but Samson caused no trouble. A couple of dogs were trained to watch him.

The article says Samson died in a fire at Bridgeport, Connecticut. His bones were collected and mounted in the American Museum of Natural History in New York City.

Chapter 13

CHILL AT ATLANTA

FOR A TOWN with a peach-picking name, Atlanta shivered through more than a fair share of miserable winters. The history of the mining camp at the head of Boise River's Middle Fork blows blue with cold. Storms that brewed in the Sawtooths whistled down the parapets of Mount Greylock, kept miners humping to cut enough stove wood, and piled deep drifts along roads to the outside world.

Although Idaho newspapers in business during Atlanta's best years contain many glowing accounts of rich mining operations and richer discoveries "just around the corner," much of the news was concerned with wicked weather. From the beginning, winters were tough. Blizzards moaned across Pleasant Valley. Below-zero temperatures clutched at hands, faces, and feet. Travelers to and from the nearest communities suffered frostbite, amputation, and death. The rigors were on a par with, and perhaps worse than, the onslaughts of refrigeration in Sawtooth Valley on the Salmon side of the jagged mountains.

Precisely how cold it was at Atlanta or Stanley in those years more than a century ago or how deep were the avalanches that smothered the passes is not known because official weather instruments were not in vogue. Residents knew it was plenty cold, maybe twenty or thirty below zero, and they knew there was a heap of snow when the mail carrier didn't arrive.

Olive Groefsema's *Elmore County, Its Historical Gleanings* quotes Fred Davis, who was born in Atlanta in 1877, as recalling seven feet of snow in Atlanta and twelve feet at Rocky Bar. Some winters, though, he said, snow was only four feet deep at Atlanta and the temperature didn't get colder than twelve below. That was a heat wave.

Bald Mountain was a particularly mean spot on the trail between Atlanta and Rocky Bar. Several tragedies of bitter memory in Atlanta's story occurred there. In the summer the trail wasn't an interstate, and in winter it was a fright. "Atlanta and Rocky Bar are connected by a wagon road," a correspondent wrote in *The Statesman* in the fall of 1876, "but the grades are of the steepest and hardly practicable for loaded teams." The paragraph went on to say that heavy equipment for the Buffalo Mine at Atlanta had been on the road nine days and had not yet covered eighteen miles. The summit was described as at least 8,000 feet, and the pitches on either side were quite difficult. And that was in the fair weather of Indian summer. In winter wagon traffic stopped. Men went by snowshoe over a dim trail. Women — with certain exceptions — stayed home.

One breed of man that had to tackle the elements, come snow or black of night, was the mail carrier. He hired out for tough, and he had to be. The Atlanta-Rocky Bar route was served by many stout mail carriers. There were numerous carriers through the years because the mortality rate was high. At least half a dozen, and probably more, perished on the trail. If they had been buried were they fell, the vicinity of Bald Mountain would be dotted with monuments.

Otto Meyer shouldered his load of letters on a January morning in 1885 and set out from Atlanta in glowering weather. He never reached Rocky Bar; he was buried in a slide. Bruno Hicks was crushed to death in a slide on Bald Mountain. Rufus Lester was killed by an avalanche on Boiler Grade. George McKinney froze to death carrying the Christmas mail in 1907. Several others, including residents on both sides of the pass, lost their lives in the line of duty.

Judge Heath of Atlanta was a victim of the cold, although he was not a carrier of the public mails; he was a lawyer. In the winter of 1899 he tried to get back to Atlanta from Rocky Bar where he had been conducting business. The *Ketchum Keystone* related what happened. "Judge Heath," the article said, "had his hands and feet frozen in undertaking to make the trip from Rocky Bar to Atlanta on snowshoes. He has been obliged to undergo amputation of four fingers of his right hand, and it is thought it may be necessary to take off the thumb, causing the old man to be a cripple for life."

One mail carrier who did survive season after season of the ordeal on Bald Mountain was Will Tate. He had some narrow escapes, but he came out whole. Tate played a role in the saga of "Peg-Leg Annie," an episode that has become a throbbing drama in Idaho history and which has been related recently with competence by Betty Penson of *The Statesman*. The Penson treatment is thorough and accurate. It is more reliable, for various reasons, than the first public report printed in Boise in May 1896.

"A sad case is reported from Elmore County," the first article in *The Statesman* said. "A woman named Hoffman lost her life through becoming exhausted while attempting to cross from Atlanta to Rocky Bar. Mrs. Thomas Morrow and the woman who succumbed undertook to make the trip on snowshoes. The mail carrier took them near the summit of Bald Mountain. They seemed to have lost their way and were much fatigued. There was a cabin nearby. The mail carrier installed them there for the night. He built a fire and gave them something to eat.

"They seemed comfortably situated and expected to get through to the Bar next day without trouble. He did not hear of their arrival, however, and on his return trip stopped at the cabin. He was astonished to find that the Hoffman woman had died during the night, apparently from exhaustion following the walk through the snow."

Amendments to the original story were printed several days later when more facts came to light. The second and more reliable account said that Anna Morrow and Emma Soaper (not Hoffman) started from Atlanta on May 15. They were caught in a storm and wandered from Friday afternoon until Sunday evening in the howling wilderness. Emma Soaper died of exhaustion. Anna Morrow wandered on in a stupor. She thought she saw a party of men in a gorge at the head of Black Warrior. She rushed to them. It was a mirage. Anna went back to the body of her companion and dragged it about a mile in an attempt to reach a habitation. She didn't know what she was doing.

Will Tate came upon her by accident as he neared the summit with his mail sacks. Anna was barely alive. Tate carried her to the summit cabin. He made her as comfortable as possible, gave her all the food he carried, and went on to Atlanta for help. A crew of willing, big-hearted men swarmed up the hill immediately. They wrapped Anna in blankets and carried her in relays to Atlanta. On

the way she mumbled please to "go after Emma." She said something to suggest, as best they could make out, that a frozen woman
was standing against a tree. Until the rescue crew had Anna under
the best available care in Atlanta, the matter of the missing woman
was not pursued. When investigation proved that there was really a
missing companion, they searched the hills and found the body of
Emma Soaper next day. (The real name is said to be Emma Von
Losh. "Soapy Emma" is a nickname.)

Anna Morrow survived. Both feet were frozen and had to be
amputated. Peg-Leg Annie became a favorite of the mining district
as a symbol of courage and victory over hardship. For many years
everyone in Atlanta and Rocky Bar knew Annie. She set up a business. Miners, lawyers, merchants and politicians stopped in for the
uplift of Annie's cheer. In her later years she moved to Boise,
where she died in 1933.

Many people walked from Atlanta to Sawtooth City, Vienna,
and Ketchum. They took the trail up Mattingly Creek and over the
divide. It was a pack trail used mostly by horses and mules, but
when a man didn't have a horse, or in winter when snowshoe traffic was the only way to go, people hoofed it. Stout fellows made the
trip to Ketchum — about seventy-five miles — in two days. The
average was three. If luck was bad it took longer. One man who
nearly didn't make it was a chap named Murphy who left Buffalo
Hump in northern Idaho for what seemed to be better prospects at
Atlanta. He walked from Buffalo Hump via Idaho City to Atlanta, a
distance of around two hundred miles. He worked a few days for
the Monarch Mine, then heard about a job at Ketchum and headed
out again. At the top of the ridge above Sawtooth City he got lost in
a snowstorm. Striking out for the Salmon River, which he knew was
somewhere below him, he missed all the mining camps and everything else except the river — he managed to fall in. A mail carrier
hauled him out in the nick of time. He rested a couple of days at
Pierson and went on to Ketchum. All in the day's routine.

Snowslides were a terror to the mail route between Ketchum
and Stanley. What was true in early days has continued into modern times. Slides are still a hazard, although the road over Galena is
much improved. Hardly a winter went by in old times without a
disaster.

David Williams, a mail carrier for several years, had several
near-misses. Early in January of 1914 he was caught between the
town of Galena and the summit while carrying mail from Ketchum

to Pierson and Stanley. There were five slides in twenty minutes; he couldn't go forward or retreat. Williams was reported missing. The Ketchum paper said he might have been buried in a huge slide. Three days later he appeared at Pierson. He said his horses had been buried up to their ears, but he got them out safely. Putting the mail on his back, he had snowshoed to Pierson. After a night's rest he went on to Stanley.

Williams was among the first ranchers in Sawtooth Valley. He operated a spread near what was later the Rocky Mountain Club. His brother, Tom, lived in a cabin a short distance away. Dave died in 1950 and is buried at Stanley. Members of his family still have property near Obsidian. Dave and Tom and one or two of Dave's sons were packers and guides for many years. They took people into the Sawtooths and up some of the peaks on scaling expeditions. Dave is credited with one of the first modern ascents of Mount Heyburn. (Never mind the Indians of ancient days and where they may have wandered.) His route has become standard. Similarly, trails picked by Tom on other peaks have since been accepted as best. Tom died in 1940 at Mackay. Mrs. Dave (Carrie) Williams was still living in Challis in 1977.

Travel in the Atlanta vicinity was quicker and more comfortable in later years than in the time of Peg-Leg Annie. A road was built down the Middle Fork to Boise. Even that route had its moments. As recently as 1944, Archie Smethurst, the late veteran stage driver, experienced one of his most difficult trips. He had a lot of experience, first with horses to Boise Basin and later in cars to various remote points.

Normally his stage run to Atlanta was one day for the round trip; sometimes he took two. The nasty one took five. There were slides all the way above Arrowrock Dam. Slides came in behind him as well as ahead of him. Dig, dig, dig; travel half a mile; dig again. A snowplow helped out a little; then the plow got stuck. Smethurst pulled his car to the protection of an overhanging rock and spent the night. Daylight came and he saw that new slides had narrowly missed his refuge. With the help of a repaired plow, Archie struggled to Atlanta next evening. It took three more days to get back.

Three passengers bound for Atlanta came through the ordeal nicely. One was a woman just out of the hospital. "We made out pretty good," Smethurst said. "Our freight was mostly beer and bread. But it was pretty cold."

Cold was the rule for Atlanta's winters and for winters in most parts of the Sawtooths. It is still cold up there, and the snow piles deep. As far as Atlanta is concerned, there was a bit of a thaw in March of 1908. That was the time the Atlanta Hotel and George Butler's general store burned. Warmed things up for a spell.

Chapter 14

DOC DURHAM

Dr. J. I. Durham was a medicine man. Sort of. He had a certificate of credentials in the healing arts and a personality that could charm warts off a frog. Kickapoo juice was his main weapon in attacking pain of toes, teeth, headbone and intermediate organs. He did quite well in subduing afflictions of the flesh and fattening his wallet until he caught a case of personal matrimonial trouble, against which nothing afforded relief but a sudden and massive application of distance.

Young Doc Durham set up his Kickapoo Sagua Remedy Company in Hailey during the fall of 1894 with drumbeats and banjo blasts. The mining community hadn't seen anything like it before, and it poured out its dollars as rapidly as he could pour his bottled potions.

Taking a stand on a portable platform in front of a tent flying the banner of his business, the fluent practitioner told the public what he was going to do. He was going to provide, in handy pocket-size flasks, a positive antidote for a multitude of ailments ranging from falling hair to flat feet. Furthermore, because of certain ingredients in his elixir — the recipe of which was a secret given to him by an Indian chief in Ohio — the miraculous juice also eased mange and glanders of horses, latent rabies in dogs, and cholera of hogs. Therefore, in case a hearer of the Kickapoo message was himself in robust health, he could do a good deed for domestic animals by investing in a jug or two.

A couple of Indian boys and two Negro lads sang songs, beat stringed instruments, and cracked jokes to gather a crowd while Doc Durham busied himself in the tent. As he clinked bottles and stirred things in a kettle, he cooed praise of the mixture he was compounding, proclaiming this particular batch the best he had ever made — just the right amount of this and that to work wonders. At the appropriate moment, when the minstrels were riding high and curiosity about the activities behind the curtain was at maximum pitch, Doc Durham took the stand. Thumb in vest, black derby on his head, a reassuring smile on his face, and a brass-knobbed cane under his arm, he launched a spiel that made women sob and caused men to step forward with open purses. Gallons of Kickapoo juice, a pint at a time, were grabbed by eager customers. At one dollar a bottle, the transaction was handsome.

On occasions when trade was slow, Doc Durham trotted out a stock of electric belts, guaranteed to stimulate, soothe, reduce weight, and enhance charm. All these attributes, the proprietor made clear, were merely additional gifts for the wise who had already toned their systems with generous dollops of the original and genuine juice.

If electric belts happened to be selling slowly, the doctor sent his Indians and Negroes into the multitude with booklets about the medicine and the show. At four bits each, they added substantially to the profit.

Response was vigorous. Not only did many customers find benefit in gulping Kickapoo juice — based on alcohol, with enough flavor and coloring to make it taste like medicine — but scores of men and women discovered physical miseries they eagerly offered to the doctor's care. Therefore Doc Durham abandoned the medicine show with its carnival atmosphere and devoted his time to the practice of internal diagnosis, surgery, and healing of broken bones. To give his patients full service at a sort of medical supermarket, he also dabbled in dentistry, pulling teeth right and left and filling the gaps with homemade dentures.

Astute in the art of public relations, he rented quarters above the *Wood River Times*, a Hailey newspaper. With Editor T. E. Picotte as his landlord and trumpet, he needed no minstrels.

For several years the *Times* bugled his triumphs. By fortunate coincidence his customers displayed uncommon knack in writing glowing tributes. An old codger happily declared he had suffered neuralgia for twenty-seven years. Doc Durham yanked a batch of molars. "I tell you I've had a good time since," the patient said.

Photo by Idaho Dept. of Tourism and Industrial Development
Hikers at Alice Lake

Another gent volunteered that he had been unable to hear or smell for quite a spell. Dr. Durham probed and tinkered. "Right away," the gentleman said, "I heard a bird, and this morning I smelled manure."

A plug from a veteran of the Indian War of '77 boosted the doctor's skills among gimpy soldiers. The old scout said he had been plagued for upwards of seventeen years with bullet wounds in the knee and shoulder. The account in the *Times* went on to relate that Doc Durham found he had a false marrow and treated it with a one-dollar prescription. A couple of weeks after the first dose he felt like a new man and regained the use of his game leg.

The newspaper, in one of a series of articles deemed worthy as news, also announced that the young doctor had effected a remarkable cure on a woman. "She suffered from a gluteal abscess of the posterior part of the os vomita which exerted pressure on the sciatic nerve in the fossa of the ilium." No problem. Having found how to spell it and locate it somewhere, Dr. Durham soon had the fossa on friendly terms with the ilium. The patient was around and about, fully capable of several paragraphs of fluent prose.

By draining a pocket behind the ear of another patient, the doc cured hemorrhage of the lungs and paralysis of the left side. His surgical specialty was in the vicinity of the mastoid. He performed at least seventeen such operations. The average took about eleven minutes, according to the stopwatch of a reporter who witnessed the handiwork. All were successful. If Doc Durham had any failures, they were not publicized. He went through his Hailey career undefeated in application of potions or use of the knife.

Doc Durham was by no means an office-bound doctor. He gave generously of his time and energy in making house calls. In fact, after he became established he was hard to find in his headquarters. When he was on deck in Hailey, he met most of his patients between 7:00 and 11:00 at night. Often for days on end he rode the woods and prairie, calling on isolated sufferers. He tended people at Soldier, Ketchum, Bellevue, and Galena. He made occasional visits to Muldoon and Carey. He expressed willingness to toss his black bag into his buggy and venture to Vienna but was not called to that outpost because Vienna was almost a ghost camp at the time.

"Rattlesnake Jack" was one of his most noted patients, not excepting the lady with a hangup in the fossa. Rattlesnake Jack (John L. Kline) was a cowboy of the Diamond Ranch, Three Creek, Owyhee County. He was kicked by a horse so far back in the mountains, he said, that it took him three days to get to a railroad. He said it was 180 miles and he crawled most of the way. That is a long crawl, with or without a broken leg.

On the advice of friends who had heard of the Hailey genius, Rattlesnake Jack went on to Wood River, this time by train because he had had enough crawling. Doc Durham took charge. In no time at all he had Jack as chipper as a jaybird.

Even more chipper was Doc Durham's department of public relations. Large headlines screamed that Rattlesnake Jack was the champion snake catcher of Wyoming, Colorado, and probably the whole world. He had earned the reputation while riding the range in a couple of states before taking a job in Idaho. He had caught dozens of rattlers with his bare right hand. He ran them down on horseback, scooped them with a lightning sweep of a naked paw, toted them alive in a saddlebag, and sold them to a medical firm. Some of their venom and other ingredients quite likely found their way into Doc Durham's Kickapoo juice. The coincidence was extraordinary. The connection was not something to be kept under a bushel, and Doc Durham's publicity agent did not.

Rattlesnake Jack's leg was hardly in a walking cast before the word got out. Jack elaborated sufficiently to keep his name public. He said, or was quoted as saying, that the biggest rattler he ever caught was six feet long, weighed six pounds, and had sixteen rattles. It may have had more, but out of respect for truth he said several had probably popped off when he whirled the reptile. He didn't want to claim things he did not know to be accurate.

Jack's services were in demand. It became fashionable to have the skin or rattles of a snake killed by the famous hunter. Live specimens snatched from their habitat at the courageous pounce of the celebrated character commanded princely sums. Jay Gould, a railroad and mining magnate who visited Wood River several times, offered Rattlesnake Jack ten dollars for a big one. Or maybe it was ten dollars a foot; stories differed. Jack caught a whopper but couldn't get it on his horse. He was still a little handicapped in spite of what he called the excellent treatment by Doc Durham — a matter he emphasized in each chapter of his adventures. He had to kill the snake or be thrown by the horse. Rather than chance another broken leg, no matter how easily Doc Durham might mend it, he choked the serpent to death. Jay Gould did not want a dead snake, so the deal fell through.

With the nation's press still panting for more stories about the robust snake charmer and the medical man who lifted him from obscurity, Rattlesnake Jack bowed out. Doc Durham timed his departure with unfailing psychology. He squeezed the last ounce of notoriety from the episode.

"Jack is not quite cured yet," he said, "but he has to get back to carry the mail to the head of the Bruneau." Without going into details that might not have stood much stirring, the sign-off statement inferred that Jack was not only a great killer of vipers but a rural postman. The sacks of letters and catalogs had apparently been piling up for about a month. It was time he resumed his appointed rounds, undismayed by gloom of night or wicked fangs. Thanks to the ministrations of Doc Durham, his broken leg was stout enough to stand the gaff. Duty called. Doc Durham would not stand in the way.

Orthodox physicians did stand in the way of Durham's continued success. The hubbub over the medicine man grated on doctors who had earned their degrees by years of professional training and who maintained dignified ethics. The brass band of their noisy brother offended them in pride and purse. They took action to calm the uproar and subdue the upstart.

A charge was filed against the Kickapoo cutup on grounds that he was practicing medicine without a license. At the trial in Bellevue, Doc Durham produced a certificate of proficiency from the American Eclectic Medical College of Cincinnati. He satisfied the court he had filed it in Bear Lake County when he entered the state. How the certificate gave him qualifications in the realm of snake medicine, minstrels, electric belts, and homemade liniment was not specified. What the court deemed adequate was that he had a diploma, whether he bought it by mail or earned it in residence. The charge was dismissed.

Not satisfied with legal vindication, Doc Durham retaliated against his chief tormentor. Citing his record in healing numerous patients and relying on support of the Durham division that sung his praises regardless of professional background, he sued Dr. N. J. Brown, a regularly constituted physician and surgeon, for a thousand dollars in damages. He said his status was wounded. The district judge — not one of his patients, by the way — heard the evidence and awarded him nothing. That left the legal score tied, zero to zero.

Still exercising his forensic and other skills, Doc Durham resumed activities with forceps and knife. He also launched into matrimony. The wedding, according to gossip prevalent at Hailey, was somewhat precipitous.

Miss Jeannette Klotz, a young lady the doctor had met in San Francisco and admired for her musical talents and other attributes, arrived in Hailey on the Fourth of July. It marked the end of independence for Doc Durham. The courtship in Wood River Valley was short, regardless of how intense or thoughtful it may have been in California and by mail. The couple first announced they would be wed August 1. They surprised everybody by being married July 8 by Judge I. N. Sullivan at the home of Editor Picotte in the presence of three witnesses.

Late in August an item in the *Hailey Times* said Dr. and Mrs.

Durham had left town. Their destination was not known. The tongue of rumor insisted the departure was not planned. There was talk then and speculation in later printed discussions that the Kickapoo doctor was kicked out if his nest by a former sweetheart who suddenly appeared from the East. Shortly after she got off the train and sized up the triangle, somebody took a shot at Doc Durham in his bedroom. It may or may not have been fired by the first love. The shot was a close miss.

Rather than risk his anatomy further (whether to jealous women or an odd patient who had not profited sufficiently from snake oil or electric belts) Doc Durham sought a healthier climate. It was just as well. If he had been punctured, it is doubtful that he could have relied on the dedicated attention of any other medical man in the vicinity.

Dr. Durham returned to Hailey in 1913 to visit his editor-benefactor, Picotte, and several former patients. Among them was George Shirley, who had received a mastoid operation many years before and credited Durham with a first-class cure. Shirley was still an advocate of Durham's talent.

Facts about the doctor's life during the years he was gone from Wood River were related in detail. He said he had quit the medicine business and shed the name of Dr. Durham soon after his departure. He now called himself A. D. Lloyd, and he lived in Fort Worth, Texas.

About a year after his marriage in Hailey, his wife died in her native Yankton, South Dakota, from whence she had gone to her musical career in San Francisco. Death of the "winsome and petite" young lady so distressed Dr. Durham that he gave up his practice, abandoned Kickapoo juice with all its trimmings, and bought a drugstore. The pharmacy venture was brief. He organized a colored regiment in Ohio and was commissioned a major. The outfit served in the Spanish-American war, and he advanced to lieutenant colonel.

Durham, or Lloyd, then became a land developer in Fort Worth and Dallas. He bought and sold property on the crest of a residential boom. Profits were rolling in nicely when he was crunched by the panic of 1907. Salvaging a few bucks, he obtained acreage in Georgia and Texas for production of cotton and onions. On the strength of that recovery, he said, he built an electric railway and a telephone company. He also had a coal mine.

The *Hailey Times* went on to relate that the erstwhile medicine man had donated a $50,000 home to the Arlington Heights Female College, a high-grade finishing school.

Durham-Lloyd said he was thrilled to be back on Wood River for a brief vacation. He said he looked forward to hunting big game in the Sawtooths. He noted considerable change in the old stamping grounds. Friends noted some change in Dr. Durham but little erosion of his flambouyant spirit. He chatted, hunted, and again went on his way.

Chapter 15

HOT SPRINGS

THE SAWTOOTHS have a lot of hot water. There are warm springs all over the place. They bubble from the ground to provide swimming, medicinal soaks, laundries, and househeating. Some are trickles; some are gushers. They gurgle from various layers of hot rock in the mysterious basement. They are so common that there are several Warm Springs creeks, causing geographical confusion on watersheds of the Wood, Salmon, Payette, and Boise rivers. For example, there is Warm Springs Creek at Ketchum. There is Warm Springs Creek at Robinson Bar. And there is Warm Springs Creek which is a tributary to the South Fork of the Payette between Lowman and Grandjean. There are many more, each named because it has, or had, a hot flow. In some cases the gush has faded to a dribble.

They are peaceful. They are not given to spectacular spouting like the geysers in Yellowstone National Park to which they may be related by geological patterns. They do their public or private duty and keep Idaho pleasantly dunked without explosive tantrums.

For many years one of the most popular public plunges was the bathhouse between Upper and Lower Stanley. It was a hub of community activity, a center for both cleanliness and information. As a source of news, it ranked second only to the post office.

For about forty years the little plunge had a scrubbing and relaxing influence on natives and visitors. Fishermen and other mountain admirers waited in line to take summer dips. Home folks soaked there the year around on Saturday nights or whenever the urge to take baths hit them.

The concrete tub was about the size of a double blanket, and was three feet deep at the lower end. It was for wading and washing; swimmers banged their heads on the wall after one stroke. The pool had no roof; it was open to the sun by day and the moon by night. Log walls with many unchinked openings afforded some protection from wind and spectators. Topless and bottomless bathing was frowned upon as a traffic hazard. Interior of the plunge was visible from the highway through gaps between logs. In spite of that, many people did wash in the nude, usually at night and separated by sex. There were two dressing rooms, with a wood stove in each. Usually there was little or no fuel. On cold days men could be observed in their long johns scrounging for fence rails and sagebrush along Valley Creek.

Sanitation was a problem. Not to the people who enjoyed the tub but because of public health standards. The plunge flunked. It did not meet antiseptic particulars. It never did. From the beginning the Stanley plunge had a coating of moss that tickled the toes and broke loose to float along with gum wrappers, bars of soap, and an occasional sock. Such flotsam was accepted as standard cargo. Men, women, and children somehow survived. The plunge was not dainty, but it sure took off the dirt and gentled the joints.

Furthermore, articles likely to be found at poolside and considered by the fastidious to be evidence of potential epidemics were actually part of the Stanley message system. If there was a cigar butt on the bench, it was a sign that the prospector from Iron Creek had been in for his bath and could presently be found at his favorite bar. If there was no tin of talcum powder in the ladies' dressing room, chances were the teacher had gone to Challis for the weekend. In case certain people didn't appear at the plunge for several weeks there was community concern. Search parties went out.

The plunge was just right for most natives and a smattering of dudes — until swarms of outsiders began to arrive and parades of tourists marched on the quaint little tub. They lined up with towels for a chance at the popular spa. Their cars caused a traffic hazard. Their lingering too long led to fights. Cleanliness was next to rowdiness on some occasions. The approved pool ceremony when there was a waiting line was a dip and a scrub, with a shout to the crowd to be patient. Dallying was bad manners, even on winter days when snow hissed into the water and a nap in the pool was particularly delicious.

Through years of increasing use the plunge suffered damage from characters inside who beat up the stoves and wrecked the furniture, and from impatient toughs on the outside who used their waiting time to rip off logs and demolish the outhouse. The traffic and destruction were more than the pool could stand. Most of the logs came down about 1970. The plunge was more open than before and not as useful. Even horse wranglers and salmon fishermen like a little privacy when they wash their tootsies.

So use had declined before the final blow fell. Health authorities condemned the place. There were too many germs. At least there was a risk of too many germs when the bacteria of Stanley amalgamated with the microbes of Chicago, Los Angeles, and Philadelphia. The plunge was torn down. It would be smart-alecky to say that some of the people in Stanley haven't had a bath since. That isn't so. Stanley has indoor plumbing and everything. Pure as a scalded thumb.

There are a number of private and semiprivate hot springs in Sawtooth Valley as well as over Galena Summit on the Wood River drainage. The owners generally like them as they are. Monkeying by outsiders is not appreciated, although certain rules must be met in the interest of public health.

Tom Williams had a private tub at his bachelor shack near Obsidian, ten miles above Stanley. It was an old cyanide tank about ten feet in diameter. Warm water from springs that also served a natatorium of the Rocky Mountain Club gave Williams a pool about three feet deep. He took baths frequently and washed his clothes there after swimming. It was a valuable asset. Tom particularly liked to sit in the water and smoke his pipe after hard days on the pack trail or at his mine on Pig Tail Creek. Aches and pains disappeared in the refreshing warmth.

Visitors made themselves useful one summer day while Williams was at his mine. As a good deed for Tom, they drained the tank, freshened the wood with chlorine, and washed the towels. They knew their host would be surprised.

He was. He came home tired and dusty and hit for the pool. The air was soon blue with prospector language, none of it complimentary. The cleanup squad had forgotten to put in the plug. The tub was dry.

Several hotels of Wood River and Salmon River took pride in their natural hot water, which was a distinctive feature and in some instances a major reason for success. The Hiawatha Hotel at Hailey was one of the first in the area to have natural hot water in the rooms for bathing and a natatorium in the basement for swimming. The system was installed in 1915 when the hotel was reopened after being closed for two years. It was originally built in 1883 by Robert Strahorn and operated at the same place under different names through Hailey's early history. It had been known as the Alturas when it closed in 1913.

An indication of the importance people put on hot water is given in this item from the *Hailey Times* in June 1900: "There being no water, there will be no baths at Hailey Hot Springs tonight. If there is any tomorrow, Baugh's Drug Store will be notified." Water from the hot springs was piped two miles to the hotel.

Guyer Hot Springs at Ketchum was established as a resort by Harry Guyer, a mining man who operated a smelter at Ketchum and had interests in several claims, including one in South America where he died in 1907. In addition to serving the public for many years, including the present, Guyer's was a social hub. In 1914 under the management of Charles Grout, the place staged lavish parties for the upper crust. Among the extravaganzas was a fancy dress ball by Mr. and Mrs. James McDonald. The Hailey paper said it was a veritable "Midsummer Night's Dream." Guests in the garb of pirates, literary figures, statesmen, and characters from Mother Goose danced until 4:30 A.M. Manager Grout went to Guyer's from the Idanha at Boise, where he was a very visible manager many years, not only because of his size — more than 250 pounds — but because of his aggressive management. Incidentally, Grout was a passenger who had to be turned down for one of the first airplane flights in Boise in April 1911. He was too fat. The plane could rise only a few feet, and the pilot, Walter Brookings, had to land.

Grout took a vigorous hand in development of tourism in the Sawtooths. He advanced a plan to link Guyer Hot Springs, the Hiawatha Hotel, and the McFall Hotel of Shoshone in a chain to encourage travel in the area. He designed package deals, including motor tours of Stanley Basin and "Sawtooth National Park." There was no park then or now, but the people on the ground referred to "Sawtooth National Park" as a reality as early as 1914. Some of Grout's plans were put into effect, but the package tour withered on the vine. There were two main reasons: poor roads and scarcity of suitable accommodations in Stanley and vicinity. Mrs. H. L. Benner, widow of a missing merchant, operated the Stanley Inn with beds for about twenty-five people and meals for more. There was a hotel at Alturas Lake run by Mr. and Mrs. Francis Law. The ancestor of Redfish Lake Lodge was in business at that lake. There were scattered overnight stations down the river between Stanley and Challis. But there was little push for outside business. A good many residents didn't want hordes of outsiders, a feeling that has carried over to modern times.

So Grout had hard sledding. His ideas, applauded by chambers of commerce in Hailey and Ketchum, were looked upon coldly in the backcountry. There were nods of agreement and shouts of anger when one chamber official in Hailey proclaimed that all the Sawtooth Park needed was good roads, more cars, and a chain of hotels a few miles apart from Galena to Yankee Fork. The proposition had a jolly ring for people who wanted the Sawtooths to make a big splash. A good many residents of the district and people who ran livestock on its Alpine meadows were not enthusiastic. In fact, they were mad as hornets.

The Idaho Fish and Game Department also had a word of caution. Fish were fairly plentiful and game could be found in many places, but each season it was necessary to plunge a little farther into the mountains to find easy pickings. With an increase in use, officers said, there would be less and less. Since the arrival of autos, they said, there had been a marked decline in fishing success. So, conservatives warned, bring in more people and develop the country, but take the step in the knowledge that the influx of humanity will gradually strangle the goose that lays the golden eggs. That was in 1916.

Heated arguments had little or nothing to do, of course, with flows of hot water at the several minor spas. Bathers and diners made use of them to an extent generally satisfactory to the proprietors.

Among the well-known oases between Stanley and Challis was Robinson Bar. Hot water at the mouth of Warm Springs Creek brought the place into early prominence as a stopping spot for travelers and a mecca for persons stricken with aches and pains. K. D. Williams was the proprietor for many years. This ad appeared weekly in the *Challis Messenger* in 1902 and later: "Medical Hot Springs at Robinson Bar at junction of Warm Springs on Salmon River eighteen miles from Clayton and fourteen miles below Custer. These springs are of a nice temperature and superior. The sportsman will find better fishing and hunting grounds than in any other part of the nation. K. D. Williams, Prop."

The proprietor wanted peace and quiet for his guests, according to an item in the Challis paper. It related that a Blackfoot man was on the trail of a gent who had run off with his wife. The manager of Robinson Bar found the allegedly adulterous pair camping at the bar. He sent them scampering. "I don't know the particulars of the case," he said, "but I don't want my premises messed up with bloodshed."

It was a thoughtful and generous attitude for management to take. Williams was also an undertaker and county coroner. He put live business first.

Chase A. Clark, an attorney, bought Robinson Bar in 1915 and ran it many years as a sideline to legal practice. Members of his family and the family of his brother, Barzilla, have had interest in ownership and management. Mrs. Frank Church, Bethine, is a daughter of Chase Clark. Because of this business involvement with Robinson Bar, U.S. Senator Frank Church, 1976 primary Democratic candidate for President and a leading member of the Foreign Relations Committee, has been criticized for his vigorous part in legislation creating the Sawtooth National Recreation Area and Wilderness. Robinson Bar is private property on the northern edge of the recreation area established by Congress in August 1972. Petty or important, political steam has blown around Senator Church. So far it has been a tempest in a teapot. However, it illustrates that the warm springs of the Sawtooths are forever boiling up surprises.

It is fitting to note here that Chase Clark became governor of Idaho and later a federal judge. Barzilla Clark was also a governor of Idaho. D. Worth Clark, family member, was a congressman and senator. Maybe there was really something in those Robinson Bar waters that K. D. Williams proclaimed as "superior."

Chapter 16

THE WHITE CLOUDS

THE WHITE CLOUDS blew their top a long time ago. Rumblings in the mountains scared lonely travelers and influenced prospectors to stay away. Uproars of the 1970s about protection of scenic values had strong influence on inclusion of the White Clouds in the Sawtooth National Recreation Area. They were faint echoes of what was going on in the majestic peaks nearly one hundred years ago.

In contrast with the verbal tumult of modern times, stemming from conflicting opinions of mining in the area, the upheaval of the 1880s was geological. It was visible and spectacular. It was a moving experience — mountains moved. How long they had been huffing and puffing is anybody's guess. Millions of years, probably. Change is still taking place. What makes the phenomenon of the White Clouds particularly exciting is that it took place within recorded times. Pioneers witnessed it and took notes for posterity. The account comes chiefly from Tom Jones of Galena, a correspondent for the *News-Miner* of Hailey in the summer of 1883. He had it firsthand from citizens of good reputation.

The alleged explosion had nothing to do with the naming of the White Clouds. They had been named much earlier because the summits looked like clouds when viewed from a distance, such as from Sawtooth Valley. They seemed to be hung in the firmament with no ties to the landscape. They still do. Many Sawtooth visitors have remarked on their resemblance to gigantic Sahara sand dunes. They are actually solid and flinty.

The 1883 upheaval happened while a group of mine developers was taking the short cut from Galena to Bayhorse. The easier but longer route was over Galena Summit to Stanley and down the Salmon River. A steeper route went from Galena northeast through the Boulder range to Galena Gulch and Germania Creek and on to the East Fork of the Salmon near Long Tom Creek. From there the trail followed the East Fork to Clayton. Miners in a hurry or with particular concern for mines on the East Fork used the trail a good deal. For a short distance it followed White Cloud Creek. The summit was about five miles from Galena.

Now hear this from Tom Jones:

"Nearly at the summit there is a high peak on the left — going from Galena. For the last four years it has from time to time seemed to have strong symptoms of volcanic action — loud rumblings and a perceptible motion of the ground in the vicinity. When occurring in the daytime, what were called clouds of smoke were seen ascending from the mountain at different points. These have taken place so often this season as to give rise to all sorts of stories as to what might take place in an actual volcanic eruption.

"Yesterday morning (September 1) Captain T. R. Wills, superintendent of the Pocahontas group on East Fork, came across the divide and stopped to rest at the Henry Collins camp, which is in full view of the peak and about a mile distant. While talking they were startled by what they first thought was a very loud clap of thunder, accompanied by a perceptible giving of the ground. The sun was shining brightly and no clouds were in sight.

"On turning around and looking towards the peak, they saw it to be smothered in what seemed to be clouds of smoke apparently coming from crevices in different places and eddying upwards as though forced up by a strong volume of gas. Thousands of rocks were tumbling down the mountain.

"Captain Wills, being familiar with volcanic disturbances from actual observation, at once took in the situation which he describes as one of the grandest he has ever witnessed of nature's wonderful workings. He says that in a little over an hour there were five of these exhibitions. They were occasioned by the disintegration of material around the bottom of the mountain. The mountain being very steep, the material gradually finds its level, leaving the ledges above projecting. They are made of partially decomposed rock. This keeps on until the overhanging weight becomes so great that they break off in large masses, carrying everything before them.

"Captain Wills says that after the clouds of dust passed away they could plainly see the large cracks that had opened on the far side of the mountain that would cause another avalanche in a short time. He gives it as his opinion that they will continue until the mountain is rounded off and the slopes will become flattened so the material will stop sliding."

The article does not specify that the mountain was Castle Peak.

Photo by Ernie Day

Castle Peak in the White Clouds

It could have been that mountain, which rises 11,815 feet and has been ranked — at least by photographers — as one of the most impressive in the country. It could have been another of the White Cloud giants. Elevations are not given. The vicinity includes Patterson, Washington, and Blackman, each more than 10,000 feet.

Blackman Peak is named for George Washington Blackman, a Negro who mined in the area for many years. Legends say he had been a slave. If so it must have been when he was a baby, because he was of middling years in the early 1930s when he was still mining. Stories that he struck it rich also seem to be exaggerated. He took a moderate living from his claim. Blackman came out several times each year for supplies. Because he paid cash and seemed to be solvent, rumors spread that he was sitting on a bonanza. He was a kindly gentleman, shy, soft-spoken, and humble. When guests came to his cabin he whipped up generous meals, including some of the finest bread ever baked in the mountains. But he would not sit with his visitors. He said his upbringing in the South did not permit it. In declining health after a long career in the White Clouds, the highly respected black citizen was "accommodated" by the Gossi family of Clayton.

The high country of the White Clouds has many lakes noted for fish. On the west side, reached partway by the Pole Creek road and on top by foot or horse, there are such jewels as Champion, Washington, Fourth of July, Deer, and Rainbow. The vicinity also includes Heart Lake, Phyllis Lake, and Six Lake Basin. Some of the lakes harbor and occasionally yield golden trout of fantastic size, as well as rainbow of more reasonable weight. Men who have landed five-pound goldens and seen their brilliant colors on snow banks edging the lakes describe the experience as "out of this world."

On the north and east sections of the White Clouds there are scores of lakes — such as the Big Boulder and Little Boulder chains — with fabulous scenic and fishing treasures. Down the main canyon between the Stanley and the Challis portions there is Warm Springs Creek, a stream of such beauty and angling fame that persons familiar with its charms have trouble telling strangers how to get there. They commonly wind up their directions by saying, "I'll get my hat and go with you."

Chapter 17

LOST FREIGHTER

THE WEEK before Christmas of 1885 not a blizzard was stirring through Wood River Valley. There was scarcely a snowflake. Ketchum was merry, taking the pulse of its mining boom as it snuggled down for the winter and finding a strong beat for future economic health. Up and down the valley, fresh tailings in scores of gulches gave evidence of brisk activity in minerals. Payrolls were substantial. More people were coming to the valley. Business was good. The new year held promise of continued happiness.

At Christmastime the weather was mild as milk. The *Ketchum Keystone* remarked that the Cougar Stage Line, M. M. Moore, proprietor, had excellent sleighing conditions to Sawtooth City and Vienna. Schedules of trips twice a week were kept as easily as they had been in the fall. There was talk of going back to the daily pattern of summer. The Ketchum and Salmon River Stage Line, H. C. Lewis, manager, carried passengers regularly. And the Ketchum Fast Freight Line, a twin of the stage service operated by the same firm, hauled merchandise with scarcely a delay because of drifts. Young bloods courted their gals in starlight to the music of sleigh bells. Small fry, released from school, coasted on the hills. The more daring were obliged to climb high for their rides. The valley floor had little snow.

The contentment was well expressed by E. H. Pierson, a mining man who snowshoed over the Sawtooths from Atlanta — two days on the trail — to find Ketchum stores offering homemade mincemeat in pails, a full line of Crosse and Blackwell's tinned and jarred delicacies, deviled and potted meats, and fancy odds and ends to tempt the appetite of an epicure. One establishment advertised a "small lot of genuine New Orleans molasses." There were well-selected stocks of china and glass for Christmas gifts. Hardware stores were well fixed in skates and pocket knives. Another retailer was particularly proud of his willow chairs as presents for households that had everything.

Of regular meats and vegetables there was a good supply. Prices were moderate for a boomtown. Butchers saw to it that plenty of beef was on hand. They dressed out scores of steers to meet the demand of a feasting public. One butcher, George White of Sawtooth City, was just finishing his preholiday chores when his knife slipped. He spent the holidays in Ketchum having his wound mended.

George J. Lewis, pharmacist, augmented his regular line of potions and pills with peppermint sticks and horehound candy. The Cornucopia Bakery and Confectionery dished up oyster stew, a special for the sleighing set. George Callahan, proprietor, also noted he would deliver bread and pastry anywhere in town. Baxter's Hotel welcomed travelers to twenty-five new rooms. Paul Baxter, owner, said the hotel had a "fine system of waterworks, good beds, and comfortable parlors." The Enterprise Restaurant, Sara Roach, manager, spread a festive board for the holidays.

Jacob's Billiard Hall distributed gifts of eggnog, beer, and cigars to old friends, including the staff of the Keystone. The newspaper acknowledged the treat and followed the thanks with a story about a billiard tournament won by William Hanna with a run of fifty-two points, for which he earned $10.

Someone traveling between Ketchum and Hailey found a coat on the road. He was so full of goodwill he announced in the paper that the loser could claim it by paying for the ad.

With what may have been a little smugness, Ketchum noted that cottontail rabbits were ripe and good eating at Blackfoot. The jest was a reference to the superior fare on Wood River, remote though it was from metropolitan cookery.

The Ketchum Literary and Dramatic Society met at the residence of Joseph Pinkham, "with a show of much interest in the forthcoming work."

And so the holidays unfolded their banners, giving no hint of coming events.

The balmy season ended in January with increasing flurries of snow, and about the middle of the month the roof fell in. Snow arrived with a vengeance. It was not an ordinary storm. In the rainy season there are cloudbursts — this was a snowburst. Unlike the waterspout that dumps its load in a flash, the snow continued hour after hour, day after day. Fat flakes smothered the valley. Ketchum got three feet; in higher country it was much deeper. Still the snow came. Shovelers were hard pressed to keep paths open in town. Road travel stopped. Teamsters called it quits. The branch railway from Shoshone to Ketchum churned a few yards at a burst, behind a groaning plow.

Stage lines and freighters took time to count noses. All drivers were present or accounted for except "Dad" Freeman, a veteran of the run between Challis and Ketchum by way of Trail Creek. At last reports before communications broke down, Dad had started for Ketchum with a mule wagon. If he was on schedule, as Dad always was, he would have reached the upper end of Lost River about the time the storm got nasty.

Old hands on the freight line figured Dad's chances were bad. Snow was beginning to slide. Big and little avalanches ripped down slopes near Ketchum, and conditions were calculated to be much worse on Trail Creek. If Freeman hadn't found shelter, he was probably a goner.

Manager Lewis sent a crew and four-horse team to open the summit and find the missing driver. The going was exceedingly tough. By nightfall the rescue party had progressed only a few miles. Unable to reach the cabin where they had intended to sleep, the men floundered in the dark through the snow.

A second relief party was sent out to find the first. At dusk on the second day a member of the crew heard a shout from a clump of pines. He staggered to the clearing and found a shack, a fire, and two men from the first rescue party. They were Gary Davis and T. B. Keller. They said they had lived on a rat. As far as they knew, they said, other members of the party were safe. They were headed for a cabin near the tollgate. The horses had been left farther down the canyon, with a small supply of grain.

Singly and in groups of two or three, the freighters slogged back to Ketchum. It was impossible, they said, to get over Trail Creek. The mountain was alive with slides. It would be suicide to try the summit. Too bad about Dad.

Concern for Freeman was presently increased with fear for the safety of other residents. Tragedies stunned the valley. Three men died in a slide at the Homestake Mine on Lake Creek. One life was lost on Boyle Mountain. A slide at Bullion trapped Mike Reagan and Tim Hawkes. Reagan was buried in fifteen feet of snow. He died soon after he was found. Hawkes survived.

In Ketchum, snow was five feet deep. A warehouse of the Idaho Forwarding Company was crushed. A slide filled a portion of the H. C. Lewis home on the lower end of Trail Creek. Many other buildings were crushed. Men driving horses hitched to flour barrels started for Sawtooth City. No word had come from Sawtooth since the storm began. The men got through to find Sawtooth doing nicely as long as nobody ventured far from his door.

People again had time to concentrate on the fate of Dad Freeman. What had happened to him?

The answer came from Challis in the first mail of two weeks. Freeman supplied the word himself. He had gone only a few miles from Challis, he wrote. He saw the storm coming and stayed at a station on Willow Creek. He was sorry, he said, to disappoint the boys who thought he was done for. He would be driving in as soon as the road opened.

Dad returned to Ketchum shortly and soon resumed trips over Trail Creek. The snow was troublesome, he agreed, but nothing to keep a man cooped up.

Chapter 18

FRITCHMAN'S MULE TRIP

TRAIL CREEK and the high country it serves have a reputation for low temperatures, tall stories, and dramatic incidents. Thermometers at the head of Summit Creek and up the draws of Phi Kappa Creek sink out of sight. The cold, gray flanks of Mount Hyndman and the frosty blankets of the Devil's Bedstead send tingling signals of hibernation. The majestic area is noted not only for its switchbacks of old, along which freight wagons toiled in pioneer days, but also for legendary spells of refrigeration which are chopped from the granite of fable.

Actual readings of thirty to fifty degrees below zero are not a patch on what tradition says happened one winter at the head of Fall Creek: An entire lake moved out of its bed to seek shelter and warmth in a grove of pines near an old sawmill. It was on a remote fork of Lost River in the same vicinity that a rainbow trout wearing earmuffs was caught on the Fourth of July.

The air is clear and charged with history on the ancient pathway over Trail Creek Summit between Ketchum and Chilly, an appropriately named terminus on the Lost River end of the link. Not the least of the historical incidents was the mule-stage adventure of the late Harry K. Fritchman, a former mayor of Boise and, at the time of his first visit to this land of enchantment, a drummer for a grocery firm.

First, a bit of background. H. C. Lewis built the wagon road over Trail Creek in 1884. It was a toll road constructed and used mostly by the Ketchum Fast Freight Line. The founder and proprietor was a son of Isaac Lewis, a member of one of the first groups to establish residence on Wood River. Isaac Lewis, travel-

ing from Montana, arrived in 1880 after an exploratory trip by
Lewis and Al Griffith. A booklet by Agnes Barry and Margaret
Doyle says the senior Lewis pitched the first tent on the present
townsite of Ketchum. The community was originally called Leadville. It soon became Ketchum in honor of David Ketchum, an early
resident of Boise Basin who went further into the mountains to
seek his fortune.

H. C. Lewis, twenty-six at the time of his transportation venture, began the freight service to provide communication with the
railroad at Blackfoot. The Ketchum Fast Freight outfit consisted of
huge wagons drawn by mules and horses. There were several way
stations and warehouses. Lewis located camps for night stopovers,
since it took two weeks for the round trip of 160 miles. The first
camp was at Trail Creek Summit at the Ketchum-Challis tollgate.
When the line was operating at full bore there were about thirty
outfits of teams and wagons on the road, serving such places as
Clayton, Challis, Bayhorse, Bonanza, and Custer. The motive
power consisted of about 200 mules, many horses, and several ox
teams.

Each wagon string usually had five units pulled by a total of
fourteen to twenty mules. The wagon boxes were sixteen feet long,
more than six feet high, and four feet wide. The back wheels were
seven feet in diameter. The wagon could carry nearly 20,000
pounds as a regular load. In one emergency a wagon came down
the grade with 24,000 pounds drawn by twenty-four mules. The
grade was a stem-winder, as many present-day drivers on the re-
built and tamed road can testify. In the beginning the grade was 12
percent. There was room for one wagon and a thin grasshopper.
Places to pass were few. On one side was the mountain, on the
other a cliff that dropped off to the suburbs of China.

The road has been improved several times. The grade has been
reduced to a gentle 7 percent. Some of the stretch near Ketchum is
oiled. Near the summit the road is rocky and rugged. There are
frequent rockslides. Trees occasionally block traffic. The road is a
political orphan, tossed around by federal, state, and county agencies that lack funds to support it. The administrative maneuvering
is as delicate as the drive up or down the road — which requires
strict attention to the wheel. Veteran fishermen who regard the vicinity as a choice retreat feel that Trail Creek is okay as it is, warts
and all — the fewer invaders the better. On the other hand there is
public clamor for a boulevard over which hordes can whiz with

Photo by Ernie Day

Little Matterhorn, a crag near Mount Hyndman

hardly time to blink at the deer and the antelope, let alone appreciate the renowned landscape.

Now the story of the Fritchman trip. Conditions were rather primitive when His Honor made his ride in the spring of 1890. They were almost as original and genuine as they were when Lewis built the road. The trip was one that a man does not forget quickly. Fritchman remembered it well. He related it to Mrs. Eva Hunt Dockery of *The Statesman* in 1929, about forty years after the event.

The stage trip he took was the first of the season. The line accepted passengers on a provisional basis. Maybe they would get through; maybe they wouldn't. You paid your fare and took your chances. The load on the day in point was made up of Mr. Lewis, Fritchman, the wife of a Clayton miner, and a ton or so of mail and express.

"It was difficult going," Fritchman said, "but we made it over the summit to the first station by noon. Here we abandoned the horses and put on six mules. It was the only stage I ever saw drawn by mules. The first two mule-team divisions were without incident.

"We came out in a big open country called Thousand Springs Valley, where we saw a big herd of antelope. Then we came to Elbow or Dickey Station — I can't remember which one, but it was the first. We had had a good deal of difficulty getting the mules hitched up at the stations we had passed, but the six they had harnessed up at this station didn't seem to have ever been harnessed before. Moreover, they didn't intend to be hitched.

"There were four men at the station, so with Lewis and myself we had a man to a mule. Having been raised on a Missouri farm, I felt right at home. The difficulty was to get all the mules headed in the same direction — no trouble at all to get them crosswise, or wrong-end-to.

"We finally pulled the coach over to the corral fence. Then we towed all the near mules over one at a time and tied them to the fence in the positions they would be if we ever got hitched, the wheeler being between the fence and the tongue. Then we brought over the other mules and lashed each to its mate. Finally we got them all on their feet, headed in the direction we wanted to go and all hitched to the coach but still tied to the fence.

"We got aboard, Lewis and the lady inside the coach. I got on the front seat with the driver. He certainly knew how to handle the ribbons. When we were all set, three of the men went inside the corral and cut the mules loose from the fence. A crack from the driver's whip and a yell from the men, and we were away to a fairly good start. That is, five of the mules got away. The other one lay down. That didn't make any difference because he had to go along anyhow. After being dragged a hundred yards he caught his feet and took off on a run with the others. The half dozen dogs at the station joined in the chase and helped make things more lively.

"The driver couldn't hold the mules. He didn't try. He just kept them heading straight down the road. In about five miles they were run down. From there to the next station they were very good mules. We had little more trouble and reached Clayton, eighty miles from Ketchum, shortly before midnight."

Ornery though the mules were, they were not as painful to Fritchman as a horse he encountered on the same trip.

"I did my work in Clayton," he said, "and went on to Custer and Bonanza. There was only one horse in town, a little white pony. I rented him and rode up to Yankee Fork and on to Custer and Bonanza. I found one store at each place, finished my work, and rode back to Clayton the next day. The little horse had only one gait and that was a gallop; I kept him at it going and coming. I hadn't ridden horseback since I left the farm two years before. The churning that horse gave me in two days I thought would put me in the hospital. When I got off at Clayton, I could hardly walk. I recovered, however, within a week, but as far as I can remember I haven't been on a horse since."

Chapter 19

CAMAS WILD MAN

THE WILD MAN of Camas Prairie was a sensation. He bared his fangs, beat his hairy chest, and terrified young and old for several seasons until his career was finished — perhaps by the blow of an ax but more likely by overexposure.

In step with tradition of the times, which sprouted a dreadful creature for every boom camp, Wood River Valley claimed the Camas terror as its own version of the celebrated Bigfoot, king of all the colossal astonishers. Bigfoot was long since gone, allegedly slain in Owyhee County and buried in an unknown grave.

Newspapers of Wood River reported sightings of a mysterious creature on the plains near Soldier. The accounts, beginning about 1881, quoted people who saw the thing as saying it was of more than average height, furry all over, furtive in its movements, scowling of countenance, and uncommunicative except for a sort of yodel. Papers of Hailey, Ketchum, and Bellevue kept on the trail of the baffling beast from time to time. Which paper had first crack is difficult to determine. The Camas wild man may have been a scoop for the *Wood River Times*. It may have been a triumph for the *Ketchum Keystone* or the *Bellevue Sun*. At any event the hairy horror got notoriety beyond territorial boundaries.

Accounts in the local press were picked up and embellished by papers all over the country. Happy reporters adopted the monster as the finest thing since Goliath. They gave him tusks and claws. They added about a foot to his height and 200 pounds to his weight, putting him right up there with Bigfoot. They hinted that he had carried off a maiden or two and that he lived on snakes. He roamed a wide swath and was liable to pop out on a stagecoach anywhere from Boise to Butte. Firsthand, I-was-there stories blossomed in Chicago and New York, although no correspondent actually set foot in Idaho.

At the peak of his popularity the Camas wild man was snuffed out. The finish was told in the *Bellevue Sun* early in February 1883. The article was widely reprinted, although not by the Wood River rivals of the *Sun*, who probably took a dim view.

The report said: "Wild Man of Camas Killed in a Desperate Struggle West of Bellevue.

"This noted personage has been well known among the old inhabitants of Idaho territory for the past ten years and of late through illustrated articles in the New York press.

"He was killed ten days ago by some parties traveling through Camas Prairie. While the travelers were camped in the foothills on the edge of the prairie, Mickelhenny went a few hundred yards from camp to kill some ducks, taking with him a shotgun loaded with large shot. Only a couple of hundred yards from camp, the Wild Man of Camas jumped up from a hiding place. After running a short distance he stopped and looked at Mickelhenny through large, clear-cut eyes for a moment. Then, with a shriek that struck terror to the hunter and caused him to shudder as the echo resounded through the forest, the man with the ferocity of a savage beast of the jungle made for Mickelhenny so fiercely that in order to insure his own safety he emptied both barrels of the gun into him. The man fell, apparently dead.

"Mickelhenny went to him when the strange being began to revive; he put his foot on the man's neck and called to his comrades to bring him an ax, which they did with all possible haste. The man escaped as they arrived, and with a pitiful moan regained his feet and started to run. The ax was thrown at him, and, as he turned his head to look back, it struck him in the center of the forehead, and he dropped lifeless to the ground.

"On examination he was found to be rather tall, with full, clear eyes and an extraordinarily large head. He appeared to be about forty-five years of age, although not a gray hair could be seen. The beautiful, wavy black hair of his head hung low down onto the body, and his bushy beard was about two and a half feet long. The body was also covered with a thick growth of hair about two inches in length. This was also black and very fine. The finger and toenails were two inches long and resembled claws more than nails.

"He was wrapped in a long robe made of rabbit skins, which, although the tailoring was not a subject of admiration, was well suited to the most bitter cold weather. The skins were sewn together with sinews.

"On examining the place from which he made his appearance, it was found that he had a very comfortable bed made of the soft bark of sagebrush. It was under an overhanging rock and well protected from the wind. Near the bed were two rabbits which had most likely been killed by stones.

"About ten years ago an insane stage driver left Boise City and has never since been heard of. The Wild Man of Camas may be the same, having taken up his abode in the desolate prairie but seldom visited by white men. He could very easily secure food there, as the country is filled with rabbits both winter and summer which can easily be killed by an expert at throwing stones. The Wild Man of Camas has, since first seen in 1873, been dreaded by lonely travelers and prospectors who will be relieved to know he is dead.

"Thus ends the life of a mysterious being, a man no one knows whom and coming from no one knows whence; a terrible specter haunting the camps of prospectors and feared as death by the red men of the forest; often seen but no attempt made to capture as he always leaped away, showing as much fear of his fellowmen as any of the animals of the forest; a being shrouded in mystery of whom nothing more will ever be known."

T. E. Picotte, editor of the *Hailey Times*, grieved more than the others. He said he had invented the wild man and the *Bellevue Sun* had no right to kill him. It was a nasty piece of business, he said "for ways that are dark and tricks that are vain."

Wood River has other unusual fauna. For instance, the pigs of Mrs. Kate Dougray. In the depth of the record cold winter of 1883, two of her fine hogs froze stiff in a pond at thirty below zero. They stayed in the ice several days. When the thaw came they popped out, none the worse for the adventure. To the astonishment of people who had seen them rigid in the ice, they resumed daily rooting for garbage behind restaurants.

Then there was the sandhill crane of Croy Gulch. Harry Smith found it hobbling around. Because of cold weather, Smith made it a pair of pants, hitched across the back with a brace of red suspenders. The crane was doing pretty well until along in January; then it died. Smith said it wasn't of cold or the croup or anything to do

Photo by Idaho Dept. of Tourism and Industrial Development
McGowan Peak and Stanley Lake Creek

with the weather. It pined away for love of a turkey. They had been pals, but the turkey became a New Year's dinner. The poor, lonesome crane turned up his toes.

It should be remembered, too, that the Sawtooth district was the setting for Foley Abbott's gas discovery. The *Ketchum Keystone* broke the news in the fall of 1882. The article follows:

"Last Sunday Foley Abbott of Sawtooth City went into the high and rugged peaks opposite the Pilgrim Mine on Beaver Gulch to kill some grouse. As the beautiful snow was about three feet deep he went on snowshoes. The trip was a hard one, as the mountain was very steep and he was obliged to take many tacks to reach the summit.

"While pausing near one of the high granite cliffs he noted there was an opening under it and thought he had found a good place to rest and be protected from the wind. So he proceeded to it. Seeing that it was dark inside and the cave appeared to be of good size, he made a torch from slivers taken from a pitch log nearby and proceeded to explore his new find.

"After going through a long, narrow, and crooked passage he found himself in a large chamber with smooth floor and perfectly dry, which was brilliantly lighted by a flame in the center. As this was the main attraction, he cautiously went to it.

"To his utter amazement he found an image of a man, made of what had the appearance of silver which he thinks it is. At the head was a helmet of peculiar pattern in which there were three imitation feathers made of gold or copper. From the mouth of the strange image proceeded the flame.

"Mr. Abbott thinks that the prehistoric and undoubtedly very intelligent race that erected it had discovered a gas jet, and that there is a communication down through the body to the solid rock from which the gas proceeds perpetually. It is an evidence that there is an immense body of coal under the mountains from which the gas proceeds. After satisfying his curiosity at the wonderful lamp he commenced a search for other objects. On the walls were hieroglyphics which he could not read. In one corner was a large human skeleton — at least nine feet high — and by it a stone tomahawk and a large crossbow, which, although it had the appearance of being perfectly sound, fell into a thousand pieces when he attempted to lift it.

"A stone mortar containing some very rich gold specimens was found, also some large pieces of ruby silver. Some backbones of salmon were scattered around, proving that the inhabitants of the cavern were salmon eaters. There were many other things in the apartment, such as arrowheads, bones of animals, a petrified human hand, etc.

"Mr. Abbott discovered an entrance into another apartment but being a little timid concluded not to proceed further into the depth of the mountain. A party is organizing in Sawtooth to explore the cave fully, and we will report all the new finds."

Alas, there were none. At the earliest opportunity Mr. Abbott climbed the hill again, this time with other men. When he reached the spot where he thought the entrance to the cave should be, he was shocked to find there had been an avalanche. The side of the mountain was gone. As he sat on a rock contemplating what might have been, the only sign of his discovery was the faint smell of gas. His companions said they could smell it, too. They told him so as they returned to Sawtooth City.

Chapter 20

WOMEN'S CLEANUP

THE BIGGEST cleanup in the Hailey mining district was made by women. Fortunes dug from the Minnie Moore, the North Star, the Croesus, the Red Elephant, and Queen of the Hills take second billing to the pure excitement Wood River ladies created in 1885.

It's all related in the *Wood River Times* during the editorship of the whimsical, free-swinging T. E. Picotte, a journalist of amazing gifts.

The episode of soft soap ranks among the cleanest stories ever told. It began when a Hailey woman advertised a soap recipe for $1. She sold a bunch. The soap turned out okay, and other ladies decided they should get in the act. Pretty soon every kitchen had a kettle of the stuff.

Church guilds had soap bazaars. Saponification societies (that's fancy for soap makers) took over from sewing circles and culture clubs. They latched onto almost all the tallow in the valley and put a dent in supplies of cocoanut oil, naphtha, perfume, acids, resins, salves, and abrasives.

They made pink soap, yellow soap, green soap, orange soap, little bitty bars, big bars, soap wheels, soap sticks, soap that smelled wonderful, and soap that smelled awful. They had enough soap to make a bigger cleanup than anything since the camp started.

A practical scientist figured it was costing the girls $6 a pound.

They sold it for about four bits and insisted they were making money for charitable causes. Pop took a beating on the bills. Women said the cost was next to nothing because they donated their time. And wasn't it wonderful to have such a clean smell everywhere and to put all that money in the treasury to buy more stuff to make more soap? Men were not so lathered up with enthusiasm. Not only were they handing out the money for ingredients of secret recipes and buying back the finished products, but they were subjected to scrubbings and scentings like they had never had before. Cleanliness was next to ridiculous.

A hog raiser on Bullion Creek was among the most distressed. Wind blew from his pigs to soap-scented parlors. He was obliged to move the animals. A reporter for the *Times* said his girl gave him a chunk of soap. In an absent-minded moment he mistook it for chewing tobacco. It was terrible.

Chinese complained. Families had so much fancy soap they washed everything at home. Laundries withered. Chinese suffered in other ways, too. One Oriental gentleman drank from a bottle he found behind the Delmonico Restaurant. It turned out to be a new kind of soap, mellowing in the sun for a bazaar. A doctor pumped him out and advised him to beware of feminine chemistry. Gin and horse liniment, okay. But not homemade soap.

The editor of the *Times* bought a jug of the stuff and washed his windows for the first time in years. The panes fell out. He made light of the matter, commenting: "Soap is so cheap even Democrats can afford to wash."

Men, women, and children were cleaner behind the ears and all over than ever before. But there were drawbacks. There was so much soap in kitchens people got sick from the film on dishes and cutlery. Every room in the house smelled like a beauty parlor. A man had to go down to the river to smoke a cigar and breathe fresh air. The town was polluted with perfume, coloring agents, bath oils, and cleaning balms.

There were barrels and bushels of soap. After they wore some of it out selling it to one another, there was a mountain left. It filled cupboards and slopped over into the streets. Getting rid of it was a problem. Boise and Silver City took a few samples and begged to be left alone.

What was the solution? "Well," said Editor Picotte, mentioning a gray mound near the Minnie Moore Mine, "that's not tailings. That's the last of the Wood River soap. Cleanest hill in the valley. We had to do it or be wiped out."

In kidding women about their soap binge, Picotte came out much more healthy than editors did on several other occasions when they tangled with the opposite sex. The soap makers accepted his jibes as clean fun. It was not so with a passenger from Shoshone. The *Ketchum Keystone* related that arrivals by train included "a little old lady whose name we did not get." Next morning a female visitor bounced into the editor's office and bopped him with her umbrella. He apologized then, and in the next issue he said: "She was certainly not a little old lady. No little old lady could be that strong."

Picotte caused the wrath of another woman. An article said: "Arizona Rose, the well-known red-headed prostitute, was arrested last night for hitting a Bellevue miner with a bottle." Next day there was a correction: "Arizona Rose, the well-known prostitute, wishes us to make clear that she is not red-headed. She is a brunette."

The editor nearly got himself into a slander suit when the paper stated that Mr. So-and-So had eloped on the evening train with Mrs. Such-and-Such. The article gave details of the alleged affair. It turned out they were not even friends. They just happened to be on the same train. However, during the legal proceedings against the paper, the parties of the first part saw each other so often that the lady divorced her husband and married Mr. So-and-So. Editor Picotte glowed publicly in the satisfaction of playing Cupid by mistake.

Apparently without misgivings and with a touch of relish, Picotte published a story about another editor, the proprietor of a weekly at Shoshone. The operator of a movie house beat up the editor for reporting that women of Shoshone deplored his distasteful offerings. As soon as he could tend his wounds, the Shoshone editor trotted to the justice of the peace to file charges. He was advised that the movie man had already pled guilty to whipping the editor and had been fined $5.

Chapter 21

THE BENNER MYSTERY

H. L. BENNER, merchant and miner, made an impression on Stanley during the years he was one of its leading citizens. He also left a mystery when he disappeared. Speculation over what happened to Benner is still a lively topic for old-time residents.

It was in 1902 that he entered the Sawtooth picture. He bought the stock of goods and building owned by Mose Storer. Thunder Mountain excitement was high. Hundreds of optimists went through Stanley on their way to this last bonanza. Many needed more supplies than they had obtained at Hailey or Ketchum, and Stanley was the last chance. Benner recognized the opportunity for immediate business and the probability of a bright future. After taking over the store, he expanded operations. He made a deal with H. C. Lewis of Ketchum whereby the Ketchum Fast Freight Line sold him a four-horse coach and fifteen carloads of goods and agreed not to operate a stage through Stanley. It was left to Benner to decide what commercial hauling there would be. He chose to stage and freight now and then.

Store business was great. Articles in the *Silver Messenger* at Challis say Benner sold $1,500 worth of goods during one month of 1902. One outfit packing to Thunder spent $500. Cash. Green citizens plunging into the mountains were a poor credit risk. Benner had been a mill superintendent in Utah and knew the uncertainties of mining. However, the outlook was good at Stanley. A correspondent for the Challis paper said: "Stanley will have a boom in the near future, and when it comes it will come to stay."

Bright prospects were based in part on the fact that many Thunder Mountain boomers lost their shirts on that adventure and dropped back to the Sawtooths for another stab. Stanley Basin appeared to be more stable than Thunder Mountain. Nothing flashy, but more likely to supply beans and bacon. By the fall of 1902 Stanley had more than 100 people. Among them was Edgar Rice Burroughs, the Tarzan man, who mined briefly on the Salmon River.

Benner added a ranch to his assets. It must have been a big one because the paper said he built six miles of fence. The correspondent tossed in the comment that "Mr. Benner is very popular with the people of Stanley." In spite of his own acreage, Benner bought hay for his stock and to sell to travelers. At one time he bought thirty-five tons of baled alfalfa from the Small Brothers. Meanwhile his mercantile business increased. Benner took on the additional job of postmaster.

Prosperity continued several years. By 1906 he was operating the Valley Creek Mine, a piece of property he acquired after it was attached by creditors. It had been an early winner and then gone into a slump. Benner, who claimed the mine owed him $5,000, became the chief owner and pulled the operation around so it was successful. At least he reported a profit of $5 per day during a sixty-day season. By that time Benner had more time for mining affairs because he had taken Jack Meacham as a partner in the store. Benner and Meacham enjoyed a big business. The store was a stopping point for freighters. They sold 100 barrels of whisky and 150 head of beef in 1905. Those items were only a couple of leaders from a wide stock, but the figures illustrate the prosperous condition.

Late in 1905 Meacham, the partner and brother-in-law, was found shot to death. The shooting was ruled accidental. Meacham was hunting at the time. It was reported that his own gun fired when he stumbled.

Facts about Benner's life ended and speculation began June 14, 1907. Benner left home about 8 o'clock in the evening for a placer camp to solicit store business. He expected to return that night.

He didn't come home. Search parties next day found his horse grazing along Salmon River. There were footprints leading to a steep bank. There was general belief that Benner had fallen in and drowned.

In July, about a month later, suggestions of "something funny" cropped up. The following was printed in the *Hailey Times*:

"The mysterious disappearance of H. L. Benner is still unexplained. George M. Smith, in from Stanley, says neither the body nor clothes have been found. It is generally believed he is not drowned but has left the country to avoid prosecution for fraud while postmaster.

"Tracks were found on a sloping bank where a man would have had to walk into water about fifteen feet deep. There were no returning tracks from the edge."

The theory that Benner skipped was spread by other papers of the area. Members of the family denied the gossip. They insisted Benner did drown. The body was not found, nor was Benner located alive at any place.

Mrs. Benner, his widow, remained in Stanley where she maintained the mercantile business for a time. She later operated a hotel and cafe.

Chapter 22

DIRTY DEEDS IN THE ROUGH

THE CATALOG of frontier murder has several entries from the Sawtooth country. In addition to the cases of Johnny-Behind-the-Rocks that resulted in an execution and the death sentence for a legislator who escaped (both related in other parts of this book) there were deeds of violence that stirred the public pulse because of the brutality of the crimes and the prominence of lawyers involved on both sides.

One of the most grisly bits of business was the killing of Julius C. Reburg (also known as Reberk and Reeberg) on the Middle Fork of Salmon River near Sheep Creek in December 1917. The shooting was the product of a triangle. Charles and Frankie Ernst had been a happy married couple. He had lived at Clayton and on Wood River. She was Frances Cooper, daughter of Tim Cooper, discoverer of the Ramshorn Mine at Bayhorse and an early settler at Stanley.

Matrimonial bliss was shattered by Reburg. He courted Frances, notwithstanding her wedding. She responded affectionately and filed for divorce. With the small son of Ernst, Frances and Julius set up housekeeping back in the bush. Boiling mad, Charles Ernst traced them. He reached the remote cabin a few days before Christmas. Reburg was outside washing his face. A rifle shot killed him. Ernst dragged the body to a haymow. That night he roped the body and buried it in a shallow grave while Frances held a candle. Then he went away with the little boy. He surrendered at Challis.

Frances stayed in the cabin a couple of weeks before going out to Three Forks and then to Salmon where Ernst was in jail with his son. The wife of the sheriff took the child home, but he screamed so much at the separation from his father she took him back to jail.

Preparations for the trial suffered a setback when it was found that the shooting took place in Valley County. Ernst and son were taken nearly 1000 roundabout miles by train to Cascade. Frances Ernst, also charged, went in another coach.

At the trial, where Ernst was represented by L. E. Glennon of Hailey and the prosecutor was Frank Kerby, Mrs. Ernst said she thought her divorce had been granted. She further suggested that she might have fired the fatal shot, not her almost-ex-husband. Both were found guilty. Charles was sentenced to ten to twenty-five years; she got five to ten. Both were pardoned after serving parts of the terms. She went to Florida.

Charles Ernst went back to prison in 1942 for assault with a deadly weapon in Lemhi County. The charge, on which he drew one to two years, was that he shot a mine manager on Napias Creek. Ernst said the miner was stealing gold from his claim at Leesburg. He blamed "a California millionaire outfit of gangsters" for robbing him of $180,000 in seventeen months.

Judge Guy Stephens, who sentenced him, said Ernst "had a bad reputation, was feared by people in his community, and was inclined to take the law into his own hands. I consider him a menace to society."

A bizarre homicide in 1913 gave Salmon River a shot of sensational adrenalin. Actually most of the excitement came in 1915, but the case began in September of 1913 when the body of a man said to be the "scion of a wealthy Eastern family" was found in a disorderly house at Mackay. The coroner said he had been drugged and robbed. There was some disappointment when the deceased turned out to be a sheepherder on a spree. Anyway, somebody had been knocked off, and an aroused community meant to find out "who done it."

One or two ladies of the night were suspected, but preliminary questioning brought forth no substantial evidence. Then in March of 1915, W. E. Welker — Professor von Welker — a musician with the Merry Makers Comedy Company, was arrested at Salmon. He had been doing a show at Mackay at the time of the crime and was believed to have been among those present when the sheepherder died. Luke A. May, private detective, was credited with cracking the case.

Solon B. Clark, county attorney, charged Welker with murder. Charges were also filed against several women as accomplices. Others were held as material witnesses. The girls had left Mackay and set up business in Hailey, Ogden, and Salmon.

Shortly before the trial was to start, the main witness, the proprietor of the resort, died in a Challis hospital. Without her testimony there was little to go on, so the charge was dismissed.

The *Hailey Times* reported that Chase Clark, defense attorney, said he was sorry the trial was cancelled because he was ready to prove that a pickled stomach which the state was going to present as the stomach of the deceased was actually from a woman who had died nine years earlier. The *Challis Messenger* said the story was a lie. Chase Clark denied it, too, and a chemist said there had been no substitution of organs.

Nevertheless, the Hailey paper repeated its intimations and backed them up with the inside tip that Clark was irresponsible, a sick man doomed to die of a wasting disease in a short time. Clark didn't take the hint. He went right on living until 1966, meanwhile serving terms as governor and federal judge.

The Buster-Brown affair at North Fork in 1913 had reverberations up and down the river. It had no connection with children's clothing or a funny-paper character. Guy Buster was the athletic, handsome, impetuous son of an influential family. He "kept company" with Mrs. Agee, housekeeper for Henry Brown who lived on Salmon River near North Fork, below Salmon City.

Mr. Brown, a rancher of middling years whose wife was away visiting relatives, told Buster to keep off. Buster told him to go fly a kite. On an April evening, Buster and Mrs. Agee met Brown on a trail. Brown repeated his warning, allegedly striking Buster with a cane. Buster shot Brown and left him dead by the side of the road. A posse gathered at North Fork to arrest Buster. The action was not needed, as Buster had gone home to notify the sheriff.

A jury at Salmon found him guilty of second-degree murder. His plea of self-defense on the contention that Brown, a much older man hobbling on a cane, was about to beat him to death with a stick was not convincing. The judge sentenced him to serve ten to thirty years. Late in 1915 the Idaho Supreme Court granted a new trial, partly because of arguments by a defense lawyer that the judge at the first trial had made errors in his instructions. The former judge was an attorney for Buster in the proceedings before the supreme court.

On change of venue, the trial was conducted at Shoshone. The jury found him not guilty "for lack of evidence" and Buster was released, meanwhile having married another woman — not Mrs. Agee — while in the Salmon jail awaiting his new trial.

(Personal note — Buster's trouble distressed me. As a boy in kindergarten at North Fork, I knew him as a friend who taught us to box and make blowguns for spit wads. He was kind to kids. To have him shoot Mr. Brown, also highly regarded, was bad enough. But to have him do it over a girl was merely stupid. A girl? Good grief! Needless to say, my father, a member of the posse, did not share my feelings.)

The killing of Vivian Hovey by Stonewall Jackson Ballinger in 1916 on a ranch about thirty miles from Salmon kept the Buster-Brown case on the front burner. Hovey was a son of C. B. Hovey, a partner of the late Henry Brown. The shooting resulted from a dispute over driving cattle through Ballinger land. Ballinger met Hovey at a gate and shot him with a rifle.

With the help of bloodhounds from Montana and a $750 reward, officers arrested Ballinger at Indianola. Ballinger, a half-breed Indian whose father was a North Fork trapper, was found guilty and sentenced to serve five to ten years. He escaped from the penitentiary.

In the winter of 1935, Frank Lobear killed Walter Estep with a rifle on Big Creek in a fight over a mining deal. Lobear was a prospector. Estep was a former ranger on the Idaho National Forest. After the shooting, Lobear told his story to "Cougar Dave" Lewis, the veteran lion hunter, who got word to the sheriff. Lewis was called as a witness at the trial — in Cascade, as was the case in the Ernst matter, because the homicide occurred on the Valley County side of the Middle Fork — but Cougar Dave died in a Boise hospital before the trial. Lobear was represented by Herman Welker and George Donart. Welker was later a U.S. senator; Donart was a state senator. Fred Taylor, presently a federal judge at Boise, was prosecuting attorney. Lobear was found guilty of manslaughter and sentenced to five to ten years. He was pardoned in 1942.

Back in 1883, "Six-Shooter-Jack" Leeb was killed on Camas Prairie near Grave Creek by a posse that surprised him in the night. Leeb was said to be a horse thief and ruffian. He had served a prison term in Montana for killing a man. Following his pardon he was traced to Idaho with stolen stock.

In 1913 Reese Clevenger was sent to prison for shooting a piano player in a Hailey bawdy house. Three years later he was pardoned on representations that he had been asleep in bed at the time and that his lawyer was drunk at the trial.

John Fallon was shot dead at Muldoon in July 1908. Joe Moran was charged with murder. The killing was the climax of an alleged cattle-rustling episode during which ranchers in Blaine County believed stock was being driven to Pahsimeroi Valley. Newspaper accounts said ranchers believed Moran was tipping off the rustlers. Fallon took a shot at him. Moran fell off his horse as if shot, then jumped up and fired several times. Fallon's shotgun had been fired at least once. Moran said: "He drawed a gun on me and I shot him."

Moran was found not guilty. Several men accused of stealing cattle were also exonerated, and the uproar subsided. James Laidlaw bought the Fallon ranch. Much of the Laidlaw property, which runs sheep and cattle, has since been sold to Mary Thomas Brooks, daughter of one U.S. senator, widow of another, and herself director of the U.S. Mint.

Laidlaw Park is a tract in and near lava beds some distance from the ranch. It is mostly grazing land.

The Broadford mining strike of 1885 was an occasion for a flood of legal papers and a freshet of violence. The excitement started when the Queen of the Hills said wages would be reduced from $4 to $3.50 per ten-hour shift. The Minnie Moore did likewise. The Miners Union called a strike about the middle of January. Some miners who went to work were beaten up. Hot heads threatened to burn property. The sheriff swore in fifty armed deputies. In February Norman Ruick, district attorney, arrested a dozen union members for conspiracy. Assaults continued. Forty more miners were arrested. James Hawley, U.S. district attorney who later became governor, appealed to the miners to cool their tempers.

Telegrams and letters, including recommendations of General George H. Roberts, later attorney general for Idaho, were fired off to Boise urging military action. Two troops of cavalry arrived at Broadford on "a practice march" April 15. The strike ended April 22. Miners returned to work at $3.50 per shift.

On the lighter side of the criminal docket:

A bartender in a Hailey saloon was struck a glancing blow by a bullet from a customer's Derringer. Angered because the shot cracked the bar mirror, he snatched the weapon and told the gunman not to play with peashooters.

Jesus Urquides, a noted packer who operated supply strings to far-flung mining camps, was sued at Ketchum in 1886 because one of his mules "fraternized" with a pack animal belonging to J. W. Bradley. The Bradley mule died. He contended the beast contracted glanders. General Roberts earned a verdict for Urquides on the grounds that the mules were just good friends and the Bradley beast was "plain sick" before their meeting.

Fairfield and Hailey had a dustup over the theft of a church by a minister of the gospel. The Reverend Max Reinhardt of Fairfield was charged with stealing the Baptist church at Soldier. He claimed he had been authorized to move the building to Fairfield. Soldier citizens who had deeded the property said that was not so. They took action against the minister.

The case was transferred from justice court in Soldier because an unprejudiced jury could not be sworn. It went to Hailey. The county attorney, by the way, was an angel — Texas Angel. The trial lasted several days and brought out that the thirty-year-old building had been used by Methodists, Baptists, Salvationists, and Followers of Christ. In spite of its ecumenical character, it was in limbo on jacks until the law spoke.

The minister was found not guilty. Angry people on both sides returned to their lives of Christian tolerance. Hailey was not amused. Blaine County was saddled with the expenses of the trial.

A sheriff of Custer County qualified for the order of Solomon in the 1940s for his handling of an explosive situation. The Blaine County sheriff phoned him that a carload of toughs was on the way to Panther Creek to shoot it out with a mob allegedly jumping a claim. The Custer officer said he would "take care of it."

He got word to the scene of the impending battle that somebody was about to blast the squatters. Several days later the Blaine sheriff called again. He said the carload of meanies had retreated through Wood River Valley like a passel of scalded cats.

"What did you do to 'em?" he asked.

"Nothing," said the sheriff of Custer. "I didn't talk to them. I didn't bother the other guys, either. Just let the grapevine know they could expect ugly company. They hightailed for Montana. No fight, no shooting. We didn't care who won. Both sides got cold feet, I guess. All foreigners. No place to waste Custer County money."

Chapter 23

JOHNNY-BEHIND-THE-ROCKS

WESTERN MEN with nicknames based on being behind something usually wind up behind the eight ball. Brief accounts of some of the characters are given in *Fragments of Villainy,* a collection of yarns by this author, published in 1959 by *The Idaho Statesman.* The Sawtooths and suburbs had several prominent Johnnies. One was a bad John; one was an untidy John; the third was an astonished John who discovered his own grave with name, date of death, and everything.

Most notorious of them all as far as Idaho is concerned was John T. Hall, the "Johnny-Behind-the-Rocks" of Vienna in old Alturas County. Actually, the episode of the Vienna Johnny has more to do with the man who killed him than it does with the minor role of the unfortunate victim whose name generally gets top billing. The chapter is traditionally labeled "the Johnny-Behind-the-Rocks story," although he was killed in the first act.

John Hall came to the Sawtooths from Eureka and Tuscorora, Nevada, where he had been a miner. Whether he was gifted in that skill or just another optimist is not known. What little the record shows indicates he was rough, ready, and unlucky. Rumor had it he shot a guy from behind a pile of rocks. One version said Johnny was shot at by a man doing likewise. At any rate, he skedaddled to

Vienna where he earned fame on two counts: He failed in the saloon business in a thirsty town; he got shot over a gal.

The gal was "Banjo Nell." Her real name is obscure. Her previous and subsequent career is likewise unknown. The few references infer she was what the nickname implies, and that does not suggest a Sunday school teacher. Members of a family now living at Payette recall that their grandfather, a mining man, met Banjo Nell on a stagecoach from Kelton, Utah, to Bullion, Idaho. He describes her as a "hard-boiled old harlot." She was loaded with parasol, luggage, and a bird in a cage. The miner had the misfortune to tip over the birdcage when the stage hit a bump. Banjo Nell gave him a dressing down in abusive language. He said that when she finished her tirade "even the dogs would not have had me."

Banjo Nell joined Johnny-Behind-the-Rocks and George Pierson in a business venture or combination of enterprises, the most visible of which was selling whisky by the shot. The less advertised activities went on in another part of the cabin without public sanction of the proprietors. Pierson was a Dane who lived most of his forty-three years on Wood River and over the hills on the headwaters of the Salmon. George and Johnny had been buddies before Banjo Nell got into the act. The triangle was not an ideal figure. Everything had been ticketyboo until Nell horned in. She did them both wrong. Neither of them did right by Nell, either, just to keep the record straight. Both claimed they loved her dearly. George let on he was married to the gal, and Johnny said he was a very close friend. She was devoted to them — and several dozen others.

In the summer of 1882, during Vienna's first boom, the trio opened a saloon with Nell as the bunny girl. In spite of such a promising outlook, the business fizzled. The reasons were not clear at the time, but they were outlined later by Pierson shortly before he died in the Quigley Gulch by request of the territory. He said he rigged out the saloon, paying for furniture and supplies out of funds he had earned swinging a pick on Smiley Creek. He said Johnny did not come through with his share.

"Johnny said my credit was good," Pierson related. "He said I could get a box of cigars and four or five gallons of whisky. I said, 'No, Johnny. I will not run into debt because I am not sure I could pay for it.'

"I went back to the Mountain King Mine and told Johnny he could have the saloon himself. He was unable to get much stock and swore vengeance on me."

With the booze store floundering for lack of financial nourishment, Pierson strained relations further by marrying Banjo Nell at
nearby Sawtooth City. At least he said they were married, making
good on the bluff he had been running right along. Johnny didn't
think well of that. It was all right to pretend wedlock, but this was
an outrage. In the space of a few days Johnny had lost his saloon
and his girl. It was enough to make a man brood, and he brooded.
Having charged up his anger with samples of saloon stock, he
barged over to have a chat with George and Nell.

George was not at home. Nell was. Johnny told her off. She told
him to go climb a rock. One thing led to another, and pretty soon
they staged a lively brawl. It was an uneven match in spite of Banjo
Nell's rugged constitution. Johnny cuffed and kicked her. Stagger-
ing across the room, she upset the stove. Johnny departed.

When George arrived a short time later, he was distressed by
the upset stove. Although it was near the end of August, a man
needed a little fire of an evening. The damage to Banjo Nell caused
further irritation. "I was very mad," George said in subsequent accounts. "My woman said, 'George, he has beaten me and he will
kill you when he sees you.' I went to Deputy Sheriff Either and
wanted Johnny arrested. He said, 'George, go home and protect
yourself but don't have a fight in the street.'"

George went back to the cabin. It wasn't long before Johnny
showed up the second time, with a pistol. George got his own gun
and waited. Johnny crept up to the door. George flung the door
open and fired. He missed. Johnny ran, and George, following him
into the trees, shot again. The bullet got Johnny in the body. He
fell dead without a word.

An angry crowd quickly gathered, growling for a lynching. Fear-
ing that he was about to be the star performer in a Vienna waltz
from an aspen bough, George Pierson surrendered to the deputy
sheriff, who took him to Sawtooth City for safety and a preliminary
hearing. As soon as possible he was escorted to Hailey, where the
grand jury indicted him for first-degree murder.

At the trial, Pierson's lawyer insisted on the right of a man to
defend his castle, an honored principle of English and American
law. It was lawful and even commendable, he said, that Pierson
protect his wife and dwelling. There was no denying that Pierson
fired the fatal shot; it was the defensible act of any red-blooded
man.

That line of thought looked promising until the attorneys for the
people shot it down. James H. Hawley, prosecutor for Alturas, and

T. D. Cahalan, an associate, poked holes in the theory. In the first place, they contended, Pierson and Banjo Nell were not really man and wife. The record showed no such marriage. The alleged wedding was a fraud; it had been dreamed up in a bar without benefit of clergy or license.

In the second place, Pierson was not defending his castle when he shot Johnny. The first shot, that did no damage, might have been okay because Johnny was threatening the premises. However Pierson chased Johnny beyond the property and killed him on public domain. Johnny was running; he posed no threat. The right to repel an invader and deal with him forcefully on home grounds did not extend to open spaces.

The jury agreed with that reasoning. It took very little time to bring in a verdict of guilty. The judge sentenced Pierson to hang. An appeal was turned down. Pierson filed a request for a new trial with the Idaho Supreme Court. Lacking hope in that direction, and being at odds with his lawyer whom he publicly described as less than competent, Pierson broke jail. He slipped out one evening wearing light clothes and slippers.

Sheriff C. H. Furey organized pursuit. He didn't know which way to look; a man on foot in the mountains left a dim trail, and the fugitive might have gone in any of a dozen directions. Reports of lone strangers trickled in from the White Clouds, from Bayhorse, from Bonanza and Galena. Pierson stayed on the loose about two weeks. Late in August 1883, his tracks were picked up on the South Fork of the Payette near Warm Springs Creek. A stranger had breakfasted with the Dowling brothers, who were on their way to Idaho City from mining claims around Cape Horn.

Officers found footprints at Jordan Bridge that seemed to be heading for Garden Valley. It was a good guess. Sheriff John Gorman of Boise County learned that Pierson had stopped at the Carpenter cabin to bake bread while the owners were away and had bought a pair of shoes at the Cathcart place. The trail led to Squaw Creek in hills north of Emmett. There the sheriff found Pierson. The convict seemed glad to surrender. He had been having a miserable time, he said. He had walked about 300 miles, mostly at night. His slippers had worn out soon after he left Hailey. His feet were sore and bleeding. They were a little better since he had obtained shoes, but the shoes were the wrong size for comfortable walking.

During his ordeal in the wilderness, Pierson said, he had lived on berries and a raw bullfrog. The bread he baked at the Carpenter ranch was the first real food he had eaten. He was hungry, cold, and dejected. Sheriff Gorman took him to jail at Idaho City and notified Sheriff Furey to come after him.

The jail was more comfortable than life in the mountains, but Pierson didn't take kindly to the quarters there, any more than he did those at Hailey. He tried to break out. Guards got wise and put him in irons. The Alturas sheriff took him back to Hailey to await the outcome of the appeal.

The Idaho Supreme Court spoke in February 1884. The verdict of guilty was sustained; there would be no second trial. The court supported the previous argument that Pierson had exceeded his rights to defend his castle when he chased Johnny into the brush. "All danger to Pierson was over," the opinion said. "Hall had withdrawn."

One justice dissented. He said Pierson had "acted as any good citizen would act" in attempting to have Hall arrested and in sending for a doctor to help Banjo Nell. He was, therefore, not very guilty.

The rest of the court found little substance in that idea. A new date for the execution was set — August 1, 1884. Governor William Bunn denied a petition for clemency. "I am unable to find sufficient reason to warrant executive interference," he said. "If the happy condition of empty jails and unused scaffolds dawns upon this territory during my occupancy of the gubernatorial chair, it must come through the behavior of the people and not by the pardoning power vested in your obedient servant."

Having exhausted all means for beating the rap, Pierson put on a show as a celebrity. He angrily denied a rumor that he had raped a nine-year-old girl some years before. He said the story was a vicious lie, and that's what it turned out to be, so far as serious investigation could determine. Pierson blamed the sensational press for defaming his character. He had killed Johnny Hall in self-defense, he said.

He objected, too, when he was ordered to have his picture taken in a railway car by "Two-Shot" Tate, a professional photographer. The sheriff said he had to, whether he liked it or not. They took him in irons to the parlor car. Whether he made faces at the camera man during the sitting, as is rumored, is not known because the pictures are rare, if preserved at all.

Early in the afternoon of August 1 a procession formed at the courthouse. A closed carriage accommodated Pierson, Sheriff Furey, two clergymen, and Pierson's attorney. Curious spectators

Photo by Ernie Day

El Capitan and Alice Lake

followed on horses and in buggies. The group moved solemnly to Quigley Gulch, then an area of wood-cutting and ranching and since distinguished by two executions. (The other hangee was 'Ah Sam', hanged September 18, 1885 for killing another Chinese.)

Pierson mounted the scaffold and spoke for about twenty minutes. He said he was about to suffer the extreme penalty of the law "not because of the crime but because of prejudice caused by my running away from jail last summer." He warned against the habit of carrying firearms. Then he went on to repeat his version of the shooting. "In all my dealings with Johnny," he said, "I did what I thought was right by a fellow man. If I had had justice I would not be here. A man's home is his castle."

At the end of his talk, Pierson said he was ready. Bishop Dan Tuttle offered a prayer. Pierson rolled a cigaret, scratched a match on his pants, and took a couple of puffs as the trap fell.

A logical question about the woman in the case deserves a postscript. What became of Banjo Nell? Not much is known. A newspaper item shortly after Pierson was arrested says she asked to go to jail with him. The sheriff refused. Public subscription raised $40 for her stage and train fare to Salt Lake City, and she departed.

A month after Pierson was executed there was another hanging at the same place. Knock Wah Choi — 'Ah Sam' — was hanged for killing a Chinese doctor at Atlanta two years earlier. Choi was a cool customer on the scaffold. "Me no likee talk," he said to the deputy sheriff who tripped the trigger.

Chapter 24

MISSING LEGISLATOR

OF THE MEMBERS of the state legislature of 1893, Paul P. Lawson of Custer County is probably one of the best remembered. His place in history has nothing to do with the laws he introduced, but it has a great deal to do with a law he broke. Lawson was convicted of murder and sentenced to hang.

The crime occurred in May 1895, two years after he concluded his services to the state. His record in Boise was uneventful. The journal shows he attended faithfully, voted on most bills, and took an average part in improving the statutory climate of his constituents. There may have been some Lawson bills of uncommon merit, but he was not long available to explain the part he played or to take credit for accomplishment.

Lawson spent a good share of his time after the session feuding with a neighbor in the little town of Houston, a place between Mackay and Arco, now little more than a memory. Whenever he met George Watson there was blood on the moon. The disagreement was a family affair. The first outbreak came when Lawson ordered Watson off his place. They met again on the street. Watson whipped the legislator. The *Challis Messenger* said Watson knocked him down several times and trod him into the mud. George McLeod, a historian of Blaine County, relates that Lawson was laid up about six weeks.

On the May day when the major action took place, evidence shows that Lawson waited at the home of a friend, knowing Watson would shortly pass that way. He did come, hiking down the highway, apparently unarmed. When Watson was a few yards away, Lawson stepped out and leveled the shotgun. Testimony at the trial conflicted as to what happened next. Lawson said Watson put a hand on his hip pocket and snarled: "Now, you old bat, I'll do you up." Lawson said he thought Watson had a gun. Other witnesses said Lawson shot Watson in the back without preliminaries. No weapon was found on the body.

The first blast, delivered either from front or rear, did not finish Watson. He staggered up and charged the legislator. A second shot ended the fight. Lawson stood guard over the body fourteen hours. He allowed nobody to approach. Finally a group of men prevailed on him to permit an inquest. He agreed to that, with the provision that he be permitted to select the jury. His committee brought in a verdict of death by shotgun wounds. Lawson didn't like the tone of it. He sent the jury back for further deliberation and accepted the second verdict of justifiable homicide.

Word of the kangaroo proceedings reached proper authorities in Challis, where friends of the deceased took offense. The coroner went to Houston for a bona fide inquest that threw out the amateur decision and held Lawson to answer for murder.

The trial came off at Challis in June. It lasted about a week. The prosecution was handled by N. M. Ruick, later U.S. district attorney; and J. C. Rogers, Custer County attorney. Lawson was represented by Presley M. Bruner, W. T. Reeves, and N. J. Sharp. The jury was out about three hours. The verdict was murder in the first degree.

The method of getting the news to the outside world caused almost as much commotion as the verdict itself. A special messenger waited at the courthouse. He scribbled notes in his book and took off for Ketchum at 1 o'clock in the morning on a bicycle. It was a period of great faith in bicycles. They were the latest thing in transportation. Bicycle togs and bicycle races were the rage from Boston to Boise. For all the merits of a two-wheeler on the flat around town, it did not prove to be the best beast for rapid travel along the ruts of Salmon and Wood rivers. The Mercury of the mountains staggered into Ketchum in the afternoon and filed his story by telegraph in time to have it in the morning papers, little more than twenty-four hours after the news broke. He made excellent time by standards of the day. There was a good deal of talk about equipping reporters in the backcountry with bikes. Most of the talk, however, came from editors. Reporters who rode the wilderness felt in their bones that a saddle horse was much better.

Judge C. O. Stockslager sentenced Lawson to hang July 26. "The prisoner received the sentence without much emotion and apparently indifferent manner," wrote the bicycle correspondent, who wheeled back to Challis and may have felt some envy for the defendent, who lolled around all day on a cot. Lawson's attorneys filed an appeal. The execution was delayed pending review of the case.

Anticipating a long stay for his most notable customer, the Custer County sheriff expressed doubts about his accommodations. The jail at Challis was a flimsy affair. Prisoners found it relatively easy to escape. On one occasion a felon burned a hole in the wall. Others had kicked down the door. Hailey had a fancy new jail with side-delivery steel doors and all the latest fixings. A deal was made with Blaine County for transfer of the legislative prisoner to this calaboose, where he could be securely detained as long as the courts debated his fate. Lawson went over the summit not on a bicycle but in a wagon because he had plenty of time.

His appeal to district court failed. Judge Stockslager reset the execution for September 25. Attorneys took the case to the Idaho Supreme Court. The appeal was filed and is duly recorded as number 602½ (the half perhaps indicating a state of suspense) but did not come before the justices.

Lawson acted on his own appeal. He broke out of jail early in September. Two masked men jumped Sheriff Benton at the courthouse in Hailey as he was locking up for the night. They bandaged his eyes, took his keys, opened Lawson's cell, extracted that gentleman, and locked the sheriff in the compartment. No other prisoners were released because there were none.

Four horses were waiting. The fugitive and three accomplices galloped into the dark. It was about an hour before the sheriff's predicament was discovered. He said he figured Lawson was heading for Canada or Mexico. He had overheard conversations to that effect.

With the search so pinpointed, posses made a stab or two in the directions of Bellevue and Ketchum and gave up. The trail was cold, and inducements were meager. Blaine County couldn't put up a reward because Lawson was Custer County business. Custer County commissioners would not meet until the following week. By that time Lawson could have been in Saskatchewan or Guadalupe.

In case anyone wants to look for Lawson, he was five feet ten inches tall, had black hair, a full beard, and weighed 225 pounds. As far as the record shows, he's going yet.

Chapter 25

LIZZIE KING

NEAR BONANZA on Yankee Fork of Salmon River there are three graves. Legend, flowering through nearly a century, insists they comprise most of boot hill, an area set aside by respectable citizens of Bonanza, as in other western towns, for the burial of flagrant sinners. Whether or not the graves were really in a place of disgrace is not established, nor is it a vital matter. The mounds are long since overgrown with pine, grass, and weeds that persist in spite of occasional efforts to tidy the spot for tourists. The graves hold the remains of three persons whose lives were full of tempest, violence, and tragedy. For better or worse, there lie Lizzie Stanley King Hawthorne, Richard King, and Robert Hawthorne.

Their relationship under laws of state and church is subject to question. The doubt was raised in legal proceedings that at various times dug at the roots of a manslaughter, a murder, and a suicide. Lizzie Stanley was probably the wife of Richard King. She may also have been the wife of Robert Hawthorne at a later date. At any rate both men loved her. One of them died in her presence; one shot her and killed himself.

Richard King was a Bonanza businessman. He was a native of London and had lived at Bodie, California, before joining the expectant tide to Yankee Fork. Like most men in Bonanza he took a hand in mining. He also dealt in real estate. His associate was William Dillon.

Early in July 1879, when a good many anxious residents feared that Sheepeater Indians would presently lay claim to the precinct by force of arms and arrows, King and Dillon squabbled over title to a cabin in Custer. The argument bloomed into a shooting in King's home. Dillon killed King. The only witness was Lizzie King, said to be the wife of the deceased. She testified that Dillon provoked the fight, produced the gun, and shot her man.

Alarmed by the first outbreak of fatal violence in the community, leading citizens arrested Dillon, rendered a do-it-yourself coroner's verdict of death by unlawful means, and packed Dillon off to Salmon for trial in district court. After due trial Dillon was found guilty and sentenced to ten years in the territorial prison in Boise.

After the homicide in her home and her appearance at the trial, Lizzie left Bonanza. She went to Butte, where in the hurly-burly of the copper camp she met handsome Bob Hawthorne. The friendship ripened. Lured by glowing accounts of fortunes ready for the picking in Idaho, Hawthorne prospected on Wood River. He struck what he said gave promise of becoming a breadwinner if not a glittering fortune. With prospects looking brighter, Lizzie returned to Bonanza in spite of sad memories of Yankee Fork. She had reason to look forward to a fresh and triumphant start as a woman of financial substance.

Hawthorne's letters from Hailey brought a series of optimistic tidings. His claim looked better and better, he said. It was in an excellent district; mines nearby were rich. His biggest problem was whether to develop the claim by himself or sell and get out. A buyer was hot for a deal. Was it wiser to take a few thousand or wait and gamble on the jackpot?

Sell, said Lizzie. Sell and take up more claims. Get the money. Meanwhile, she started a nest egg of her own. Relying on credit backed by the sure thing Bob had by the tail, and helped by Bonanza friends, Lizzie opened the Yankee Fork Dance Hall and Saloon. The venture lifted more eyebrows than mortgages. Few women engaged in business at that time and place. Traffic in liquor and entertainment was tolerated and generously supported, but it was no enterprise for a lady. The better element of Bonanza City twittered in amazement as the widow kicked up her heels. Money did not pour into the saloon. Debts piled up. Whispers about Lizzie mounted to a roar.

She appealed to Hawthorne to make haste. Sell the claims and come to Bonanza, she urged. Bob came quickly and in glory. Everything was grand. Not only had he picked up a nice bit of money

on Wood River but had just had word from England of an unexpected $1,000 windfall. The money was the first of several hand-
some sums from an estate just distributed. They were well fixed, he
said. No more worry; no more penny-pinching. Let Bonanza turn
up its nose at you. Who cares? We'll buy the place. We'll pay off
the debt on the saloon. Then we'll leave town. We'll take a trip to
England. Together we will see the world.

Glowing with happiness, Lizzie decorated her establishment for
a wedding. She scrubbed the floor and put up frilly curtains. She
brought in a new stock of fancy hats for the millinery corner of her
multipurpose shop. Her dancing girls brought buckets of wild
flowers. With a bar mirror for a backdrop and in the presence of a
few friends, Lizzie King and Robert Hawthorne pledged loyalty to
each other on an August afternoon in 1880. The *Yankee Fork
Herald* called it a marriage.

Bliss reigned. As radiant as any bride who walked down the
aisle to the music of a cathedral organ, Lizzie Hawthorne trod the
walks of Bonanza. Her presence brought a distinct thaw in areas
recently cool. Respectable people smiled at her; merchants welcomed her trade. The word was around that Mr. and Mrs. Hawthorne were rich. What a charming couple! Too bad they would not
stay long.

The scheduled date of departure was the middle of August.
There was just time to tidy up a few business matters before tod-
dling off to London. On the morning of August 11, Lizzie blew
herself to a new bonnet. It was to be a surprise to Bob.

She skipped up to the bedroom. As she was adjusting the hat in
front of a mirror, she heard a tap at the door. Bob stepped in. From
a coat pocket he took a Bristish bulldog revolver. He shot his bride
three times. He turned the short barrel to his head and missed. He
then shot himself twice in the neck. Mr. and Mrs. Hawthorne died
quickly.

The reason for the shocking act soon came to the public ear.
Hawthorne, it was revealed, had scant funds. His talk of estates and
dividends was pure malarkey. He had put up a false front with no
collateral. On the day Lizzie put on the new bonnet he discovered
the jig was up. While Lizzie was choosing the hat he was trying to
buy her a dress. He offered a check. The merchant turned it down.
There had been a quiet investigation of Hawthorne's finances. The
reports from Wood River and the outside world were black. The
payment from England was not only delayed, it was a figment of
fancy.

The Yankee Fork Dance Hall and Saloon closed for the funeral. It was a short ceremony. Mr. and Mrs. Hawthorne were buried close to the grave of Richard King.

Bonanza returned to its normal pace as the tragedy faded into memory. A year later the details were dusted off and paraded again. William Dillon asked a pardon for killing Richard King. Colonel W. H. Broadhead, who had prepared papers for Dillon's arrest, said there was wide discrepancy between what Lizzie had told him immediately after the shooting and what she said in court. Lizzie was termed a "disreputable character." The statement said little or no weight should have been attached to her testimony. District Attorney James Hawley joined in the request. The marriage of Lizzie and Dick was questioned. Citizens who had been silent before said King had threatened Dillon before the fatal argument. County commissioners, territorial legislators, and other men of repute praised the character of Dillon. The slaying, they said, was self-defense.

Governor Mason Brayman granted a pardon.

A romantic note is added to the chapter by Ethel Yarber in her book, *Land of the Yankee Fork.* She says Charles Franklin, a prominent mining man, had been in love with Lizzie. He had helped her in business and was disappointed when she married Hawthorne. He died several years later in a lonely cabin at Stanley, allegedly of heartbreak.

Chapter 26

DEATH OF A TEAMSTER

HENRY MCDONALD wrote poor letters. He is known in Idaho criminal history for other things, but his notoriety at Silver City, Boise, and a portion of the Sawtooths does not erase his blunders as a correspondent. If there were a contest for miserable letters, McDonald would stand high in the blue-ribbon group. In a sense, he wrote himself to death. If he had known more about the mails and the geography of the Sawtooths, things might have turned out differently. He might have escaped the hangman.

The McDonald case is the most notorious crime in the records of Owyhee County. It touches the Sawtooths in only one of its episodes, but that connection is sufficient to make it part of the saga.

The story is full of mystery, moonlight, bleached bones on the prairie, rolling wagons, cops and robbers, and the unfortunate letters. The letters are particularly significant.

Late in September 1880, George Myers, a gray-haired, whiskered freighter known as "Old George" because he was about 56 and wore one dirty shirt all summer, disappeared on the road between Boise and Kelton, Utah. He was last seen traveling with Henry McDonald, a young teamster. McDonald presently showed up on the way back from Kelton with a load of freight on Myers's wagons. He said he had bought the outfit from the old man, paying

$600 cash and signing a note for the balance amounting to $800. That was odd, because McDonald had not been known to have more than $50 in one bundle for a number of years. He was reasonably industrious, but nobody believed he had put aside $600 for a rainy day.

The finger of suspicion pointed so straight, and Myers remained so strangely absent, that Sheriff Joe Oldham moseyed to Mayfield to have a talk with McDonald. Where, he asked, was the old man? McDonald couldn't say for sure. Maybe he had taken off for Oregon. Yes, that was it. Myers went to Oregon to look for a horse he had lost in the Bannock Indian War. McDonald recollected that a day after he bought the outfit they met people who told Myers where the horse might be. He had gone after it.

Notwithstanding the lost horse and the possibility that the old man might be hale and hearty in parts unknown, the sheriff jailed McDonald at Boise. It was very unfair, McDonald said; it was all a mistake. He had bought the team and wagon. Myers would show up any day. Even if Myers did not come in person he would write. A letter was expected.

A letter did come to Boise. It was received by William Morlatt, a freighter who lived on the Placerville road about eighteen miles from Boise near the Rossi tollgate. Myers had kept stock at the Morlatt place. The letter was dated October 23 at Salmon Falls, nearly a month after the old man disappeared.

"I have sold my team too Henry McDonald," it said, "and have got track of that horse of mine and am going to find him. I may go down to Portland, Ore. if I don't find him and come back by Kelton. I will get a team from McDonald to come home if he don't want to load there. I want you to get that colt that is halter broke and let McDonald have him. I will give him an order for him and I want you to look out for the horses until I get back. Yours truely, George Myers."

Morlatt said the letter had come several days after he turned the halter-broke colt over to McDonald. He was still waiting for the order that did not arrive. He was still waiting for it several weeks after McDonald was jailed. Morlatt also told officers that the letter he did get was peculiar; the signature was not that of George Myers.

Tom Cahalan, district attorney, refrained from informing Henry McDonald that the law knew about the letter. Instead, he pounded again on the question: What had become of the old man? McDonald had a new flash of recollection. There were many hard

characters on the Kelton road. It was quite likely they had robbed
the old boy. Maybe they knocked him in the head. They could
have buried him in the sagebrush. It's a big country out there; nobody would ever find him. As a matter of fact, McDonald said, he
had been robbed himself the day after Myers sold him the outfit
and went off someplace. A couple of mean guys held a gun on him
and took $35. All he had left was $5 they overlooked in his watch
pocket.

The story was a little late, but better late than never. Territorial
officers were checking into it when fresh evidence developed.
Freighters who had met Myers and McDonald said the two were
fighting about a dog. They said there were angry words, and somebody went for a gun. At the next camp, they said, Myers did not
appear. They asked McDonald about it and he said the old man
chewed him out because of the dog. He said Myers had the dog on
a short leash and it kept falling out of the wagon and dragging its
hind legs. He said he told Myers to put the dog in the wagon and
quit dragging him. Myers went for his pistol in the toolbox and fell
under the wagon. A wheel ran over him.

McDonald said he was fixing to take care of the old man when
three riders came up. They told him they knew Myers and would
look after him. They told him to go on, so he did. He didn't wait to
find out how badly the old man was hurt. It looked like the wheel
ran over his head.

That was the substance of the freighters' revelation. The account, like the letter, was kept from McDonald. He stoutly insisted
that a message would come from the old man, putting a finish to
the uncomfortable affair. In spite of his story, the justice court held
McDonald for the grand jury.

The prisoner got busy with his correspondence. Being short in
the arts of writing, he enlisted the aid of Bill Glines, a cellmate
serving a short term for a minor offense. Glines furnished paper,
held a candle, and coached McDonald. Between them they
whipped out a batch of letters. All went to the same man, a bartender at Kelton. There were several enclosures and a covering note.

"Dear George," the covering letter said. "I am in a tite place. If
I have to stay for the grand jury I am gone for good. Now doo mee a
favor, for this does depend on my life and I will make it all rite
with you when I see you. George, be sure and see some of Myers
hand write and sine his name as near like it as you can. George
now don't fail and don't write anything but the affair between me
and Myers because the sheriff opens letters and reads them."

Photo by Ernie Day

Beef on range in Sawtooth Valley

The first enclosure was as follows:

"Willow Creek, November 1, 1880. Mister Henry McDonald, Sir: I am now at Willow Creek. I have bought a span of mules and wagon and want to traid for the horses if you want to traid for them. Well, I hope you get the colt all rite. I will pay Mister Morlatt for getting him to you. I may go up to the Dalles and I may go to the railroad and if you want the mules you can have them. Well, I haven't much to say this time. I hope you had a good trip. Yours truely, George Myers."

The second enclosure said this:

"Toris, November 18. Mister Henry McDonald, Sir: I am now at Toris and am a little under the weather and I want to get down to Ward as soon as I can and then I will be coming to Kelton and see you and straighten out the business between you and me. And then I am going to Boise City. I hope you had a good trip and got along well. Yours truely, George Myers."

There was one further message to the bartender at Kelton:

"George — be shure and get his shipment card and see where he signs his name and get it as near as you can. I shall go to hell if you don't do this for me."

McDonald sealed the envelope and gave it to his cellmate. The letter did not get to Kelton. It did not even reach the post office. It was handed directly to the sheriff. McDonald roared. He said unpleasant things about his jail partner, and that man was happy to be moved. "I did not stay in jail but a few minutes after the jailer came," he said.

Having flunked the course in communications, McDonald took heart in the fact that Myer's body had not been found — if indeed he was dead. Without a body, the charge of murder was thin. Nevertheless, the prisoner's prospects were not bright. McDonald threw away his pen and concentrated on a soup spoon as a better implement for obtaining freedom. He started digging a tunnel under his bed with mealtime tools. He hid his excavations with spare clothing.

While he was digging he had additional reason to get out of there. Four stockmen hunting cattle on the Kelton road found a shirt, pants, and bones. The discovery was near the intersection of the Kelton road and the Toano cutoff between what are now Glenns Ferry and Twin Falls. Henry Pierce, one of the stockmen, discovered enough evidence to convince the coroner and prosecutor that George Myers was dead and had been dead since September. It was extremely doubtful, to say the least, that Myers could have written letters from Kelton and from points in Oregon more than a month after his skull was crushed and his body buried in a shallow grave.

The district attorney informed McDonald he would be tried for first-degree murder in Owyhee County. The defendant's first reaction was that Owyhee did not have jurisdiction. He said the grave of whoever it was — certainly not Myers — was in Cassia County. The objection was technical. Whether the body was in Owyhee or Cassia, geography would not delay justice long. With that thought in mind, McDonald dug furiously until, in April, the jailer halted the enterprise. He said he had been hep to the tunnel for some weeks and felt that McDonald had moved about all the ground the county could spare. McDonald was moved to another cell, and the tunnel was filled.

Two crushing defeats — one with his literary excursion and the other with spoons — might have discouraged the average prisoner. But McDonald tried again. In May he opened the jail door, which nobody was watching at the time. He mounted a horse a few rods away that just happened to be conveniently saddled, provisioned, and armed, and galloped for Boise Ridge.

The only witness to the flight said McDonald fell off when the horse jumped a ditch on the fort grounds. The tumble was of little consequence. McDonald climbed on again and galloped into the mountains. He made his way up the Middle Fork to Atlanta. After a short pause he plunged on into the Sawtooths where, up to that time, only Indians and a few miners had ventured. McDonald didn't know the territory, but he didn't care. Anything was better than sticking around in jail. He soon ran into deep snow. He turned his horse loose and tried to follow a difficult trail on foot. The going was very tough. His small supply of food gave out. Cold weather chilled him to the bone. Huge drifts delayed his painful progress to headwaters of the Salmon River. He tossed up a lean-to and waited.

Meanwhile, back in Boise, jailer Jerry Plume, smarting with chagrin at the escape, loaded a horse with provisions and gave chase. He picked up clues here and there along Boise River and followed tracks to the divide. He then sniffed around among early spring prospectors and found McDonald's hideout. The fugitive surrendered without a fight. He was ready to call it quits for something to eat and a warm place to sleep. Plume took McDonald to Rocky Bar — no easy jaunt — and turned him over to the sheriff of Alturas County for transfer by wagon to Boise. McDonald was in irons and in a very tough pickle indeed.

Soon after his return to custody, a survey of the Toano junction proved that Myers's grave was in Owyhee County. Silver City stashed the prisoner in its substantial lockup near old Champion Hall, from which felons found little point in digging because their cells were in a cave. McDonald settled in for the duration.

His trial took several days. Witnesses for the territory piled up a crushing load of testimony. The evidence established that McDonald, a teamster of modest means, had gone out with Myers coveting his freight outfit and had returned with the team and wagons. Moreover, he had told several inconsistent stories about the absence of Myers. Story number one was that Myers had gone to Oregon. Story number two said the old man had been done in by robbers. Third: Myers had gone on to Kelton and been taken ill after writing a series of letters clearing McDonald. Fourth: He had died of injuries when he fell off a wagon.

McDonald explained everything when he got on the stand. In a long statement he patched holes and darned rips. Some of his earlier concoctions, he said, were not quite true. Having had time to review the entire matter in light of unfortunate developments and in prospect of the gallows, he realized he had been too imaginative. He had lied, he said, because he was afraid a couple of guys would kill him if he told the truth.

It was actually this way, he told the court:

He wanted to buy Myers's outfit. He knew the old man wanted to sell. He learned Myers was headed for Kelton, so he quit his job with another freighter, bought a ticket for Rattlesnake on the Overland Road, and caught up with Myers there. They went on together several days. He made a deal with Myers. He paid some money down and agreed to sign papers for the whole business when they got to Salmon Falls.

After selling the team and wagon, McDonald said, Myers started nipping a jug. He talked mean. He was hard to get along with. Myers had a dog. It chased rabbits and whatnot. Every so often they had to wait for the dog. It was so worn out it could hardly navigate but it kept jumping out of the wagon. Myers finally tied it in with ropes. One rope came off and the dog jumped out again. The remaining rope was so short the dog dragged on its hind legs.

"I said turn him loose or put him back in the wagon," McDonald said. "Myers said to mind my own business; he would take care of the dog.

"I told him again to go easy on the dog, and he went for a six-shooter in the jockey box. Myers fell off. His right leg was under the doubletree and his left leg between the doubletrees when the wagon hit a chuck hole. He caught hold of the breeching of the harness which scared the mules and they went to kicking. Before I could get the brake on, the mules kicked him loose. The front wheel of the lead wagon ran over part of his body. The hind wheel, being locked with the brake, crowded him along in front of the wheel for ten or fifteen steps before I could get the team stopped.

"Len Lewis and Frank Kellet rode in before I got Myers out from under the wheel. Lewis said: 'What's the matter?' I told him Myers wanted me to leave the dog travel the way he was tied and he went to get his six-shooter and fell off the wagon. Mr. Kellet and myself took Myers from under the wagon wheel. I asked him to help put Myers in the wagon so I could take him to Salmon Falls. He said I had better leave Myers where he was and that they would take care of him. I told him no, that I wanted to take him to the station. Mr. Lewis and Mr. Kellet stepped back and had a talk for two or three minutes.

"Lewis said if I didn't leave Myers for them to take care of it would be so much worse for me. I asked them how I could account for Myers. They told me I should say he had gone with those folks down toward Oregon. Mr. Lewis said that Mr. Glenn had been trying for two or three years to get him in trouble and they would say that Gus Glenn was the cause of Mr. Myers's death. They insisted I should leave him with them and they would fix it all right for me to go about my business. I then rode to Salmon Falls. I could not state the real facts because I was afraid of what these men told me."

The narrative did not catch the prosecution by surprise. Intimations of the scenario had leaked out while McDonald was in jail in Boise. In rebuttal, the territory produced Mr. Lewis. He proved he was not near the scene of the crime. As for Kellet, he was not known. Lewis had never heard of him; neither had anybody else within knowledge of the court. The prosecution branded the tale a fancy piece of fiction. The jury thought so, too. McDonald was found guilty. He was sentenced to hang in August.

An appeal was heard by the state supreme court. The judgment was affirmed and a new date set for the execution. McDonald was hanged on a rainy October afternoon in the Ruby City cemetery. Several hundred people watched the only legal execution in Owyhee County. An often-repeated story relates a remark by McDonald while he waited in a wagon for the procession to the gallows. A late-comer dashed up. "Take your time," McDonald said. "There won't be much going on before I get there."

The *Owyhee Avalanche,* a Silver City newspaper, said McDonald was composed and unemotional in his final hours. Whatever letters he may have written just before the execution remained private. Officers did not intercept his communications. There was no longer any point in expecting a letter from George Myers.

Execution was efficient. Officers performed their grim duty with dispatch. A "recollection" that a band played "Down Went McGinty" when the trap sprung is probably fictional. There is nothing to support it in contemporary accounts.

McDonald was buried in the cemetery a short distance from the gallows.

Chapter 27

CHIPS EVANS

SHOOTING PEOPLE, even bad guys who deserved to die, was not a way to make friends and influence juries, even in Idaho territorial days. Charles ("Chips") Evans took a whirl at it in an area on the fringe of the Sawtooths and reaped a whirlwind of justice. The judge who tried the case said the man Evans killed was "dreadfully low and base" but that was no excuse for murder. Chips Evans was just as mean, probably meaner. And crafty as a nest of owls.

The shooting happened on Big Creek in November 1886. Several miners were on an expedition into the bush. The most disliked of the lot was James McKee. Testimony at the trial suggested he would have won no popularity contests or awards for good citizenship. His companions, driven beyond patience by his ugly nature, wanted to get rid of him. Whether or not there was an understanding that he should be done in was not established, but there was common belief that few tears were shed when opportunity presented itself.

McKee got into a heated argument with Edward Lyon and Caleb Davis. Somebody — perhaps McKee — shot and wounded Davis. Charles Evans shot McKee, and the shot was fatal.

Knowing the ruction would create notoriety and inquiry, Evans hastened to Salmon City, some forty miles away, and swore out a complaint against McKee, then dying from his gunshot. He also charged Lyon with shooting Davis. Evans had the brass and the cunning to charge the victim with a capital crime when there were witnesses alive who were likely to talk when matters came to a showdown.

The sheriff went back with Evans to arrest Lyon. He would have arrested McKee, too, but that customer was dead. The sheriff tied Lyon on a horse and led the horse personally. Behind them rode Thomas McKinney, Sam Vinson, and Chip Evans. A few miles down the trail the sheriff had a surprise. At a switchback the three followers dropped out of sight. The officer wondered what caused the delay. He didn't have long to wait.

They jumped him from the front, having raced ahead through a clearing into a rocky ambush. Vinson held a gun on the sheriff; one of the other men shot Lyon three times. He could not defend himself, being unarmed and tied to the saddle. As the bullets slammed into his body, he slumped. He rolled to one side, head down, with his feet roped to the stirrups. McKinney and Davis came close to see whether the job was finished. They found no sign of life. They then ordered the sheriff to ride on alone to Salmon, which he did. Confident that the verdict would be that Lyon was killed resisting an officer, no matter what the sheriff said, they had a drink and went about their business. It was their word against the sheriff's if they were apprehended. Furthermore, they had saved the county the cost of eliminating a murderer or two.

Their clever ploy didn't quite come off. Lyon was not dead. In spite of the shots, which would have killed almost anybody, he refused to die. Several days after the conspirators arrived in Salmon, cocky and talkative, Lyon arrived, too. He was quite distressed by the treatment he had received. He had played dead on the horse, he said, because he wanted the gang to think he was done for. He had held his breath as he hung in the saddle. He was so nearly dead it wasn't difficult to put on an act. After the sheriff and the gunmen left, he managed to untie his feet. He wandered three days before miners found him and brought him to town for medical care and a chat with the prosecuting attorney.

The entire mess, from unsavory beginning to shocking conclusion, was aired before a grand jury. The jurors chose to throw out the charge against Lyon for shooting Caleb Davis; there was reasonable doubt that the right man was accused. Chips Evans was indicted for second-degree murder in the killing of McKee. Vinson was tried, found guilty of assault, and sentenced to fourteen years.

McKinney was charged with shooting Lyon with intent to kill. Admitted to bail, he left the jurisdiction.

Evans denied the murder rap. His trial was the main event of the April 1887 term of territorial court at Salmon City. A reporter for the *Salt Lake Tribune* expressed the general excitement when he said, "The affair has created a great deal of feeling in this region."

Evans advanced thin arguments in his defense. His main excuse was that he was acting in the cause of justice as a good citizen when he killed McKee. He shot the old buzzard, he said, to prevent him from taking the life of another. The jury did not buy that. Neither did the Idaho Supreme Court, to which the point was referred on appeal.

The most dramatic moment of the proceeding was the pronouncement of sentence by Judge James B. Hays. His language blistered the convicted man:

"You have been indicted for the crime of murder. You have been found guilty by a jury of your countrymen. I had serious doubts as to whether I did not commit an error when I instructed the jury that they could not find you guilty of murder in the first degree. I have the consolation that if I have erred I have done so on the side of mercy, although I am not sure but what, if the question had been submitted solely to the jury, it would have been murder in the first degree, and then the dreadful penalty would have to be pronounced against you and inflicted on you.

"I have listened to the details of the crime and have found nothing in your conduct to palliate your guilt. There was much in the trial to disgust and shock every good citizen. The man who was killed was dreadfully low and base, too low to be fit for any society, and the testimony corroborates it, but it is no excuse for your crime. You have violated that ancient law, 'thou shalt not kill.' It has been given by God to the human family and by them has been held as such a law for countless ages. You have killed your fellowman without a moment's warning in his weakness and baseness.

"There is nothing about you to commend itself to the favorable consideration of this court. You acted with a baseness that was fearful, and the degree of wickedness you showed at the trial showed you possessed of a heart dead to every noble impulse. You are at heart a double murderer. You killed McKee. You have not denied it on the stand except so far as the law denied it for you. Your counsel helped you out as far as concerns the attempted murder of Lyon.

Had you succeeded in that, nothing would have saved you. The death penalty would have been inflicted.

"I have inquired into your past record, and while you have not been a desperate man you have been a meddlesome one, of an officious and interfering character, which in years past, I understand, gave you the nickname by which you are known. You have gone from bad to worse until you now stand a convicted murderer. I am thus merciless, because the law does not ask you to be a good citizen — it commands you to be one. It will control you by brute force. If you should endeavor to escape from officers of the law it will be their duty to slay you as they would slay a wild beast. This language is harsh and severe, I am aware, but I want you to understand your position, and you must and shall submit.

"The judgment of this court, Charles Evans, is that you be imprisoned at hard labor in the territorial prison for the full term of your natural life. Society cannot afford to be bothered with you any more."

During the delivery of the sentence, a reporter said, "the court-room was crowded with men who sat with bated breath and seemed glad when the judge was through because of the burning language and the impressive manner in which he spoke. He has made crime in this district a terrible thing, and in giving criminals the full extent of the law he has inspired a feeling of safety among citizens."

Chapter 28

CLAYTON DANKS

HE WAS NOT really a bad man. In the roster of Idaho criminals Clayton Danks never attained the notoriety of Brocky Jack, the laughing stage robber, or John Wheeler, the braggart of Bigfoot fame, or "Diamond-Field" Jack Davis, the mercenary gunman of livestock wars. He was a bush-league felon, a fairly late comer to the fraternity of outlaws and an impulsive gent whose career as an apprentice butcher might never have been interrupted, or his subsequent deportment be worth recollecting, if it had not been for some striking incidents in his extraordinary wrestle with the law.

The Danks case is an example of the marksmanship sometimes exhibited in old western gunfights that gives the answer to small boys of the current generation who wonder, while watching prolonged hailstorms of lead on television, why nobody gets hit: They didn't shoot worth a darn.

Of course, there were exceptions. Hugh Whitney shot the trigger finger off the hand of a bridge guard at seventy-five yards while making a getaway in eastern Idaho. An Indian scout shot Buffalo Horn at a creditable distance in a battle near Silver City. A hothead at Graham killed two men with three shots, although the accomplishment can hardly be scored as a triumph, since the shooting took place in a small saloon and the third shot hit an innocent bystander across the street. "Wild Bill" Johnson of Albion, who specialized in homemade money, enjoyed a reputation as a good shot, but he shot off his mouth more than his revolver and talked himself into prison.

Most of the Dead-Eye-Dicks didn't, or couldn't, hit a washtub at thirty paces. And if something the size of a washtub happened to be armed and angry, they didn't come close. A large majority of Idaho homicides caused by firearms were the product of shots fired point-blank. A man who placed the muzzle of his gun against his opponent's chest was not a marksman.

Clayton Danks did not claim to be a gunman. Neither did the men who carried on a running war with him across the state. In the public mind, however, desperado and possemen were cloaked with the mantle of Daniel Boone. As the skirmishes progressed from county to county like a traveling Buffalo Bill show, the reputed dexterity of the participants grew and their embarrassment in falling short of their unsought status bloomed blush red.

The number of jurisdictions disturbed by Danks in his adventures of the spring of 1909 was almost as remarkable as the abundance of bullets spent in his behalf. The show began in Canyon County. Somebody stole several horses. A John Doe warrant was issued, nominating a character about five feet nine, 170 pounds, brown hair, blue eyes, wearing light corduroy pants and a light hat with a half-inch strap band. He was reputed to be armed and ornery. Canyon County offered $50 reward.

Sheriff G. P. Taylor of Blaine County got word on a Sunday afternoon in May that a customer filling the description was headed for Hailey. It was a reliable tip. John Doe rode into town leading a packhorse. Sheriff Taylor and Deputy Hart jumped into a buggy and caught up with him at the lower end of Main Street. Taylor told him to get off his horse, and he did so. Leaping to the ground on the offside, he drew his pistol and commenced hostilities. Taylor and Hart piled out of the buggy. Lead flew. A widely copied report of the encounter said fourteen shots were fired. One tore a hole in the sheriff's coat sleeve, but he was not injured. Neither was John Doe.

The desperado — identified as such immediately after the exercises — hit for the hills without his horses. The deputy sheriff went after him. John Doe had the edge. With the advantage of concealment and a head start, he distanced the law and presently scared the daylights out of two young ladies riding down a country lane. He took their old white horse. It wasn't much of a horse. He rode it to the Wondersheck ranch, abandoned it, and stole a horse and buggy. A rancher there took two shots at John Doe and missed both times. (If these shots are counted, the total for the series of battles goes up to thirty. They are not accepted as part of the war because Danks did not reply. Only exchanges are tallied.)

John Doe drove the buggy to Broadford and abandoned it in a fence corner. Young Wondersheck rode up to see what was happening to his buggy. The desperado took the boy's horse at the

Photo by Ernie Day

Snowyside Peak and Twin Lakes

point of a gun. Sheriff Taylor arrived a few minutes later. He trailed John Doe to a crossing of Rock Creek, found the trail on the other side, and followed it to the Rube Pressie place where John Doe had switched horses again.

The multiple relays confounded the pursuit. The sheriff went back to Hailey. Blaine County offered $50 reward — the head money was piling up. With $100 for his scalp and any number of hoss thieveries in his wake, John Doe was a weekend sensation.

He had abandoned a good outfit when he ran away from his warm welcome in Hailey. Officers found a fine saddle, hair rope, and field glasses on the horse. The packhorse carried provisions and blankets for a long outing. Somewhere along his hurried tour from Hailey to Broadford, John Doe left word he would be back for his horses and outfit. The sheriff waited for him to put in a claim, but there was no further action on the Hailey front.

The next act was at Bruneau. A man robbed Hodge's Saloon. He was discovered before he could get a horse from the stable, and he had to take off on foot. A group of four sighted him and began long-distance rifle fire. The shooters were led by Roy Hodge. He identified John Doe as Clayton Danks, a former resident of Bruneau — a stockhand and apprentice butcher with a year's education at a college in Corvallis, Oregon.

In the first phase of the Bruneau battle nobody was hurt. The chase continued to Loveridge Ferry on the Snake, fifteen miles from Bruneau. Danks was cornered there. He kept firing until a shot by Hodge shattered his right shoulder. He held up his left hand in surrender.

Sheriff M. M. Kreig put him on a train at Mountain Home, headed for Nampa on the first leg of a journey to Silver City, the seat of Owyhee County. He was wanted in three counties, but authorities deemed it best to jail him at Silver City until they could decide which charge to press first.

Two officers and Danks reached Nampa at midnight. They lodged him in a room on the second floor of a hotel. The officers bedded down for the night between Danks and the stairs. Security was presumed adequate — besides, the prisoner had a broken shoulder. At 2 A.M. a couple of women outside the hotel saw somebody dangling from a second-story window. They didn't know whether he was going up or down, but they thought it might be a robbery. One woman watched while the other notified the night clerk. It was too late; Danks was out and away. He had made a rope of bedding, tied it to the bed, and slipped to the ground — with one arm in a sling.

He had a fifteen minute lead on the law. He left no trail, and the hunt was futile. Officers did not get their man. On the evening of the same day, H. A. Zimmer, who farmed a mile east of Nampa, saw someone skulking behind a shed. The stranger ran, but Zimmer caught him. The visitor said he was Clayton Danks and he was too tired to run further. Zimmer turned him over to the law and collected $50 reward.

At the end of his high jinks, and suffering sore feet as well as a wounded shoulder, Danks called it quits. Selecting from a sheaf of alleged felonies, the law charged him with assault to commit murder. The assault was on the person of Sheriff Taylor who was shot in the sleeve. Danks admitted guilt in court at Twin Falls. Judge Edward Walters sentenced him to serve one to fourteen years in the state prison. He was received as Clabe Danks, a well-built man of 29, scarred by many wounds: He had a scar over his left eye, a scar on his left jaw, a scar on his right thumb, three scars inside the right knee, a scar on the left knee, and an ax scar on his right foot. His right ankle was broken and enlarged. There was a scar behind his right ear, a bullet scar on his right shoulder, and a burn on the left wrist.

He was a good prisoner. After two years he was paroled to Lemhi County. In later years he became a peace officer in eastern Idaho, serving with vigor and fidelity.

Chapter 29

SILVER MOUNTAIN

PITT SMITH set a record for Idaho law enforcement. He was sworn in at 9 o'clock in the morning and went out of the deputy sheriff business, feet first, the same night. He was shot to death at Silver Mountain (also known as Graham) trying to make his first arrest, thereby establishing the championship for the shortest term with a star.

The fight in which he died rocked the mining camp in Boise County, just over the line from Elmore County, once a part of the old Sawtooth empire of Alturas. In fact, Elmore had pressed claim to Silver Mountain shortly before the fracas. After the shooting and the expenses of cleaning it up, the Elmore commissioners wanted no part of it.

Silver Mountain was a rip-roaring clutch of humanity destined to outrageous fortune from the first bite of the pick. It boomed out of nothing in the summer of 1888. Miners struck ore on the North Fork of Boise River. Matt Graham, a mining magnate of Boise Basin, Hailey, and London, provided financial muscle. He supplied the name and a mascot in the form of the largest dog in the territory — and he lost a fortune. Silver Mountain roared, sputtered, and died.

The roaring started not long before Pitt Smith arrived. "This is getting to be an enterprising camp," wrote a correspondent for the

Idaho World at Idaho City who signed himself "Olie." "Six saloons are already in and more coming. There are two dance halls in camp and two boardinghouses. Jas. Moriarty's is the larger, with room for 150 boarders. Mrs. Austin has two who will surely eat her out of house and home. Wood hauling has commenced in earnest and many teams are engaged. Here are to be found all the elements of a new camp with humanity shown at its worst side."

The raw elements exploded June 29. The *World* called it "one of the bloodiest shooting affairs that ever took place in the country."

Henry L. ("Tobe") Pitts from Boise, about 28, went on a drinking spree with William Ninemier, a freighter of many years' experience in Owyhee, Ada, and Boise counties. As a climax to their frolic, Pitts hit Ninemier over the head with a brace and bit. It did not augur for friendly relations, and retribution was not long in coming. Bill Ninemier and his brother, Ben, recruited Sam Wilson, their half-brother, for a call on Mr. Pitts. They found Pitts at a card table in Tom Combs's saloon. One man stepped behind him with a drawn revolver. Two stood in front challenging him to fight. They called Pitts a coward. Pitts may have been something short of the All-American boy, but he was no idiot. He shoved back his chair and dove for the bar. The man behind him fired. Pitts went down with a bullet in his back. Although dying, he pulled his gun with his left hand and jerked the trigger. The shot hit his own right hand.

John Townsend, an innocent bystander, leaped for the door. He caught a fatal bullet in the back. Other persons present ducked behind the bar. One scuttled into the woodbox.

Pitt Smith, the brand new deputy sheriff, heard the commotion from the other end of the street. He was unarmed. Nevertheless, he ran to the saloon and said: "Men, I command the peace."

A shot ripped into his side. After he fell, another shot hit his right arm. He lay groaning in the dust. The killers commanded Combs, the saloonkeeper, to kneel on the floor. They kept him there five minutes before allowing anyone to approach Smith. Friends then carried the deputy to the company store, where he died half an hour later.

The Ninemiers and Wilson stalked the town, daring arrest and threatening to shoot the first man who stepped up. Nobody stepped. The three gunmen left town in the morning; Sheriff Carey Havird arrived in the afternoon. He had had adventures on the way from Idaho City.

He said he had met and arrested Ben Ninemier. While the prisoner was on the way back to the county seat in custody of a deputy, Havird had been ambushed by Wilson and Bill Ninemier. They advised the sheriff to clear out, which he did. He went to Graham and raised a posse of thirty or forty men to scour the country. They turned up no prisoners.

Meanwhile a fourth casualty developed. George Hardin complained of a splitting headache. A reconstruction of the shooting established that the bullet that went through Townsend glanced off a rock and creased Hardin's forehead.

Justice court freed Ben Ninemier, who said he had not fired the fatal shots and that he had saved at least one life by preventing Wilson from potting another bystander. Ninemier resumed his freighting from Boise to Banner and from Banner to Graham. A year later, a grand jury, not satisfied with the first proceedings, indicted him as an accomplice in the murders. A trial jury found him innocent.

In August 1889, more than a year after the massacre, a sheriff in Texas read a poster offering $500 reward for Sam Wilson. He wired that he had the man. Sheriff Havird decided he wasn't the officer to go down and complete the identification because the only glimpse he had caught of the outlaw was over the business end of Wilson's pistol. Ada County Sheriff Orlando ("Rube") Robbins, a noted Indian scout and lawman, knew Wilson and said he would go. He took with him James McKay of Banner, another citizen who knew the fugitive.

They discovered it was just another Texas brag. The confessed killer wasn't Wilson. He said he had killed Pitt Smith, Tobe Pitts, and John Townsend, but he was rather vague about the particulars and the geography. On closer examination he admitted he had made up the story because he wanted a free trip to Idaho. They slapped him back into the Texas calaboose for obstructing justice. It didn't pay to impersonate a genuine, bottle-blown Idaho badman.

Wilson was never apprehended. Bill Ninemier turned himself in at Boise about twenty years later when he returned to visit his dying mother. Bill was himself suffering a terminal disease.

The unpleasantness in Tom Combs's saloon wrapped up Silver Mountain's bloodiness. The entire camp presently fizzled, but not without a blast or two. The boys staged a New Year's Eve celebration in 1888 that jarred peaks as far away as Atlanta. They gathered a supply of dynamite in Shanahan and Stanley's Saloon to dry out for midnight fun. It caught fire. Men left in a hurry, taking doors and windows with them. The explosion ripped the building apart, shook several others, and injured one miner.

In March the *Idaho World* said Silver Mountain was on its last legs. Most people were sitting around whittling. The correspondent wrote: "Tom Graney is in his saloon reading a four-cent novel while two men quarrel over a card game for a dime's worth of chewing tobacco."

A semblance of excitement returned when Sheriff Havird was arrested for saving Graham from a forest fire. The actual charge was setting a blaze in the timber, but he insisted he had started a backfire to keep the place from going up in flames. There were hot accusations of spite. In its wrath, the *World* declared: "The most worthless official in Idaho is the timber agent."

Notwithstanding the slings and arrows, Havird kept the peace in Graham. He arrested a pickpocket for lifting $230, collared a horse thief who said he was just holding the beast as security for a loan, and caused a jail to be erected with Jess Pollard as landlord and J. D. Agnew as justice of the peace to see that he had boarders.

By the end of 1888 the camp was down to 75 men from a peak of 400. The mill was idle. "There are so many rumors afloat in regard to the company," the *World* said, "that the program of operations is very much mystified." Matt Graham, Jr. went from Silver Mountain to London and back. George Thorn and Vivian Thorn came from London. There were reports of new operations in the Julia and the Cleveland diggins, main sources of ore. In May 1889 Sheriff Havird reported six men were draining the mine so experts sent out by the English company could examine it. A new body of gold and silver was reported in the vicinity. Big things were in the offing "next spring."

Death came to the camp in November 1889. It was a melancholy death, not as dramatic as the killing of Pitt Smith. Sheriff Havird was in on the rites, as he had been on most of the events. In a period of five days the chapter was closed.

November 19 — Ben Ninemier pleaded not guilty.

November 21 — Ninemier found innocent in district court.

November 22 — A. J. Penner sentenced to three years in prison for stealing $230 from Rolley Oakes at Graham.

November 22 — The Silver Mountain mill sold for $9,500 at a sheriff's sale. Estimated original cost $350,000. Thirteen mines, buildings, etc., sold under the same auspices for $500. Estimated investment $1,000,000.

November 23 — A. J. Penner tossed a roll of greenbacks in the jail stove, remarking: "There's something they won't get."

Silver Mountain died young of overfeeding. A great deal went in; scarcely anything came out. The mines were rich in optimism, poor in production. Bones of the old camp are still visible. Fishermen and hunters find decaying boards from Tom Combs's saloon and colored bottles under the ruins of the superintendent's house.

Chapter 30

CONFESSIONS OF A
SAWTOOTH LOVER

My love affair with the Sawtooths began with a flat tire on a touring car in the heat of a summer day more than fifty years ago. It is quite likely that the connection would have been established at another time and by other means because we were meant for each other. However, the magic of love at first sight took hold when I first saw snowcapped peaks in the distance on a hazy afternoon early in the 1920s. They pulled like magnets.

Mr. Brown, owner and driver of the car, said they were the Sawtooths. He said some other things, too, but they were mainly addressed to a tire iron that slipped off the clincher rim and bruised his thumb. He was not in a mood for admiring scenery. I asked him the name of the most prominent mountain.

"Kid," he said, "I don't know. Maybe Hyndman, maybe Glassford. Now get out of the way. If I don't get this tire changed we'll never get near them."

He did change the tire and we did get to the mountains, at least to the timbered slopes at their feet. It was a smooth trip. We made it from Rupert to Baker Creek, all of 160 miles, in one day with only three flats and a short stop in Hailey to fix a thingumajig on the spark advancer. The road was dusty, full of chuckholes and, in some stretches, surfaced with gravel the size of footballs. But we purred along merrily to Valhalla in the pines.

Mr. Brown — I didn't know his first name then, but later inquiry suggests it was Amon — was a generous and thoughtful citizen. He must have been rich, because he had a touring car and a tent. I did not know his business. He probably had a band of sheep on the headwaters of Wood River, because he spoke of supplies for herders. He also talked about tunnels and tailings, so he may have been interested in a mine. Such details were of no consequence to me or his son, who was also in his early teens. What mattered was that we were going camping. And in the Sawtooths.

There were five of us: Mr. Brown, Mrs. Brown, my mother, and two boys. There was also a tent lashed to a mound of bedding. Running boards and rear bumper bulged with boxes of groceries and skillets. We went first class — everything but a kitchen sink.

About the only thing we didn't take was my French horn. When the trip was suggested, my father, who had an ear for music but no skills in that line, urged that we take it along. He had heard me practicing at home and probably hoped we might lose the instrument. He said my tooting in the forest should keep off wolves and wampus cats. Even when it was decided there was no room for the horn he did not change his mind about passing up the chance for an outing on pine boughs.

We pitched the tent near the mouth of Baker Creek. In current times there is a Forest Service camp there, with tables and other conveniences. At that season we made our own. Mr. Brown obtained lumber from Easley to wall up the tent for cooking and dining and sleeping quarters for the women. Young Brown — "Buster" naturally — and I threw our blankets on the ground. Branches and roots were a comfortable mattress.

Mr. Brown cranked up the car and departed on his business early next morning, leaving the rest of us to our own devices for a week. The first thing I decided to do was climb Galena Peak. After that I would take on Easley and Boulder. All three were handy and handsome in their rugged grandeur. Galena was first choice because it was nearest, so I climbed it. Well, I got about half a mile. My alibi for not reaching the summit was a turned ankle. Although no injury was apparent to the other members of the camping party when I got back, I explained that I might have sprained an ankle if I had gone farther and I didn't want them to worry about me.

That first attempt to snuggle up to one of the Sawtooths (no quibbling, please, that Galena Peak is not a genuine Sawtooth) was recalled years later when I was helping with a 4-H camp at Easley. Right after breakfast on the first morning a small boy from Burley announced he was going to climb Easley Peak. He said he would be back for dinner. I watched him hike up the sage-clad foothills. He was back before lunch. He said he had forgotten his canteen. The mountain summits, I noted with satisfaction, are just as alluring and just as far away today as they were years ago. As a poet said, "A man's reach must exceed his grasp or what's a heaven for?" Heaven, or at least a suburb thereof, must be located in the Sawtooths. Indians thought so.

Details of what we did on the Baker Creek camping trip half a century ago are fogged by time. Except for vivid recollections of how we got there and my admiration for the mountains, I do not remember specific activities. Fishing was so good it was taken for granted. We caught dozens, frequently two at a time on tandem hooks dangled from cheap line on homemade poles. We ate trout and mutton and huckleberry shortcake. We swam at Easly Hot Springs and hiked up Baker Creek to visit the few campers in an area that is today filled with summer cottages.

Most of all, I wanted to climb a peak. As that was not possible, I looked at the mountains, particularly at dawn and sunset when their colors were most spectacular and inspiring. Second of all, young Brown and I wanted a ride to Galena Summit. That was the equivalent of going to the North Pole as something to tell about when school started. We didn't get to the summit, either. When Mr. Brown came for us we asked him to drive over the summit just so we could say we had done it. He said that would be ridiculous. It was out of the way home by a long jump; he hadn't lost anything in Stanley Basin and wasn't about to go there unless he had to, which he didn't. Besides, he couldn't climb the grade without turning around and backing up, a standard practice for many cars. Backwards or sideways sounded all right to us boys; anything to get to Galena as a matter of pride. But Brown declined. As a concession, though, he drove us to Russian John ranger station to see "Russian John," an early inhabitant and part-time guard for whom the station is named. Russian John was not there. Whether he was still in the area at that time we did not learn. We did hear stories about Russian John. It seems he sometimes got a snootful and made the brig at Hailey. He was also nominated as the man who scared the pants off a sheepherder on Owl Creek. The herder had his washing — long johns and stuff — hung on a line between two trees. Russian John came along on his horse in the dark. He got tangled in the laundry. The herder awoke to see a terrifying sight. He ran to the store at Galena with a report that a ghost on horseback was after him.

I do not remember the trip back to Rupert from Baker Creek. We must not have had many flats or taken wrong turns because we again made it in one day. I do recall a stiff neck from turning

around to look at the peaks as long as the slightest slivers were
visible. I thought of them as *my* mountains. I wanted very much to
be near them, and I was afraid I might never reach their doorstep
again.

But I did. Again and again.

The next phase of the courtship was several years later. I call it
the B. S. Martin adventure. It is also the "Bull" Disney fishing trip.
If this account seems too full of personal trivia, skip it and turn to
more objective chapters of Sawtooth history. However, I believe it
is useful and proper to give reasons for my interest in the area —
qualifications for the right to speak, in other words. I do not claim
to know a whole heap about the country, but I take a back seat to
none in my affection and respect.

The Martin-Disney trip was made to the headwaters of Lost
River. W. H. Disney, a Rupert merchant; his son, Dwight, then a
student at the University of Idaho; and my father, the Reverend B.
C. d'Easum, an Episcopal priest and English teacher, let me join
them on an outing that was expected to last a week. For two of us it
lasted nearly all summer. It was prolonged because of car trouble.
We camped the first night on Trail Creek, near the present site of
Sun Valley. We declined a chance to bed down on the old Brass
ranch in favor of a spot not far from today's Sun Valley Trail Creek
cabin. Next morning, after a breakfast of fish, we started up the
Trail Creek grade. The road, still a twisty dinger, was then narrow
and steep. It had been built for freight teams and may have been
okay for mules but was no bargain for cars. I walked most of the
way to watch for approaching traffic. Turnouts were few; somebody
had to look for autos and choose the best place to pass. There is a
drop to China on one side, a cliff on the other, and nothing in the
middle but a track for a narrow-minded gopher.

At about the fourth bend the boiling Reo rammed the hill.
Tinkering disclosed an impediment in the steering gear. It would
not turn to the left. We limped along, backing and tacking around
hairpins to reach the summit. No help was available so we crawled
down to a camping place on Lost River. Then Dwight Disney
coaxed the auto to Mackay, again with me riding shotgun and
scouting against collisions. We left our dads in camp.

A Mackay garage diagnosed the ailment but said it would take a
week or two to get a new ring gear. Dwight stayed at Mackay to sit
with the sick Reo and wait for rescue transportation summoned
from home. I hiked back to camp. Mount Caleb, Leatherman Peak,
and Mount Borah loomed as comforting sentinels along the way,

and a trucker gave me a lift. But the night was pitch black as I walked the last five miles from Chilly up Lost River. Range cattle snorted from bed-grounds. Coyotes sang. I struck matches to let bulls and beasts know I was a human being, unafraid. If they could have smelled my fear, as studies say animals can, they would have known I was the most frightened 15-year-old in the country. I lit up my first cigaret, a One-Eleven from a pack the truck driver had given me under the assumption (not discouraged on my part) that I was an adult. I coughed and gagged. I thought I had instant tuberculosis, a fate worse than being gored by a bull or eaten by coyotes.

The coughing aroused something in the brush. A figure emerged and said: "Who's there?" It was my father; I was back in camp. The welcome was warm and remarkable, in retrospect, because there was no comment on cigaret smoking.

In a couple of days a car from Rupert took our dads home. Dwight and I stayed in the hills until the Reo was repaired. Happy to say, it was a long job.

The B. S. Martin phase began when the wait started. Martin dropped in to visit. He was a talkative codger, full of ripe anecdotes and salty language. If his conversation had been on tape it would have contained many deleted expletives. Apparently he gave us the benefit of his company because he wanted someone to talk to, saw our fire, and joined us. Noting that we were camping in the open and that a storm was blowing in from Mount Borah, he invited us to his cabin. Having no pressing engagements we gladly went along. Martin hauled our gear in his truck up Fall Creek to his shack on the edge of a little lake. He had more provisions than we did and seemed glad to share them.

He said he was custodian of a mine that had been sold to Henry Ford. The amount was half a million or some such. His property was one of several claims on the Red Ball string. We knew better, of course, and winked behind his back as he spun his windies. Later inquiry, though, showed that Ford had bought the mine for a substantial sum. B. S. Martin, who earned his initials for baloney, was telling the truth in that respect.

His stories about the mountains were something else. He said that when the lake (from which he got his water and in which he bathed once or twice a summer) was frozen solid in winter he harvested chunks of ice loaded with trout. Some winters, he said, he lived on frozen fish, chipping out a rainbow from time to time in his icehouse. He further claimed that Lost River got its original supply of trout from another lake in the vicinity that fell into the valley and gradually melted. For evidence he showed us a dry bed between cliffs where a lake had once been.

Regardless of the hokum in his ice accounts, the remaining lake had abundant fish. We rigged up a raft and caught as many as we wanted. They responded to flies, worms, grasshoppers, cigaret butts, or bits of hotcake. Sometimes they would take a bare hook. Martin said it was fine we were harvesting a few; the lake had too many for the food supply. The trout used to be big, now there were hardly any over two pounds.

The subject that most agitated Martin was sheep. He said he hated them with a passion. The stinking mountain maggots, he said, were ruining the country. First thing every morning he stepped to the edge of his porch and glassed the valley. If he saw sheep he raged.

"Damn," he said one dawn, standing in his underwear and waving a skillet as though he were going to hurl it among the ancient enemy. "Band of 'em got in. Hell of a note. Dust and stink. Dirty up the creek. By God, I'll show 'em. They know better than to get in my territory."

He paused to take another look and gather steam.

"Tell you what I'm going to do. I'm going to set off a charge that'll turn a whole mountain of rocks on them. Bury the bastards. See if I don't."

He put the skillet on the stove and cracked a couple of eggs into it, suggesting that he would delight in treating a couple of lambs the same way.

Then he said, "I'll go down and tell Pedro to get his lice out of here pronto. If he doesn't do it I'll probably break his neck before I blast the sheep."

After a quick breakfast he hiked down the hill. We didn't see him all day. We didn't hear any shots or blasts. In the evening Martin came back with half a lamb.

"Put the fear in Pedro," he said. "Told him off plenty good. He made savvy quick. Gave me this lamb if I didn't blow him to hell. You can eat this mutton if you want it. I never touch the stuff."

We fried chops for dinner and had several roasts later. We noted that Martin ate his share, although he insisted the meat on his plate was beef he had saved from an earlier meal.

When we went to the valley we found the sheepherder calmly playing a stringed instrument and obviously in good health. We asked him how he escaped Martin's wrath.

"No trouble," he said. "Big talk. Get along fine. He tells me go away. I tell him go to hell. We have drink of wine together. Good friends."

"But he scared you into giving him half a lamb?"

"He bought it," the herder said. "Bought a lamb in spring. Pretty small. Bigger now. He get half a bigger one to make up. You tell my friend B. S. Martin he is *loco de cabesa*. No fight. No shoot. He give me bullets to kill coyote. You like sip wine?"

We said nothing about the meeting to Martin. He continued to bluster about sheep and what he would do to them. On the morning we bid him goodbye he was out on his porch again in his underwear spouting curses on all flocks.

Through some sort of moccasin telegraph we got word that the Reo was ready. We hitched a ride to Mackay and drove home without further incident — unless camping in an inviting grove at Hailey and waking up to find it was the public square counts as an incident.

Again I hadn't climbed a Sawtooth, but I had been close to Hyndman and Devil's Bedstead. I had felt the spell of the mountains by being among them. I had smelled their smells and heard their language. I knew them better and was ready to clinch the engagement.

The first closeup look I had at the Sawtooths was a disappointment. It was spitting snow at Stanley on a late fall day in 1931 when I arrived there with three other young men from eastern Idaho. Clouds filled the sky. All I could make out in the way of a peak was a dingy bump above Valley Creek. I said the Sawtooths didn't amount to much. A native told me I wasn't looking at the Sawtooths; they were up the other way, hidden in mist. It was a sour beginning for an experience that brightened and ripened. The sun did come out, and during a sparkling winter the mountains proved all they were cracked up to be and then some.

The four of us, all unemployed, had chosen Stanley Basin as a place to ride out the Great Depression. By spring, we figured, the economy would be robust again and our services would be required to turn wheels of industry. Meanwhile we would live with nature, sample the joys of mountain men, be tough hombres in the tall sticks.

We figured that by pooling our resources we would have enough money to feed ourselves indefinitely. The assortment of provisions — flour, sugar, canned corn, a sack of potatoes, slab of bacon, half a gallon of syrup, ten pounds of dried prunes, two pounds of coffee, a carton of candy bars, a case of peaches, and two hams, plus a few odds and ends — came to $60. That presented a problem, because our combined wealth was $75 and we needed cash to pay for transportation to Stanley. So we eliminated half the peaches and the candy. Boxed for auto freight, the groceries seemed enough for an army. The tab for freight — cash in advance — sounded like the war debt. We got around that by charging the groceries, after a modest down payment.

Housing for the winter would be easy. Two of the men in our party had met Tom Williams — miner, hunting guide, and confirmed bachelor — while fighting fire during the summer. In response to a letter proposing that we stay with him, he invited us. "Invited" is not quite the word. He said he guessed he could put us up if we thought we could stand it and if we would provide our own board. Clear sailing. We had nearly sixty bucks worth of grub; Old Tom should be delighted at the prospect of eating like a king on our bounty.

Getting to Stanley and to Tom's cabin at Obsidian, ten miles up the Salmon, was a matter of stages. The four of us scrounged a ride in a truck to Challis. The closed body contained onions, furniture, and pieces of mining machinery. Two of us rode in the cab with "Slow Jim," the driver. The other two bounced around among the onions. It was dark and stuffy back there, and the view was limited. We changed off from time to time to avoid suffocation and give the prisoners a chance at the scenery. Slow Jim, a man of few words, asked where we were bound. When we told him, he wanted to know whether he should pick us up in a couple of days for the return to Idaho Falls. He thought we were nuts. Why anybody would want to spend a winter at Stanley beat him. He had his belly full of the country. Any man in his right mind would get out of there and go to Salt Lake City or Reno. When I quipped that we wanted to get next to the Sawtooths "because they are there," he glared at me and gnawed off a hunk of chewing tobacco.

In the afternoon he unloaded us at Challis, where we splurged on a $3 hotel room with two double beds — our final luxury before plunging into the primitive. The fire escape from the second-story room, we noted with amusement, was a coil of rope tied to a bed. We had a lot of fun with that.

Dinner and breakfast, family style, were excellent at six bits apiece. The regular boarders greeted us with suspicion, saying little but "pass the potatoes." Home folks, we learned, do not warm

Dick d'Easum and Mercer Kerr at Obsidian in the winter of 1931

up to outsiders until they know more about them, and maybe not then.

But there was warmth, of a sort, at dinner. There were jars of pickled peppers on the table. Nobody took any until one of us dudes made the move. "Hot?" he asked. "Might be," said the native. The freshman popped one into his mouth. He immediately jumped up and dashed for the street.

"Told you it might be hot," said the regular. "We never eat 'em."

In the morning, following a big breakfast, we took the stage to Stanley. The fare was shaded a little, I believe, by driver Bill Centauras, who had an idea we were strapped. Nevertheless, it reduced our treasury to the vanishing point. I had four bits when we reached Stanley. I still had the coin when I left much later because there was little chance to spend it. The price of anything was more than that, so I went without and kept my money. The best things in Stanley were free. The people, God bless them, were so kind we didn't starve or freeze. We had a ball. Most of the citizens in Stanley and Lower Stanley gradually thawed to us and gave friendly welcome.

Our arrival at Tom Williams's cabin was at a poor time. His favorite dog was dying on the back porch; it had been poisoned. Tom greeted us as warmly as circumstances justified. He told us where we would sleep and said dinner would be about six — or earlier if we wanted to break out some of our groceries. He was taken aback when we said our supplies had not come and might not be delivered for several days. He might have hit the ceiling, but he was so concerned about the dog that all he said was, "Hell fire. You'll have to eat some of my cooking."

The dog died while we were getting acquainted with the cabin. We offered to help Tom bury the dog, but he said he would rather do it himself. It was no time to intrude.

At dinner, cooked by Tom, we had a better chance to introduce ourselves. There was Jim Kelly, a big, easygoing man of many mechanical skills and a gift for charming people out of their back teeth. He had many jobs, but money melted in his hands and he was perpetually broke. His million-dollar smile was collateral for almost anything he wanted to buy or do.

There was hot-shot, Bill Petersen, raccoon-coated, whizbanging, knock-'em-dead lad from a prosperous background. He was the take-charge type with most of, if not all, the answers. The quick quip was his conversational style. Those of us who knew him well accepted the bluff as veneer. The real Bill was a solid citizen, a man to tie to in a pinch — or in a mountain shack.

There was Mercer Kerr, droll, spectacled, witty, and phlegmatic. He moved and talked slowly. He saved his energy for something essential; he saved his words for pertinent comment. He thought a lot. He thought and talked best sitting down, a posture geared to his philosophy. With owlish grin and twitching eyebrows he teased society. Moody at times, he bounced quickly to high spirits. Poet and pixie wrestled in his giblets. Dynamo he was not, but dependable he was.

As the most recently employed member of the quartet — except Petersen, who had been engaged in some sort of advisory capacity in his father's furniture store — I was banker for the enterprise. Some bank! After groceries, stage tickets, and the stay in Challis it was in the red. My last check as reporter for an Idaho Falls newspaper had come when the paper consolidated with the opposition. The money had gone like dew in the morning sun — all but the final four bits.

Tom Williams was a graying, bristly-whiskered character in baggy wool pants hitched to broad suspenders above a lumberjack shirt, the tail of which usually sneaked out. He had been in Stanley Basin many years and knew everybody up and down the creek. He had wrangled with most on some issue or other and had sided with others in different community scrapes. He smoked a curved-stem pipe constantly. His favorite tobacco was Peerless, a mixture that seemed to be made of bark and molasses and smelled like burning feathers. When Tom didn't smoke he chewed. Spitting trips to the door helped ventilate the house.

Tom and his brother, Dave, who had a ranch two miles away, had been in the Sawtooths since the early 1900s. Dave had a family, but Tom lived alone. Tom mined a little. He took dudes on fishing and hunting trips. He helped the Forest Service and game department plant fish in lakes. He did carpentry when he felt like it. He went to town and bayed at the moon when he was ready — and had the price.

Tom was no yokel, no empty-skulled, quaint pigeon for tourists. He spun yarns and went through the motions of rusticity because it was good for his income and the success of dude ranches for whom he often worked. In his cabin on free days he read a great deal. He had a library including many classics presented by the sportsmen he guided on goat, elk, deer, and sheep hunts. He knew a lot of history and had a smattering of knowledge about opera. His formal schooling had ended early. What he picked up later was all he needed for a well-rounded education.

Domestic arrangements of the Williams diggings were simple. The kitchen was dining room and parlor. It was the only room with heat. A cooking range furnished all the warmth in the cabin. Attached to the kitchen was a storeroom stuffed with saddles, coyote traps, and mining tools. Beyond the tack room was a bedroom with a small window that did not open. There was no need to open it because fresh air came through gaps between the logs. Tom's bed was in that room. It was more of a nest than a bed; he made it once or twice a season, shoving the lumps around to fit his contours. Two of us were assigned to cots in his sanctum. The other two slept in the storeroom. Accommodations were adequate if not palatial.

There was no plumbing. Water was fetched from the river in buckets. A reservoir in the kitchen stove heated water for washing dishes and faces. The bathroom — really a bathroom — was a wooden tank, open to the skies, a short distance behind the wood shed. A hot spring kept it full enough for luxurious baths. The outhouse was a separate structure. The door faced the Rocky Mountain Club, several hundred yards away across the road. Tom said he originally built it facing the river but turned it around so he had a handy vantage point to watch the dudes. Morning observations, he said, gave him all the information he needed about goings and comings without necessity of a hike to the club.

Tom cooked our meals. At first he said he would show us the ropes and then let us take over. The arrangement did not work out, for several reasons. In the first place, Tom liked to cook and was good at it. He knew where everything was. In the second place, none of us could hack it. We burned the gravy and messed up the hotcakes. In the third place, our supplies did not come for several days. Tom figured that as he was furnishing all the food he would cook it. He had groceries enough for himself to last the winter, but it was dismaying how much four guests could put away. Furthermore, when our boxes and sacks did show up — by mail stage from Stanley — they ran out in a couple of weeks. Our provisions vanished like a puff of smoke.

Tom decreed two meals a day: breakfast early and dinner in the shank of the afternoon. Fare was usually the same every day. Tom got up at dawn to mix hotcakes, often spilling tobacco crumbs in the batter. He passed them off as raisins and nobody suffered. For dinner we had potatoes and fried meat. For a few days we had cheese. The slab quickly disappeared. The meat was venison. Tom had about half a deer frozen in the woodshed. That supply ran out before Christmas. We trapped a couple of snowshoe rabbits and made a stew. Tom wouldn't eat it. He said the time had come to get more real meat.

He took his rifle and went to visit a friend at Obsidian. In the afternoon we heard shooting — a regular war. There must have been twenty shots. We got a sled to help Tom bring in what we thought must be a half a dozen deer. Tom met us. He said not to bother with the hauling; he had missed every time. We ate rabbit stew for several more days. Then one evening when we got back from playing Mah-Jongg and working out with a bow and arrow set at the Rocky Mountain Club — then vacant — we found two carcasses in the woodshed. Tom said he had obtained a couple of calves from a neighbor. The meat tasted just like the deer we had been eating. Tom said it was remarkable how veal and venison were similar. It was a blow to our spirits. We had thought we were becoming members of the community, but it was obvious that Tom didn't trust us.

A glaring reason why we were suspect soon came to light. I was getting mail addressed to Lieutenant d'Easum. The official U.S.A. folders contained correspondence courses of the infantry reserve. The postmaster at Stanley, the mail carrier, and almost everyone else between Challis and Galena Summit probably guessed I was a cop or an undercover agent for the prohibition staff. It was very hard for any of us to buy a drink in Stanley, although some excellent moonshine was on the market. The gents took no chances on the lieutenant or his buddies. Tom, who liked a drop now and then for his health, got around the boycott by asking a pal to send a dollop of medicine on the stage. The medicine was duly transported. Half a gallon seemed a substantial prescription; however, it proved good for whatever ailed Tom, and it helped the rest of us ward off the chills and fever of zero weather. The mailman didn't charge for postage. He said he had taken the stamp money from the medicine bottle — about half an inch.

Life at Tom's cabin was full of surprising adventures for city boys. We tried trapping and caught one mink and the neighbor's dog twice. Our hide-curing method ruined the mink skin. The dog recovered quickly both times, but we abandoned the trapline for fear of fatal repetition.

Bill Petersen rigged up a radio operated by a wet battery salvaged from a car at the Rocky Mountain Club. It squawked and whined but brought us "Amos 'n' Andy" and fragments of news.

We ran it all hours of the night until Tom put his foot down. He was used to turning in early and didn't like racket disturbing his sleep. Furthermore, we didn't have enough fuel for the gas lantern to waste it on night life.

We engaged in a marathon Hearts tournament. Poker was Tom's game, but nobody had money. He said playing poker for fun was like picking flowers. The rest of us settled on Hearts at a hypothetical dollar a point. We kept track daily in pencil marks on the kitchen wall. At the end of the competition everybody owed everybody else about $4,000, not a dime of which was paid. The accounts were still visible behind the stove when Tom's shack was torn down some years later in a "landscape improvement" project.

On sunny days we floundered in the snow, hiking on snowshoes to various points of interest, usually no more than a mile and frequently no farther than the outhouse. Snow was deep and the weather was cold as sin. It was so cold one blustery day that a horse Tom kept as a retiree tried to get into the cabin. It leaned its rump against the bedroom window, breaking the pane. Cardboard nailed over the hole didn't do much good. The guy who slept in that corner often had a drift on his bed.

Tom reeled off a string of stories when he was in a happy mood, commonly when he was cooking breakfast and the radio was disconnected. The yarns were an added bonus for early rising. Lads who didn't get up until noon not only missed their hotcakes but lost out on Tom's tales. He was full of salty yarns, baloney, and considerable factual information about the Sawtooths. If we had had a tape recorder the monologues would be priceless today, with or without censorship. Like the one about his cat with a wooden leg with which it conked mice on the head.

Sawtooth peaks were not visible from Tom's cabin. On fair days we could see Decker Peak and one or two other humps in that sector, but we had to go to the porch of the Rocky Mountain Club for a glimpse of the big crags behind Redfish Lake. After one such artistic mission we decided to approach the range. We snowshoed up Huckleberry Creek to a small clearing. There a couple of us turned back. I went on. A storm struck. No problem — I had been a Boy Scout and knew all about the north side of a tree.

For about an hour I waddled through the forest. I happily tossed a snowball against a pine and whistled into the vastness. Presently I came upon snowshoe tracks. One of the other guys, I thought, had cut over the hill and got ahead of me. A mile or so further I noticed a tree that had been hit with a snowball. That was strange. Also sort of familiar. I measured my tracks with those left by the other guy. Perfect fit. They were my own; I had been going in a circle. A pretty how-do-you-do. I didn't know where I was, and it was getting dark. Don't panic, I told myself. But I did panic. I set off on a snowshoe trot that brought me to a wide open space. It was not inviting or at all familiar. I turned around and eventually picked up the trail where I had gone wrong.

When I staggered back to the cabin it was nearly midnight. Tom was putting on his snowshoes to look for me. "I didn't figure you were lost," he lied, "but guessed you might be ready for a sandwich."

Comparison of distances, time on the trail, and approximate directions established that I had wandered to the shore of frozen Redfish Lake. I have admired it more on many subsequent visits.

One of the big surprises of the winter was a knock on the door one night just as Tom was turning off the lamp. The unexpected visitor was Ole Johnson, an old friend of Toms. He said he had come from Ketchum that day on snowshoes, a jaunt of more than fifty miles. He would appreciate bed and board if he wouldn't be putting Tom out. Of course, if we were short he would sleep in the woodshed and eat his own rations. Tom gladly made room and cooked him a meal.

We immediately began asking questions.

"Where are you going?"

"Down the valley a piece."

"How far?"

"Few miles."

"Got a mine?"

"Maybe."

"Gold?"

"Could be. Cold weather, isn't it?"

"Going to work the mine this winter?"

Tom shuffled his feet, clattered stove lids and said: "Get some wood."

One of us started for the door.

"All of you get wood," Tom said. "Cold in here."

We went to the shed in a bunch. Tom joined us.

"Keep your goldarned traps shut," he stormed. "Don't ask Ole what he's doing or where he's doing it. Don't pester him with a lot of questions about his business. If he wants to tell you, he'll tell you. It's a wonder he didn't knock your blocks off."

We filed back in, chatted with Ole about temperatures and the price of potatoes, and went to bed. Tom and Ole talked long into the night. In the morning Ole was gone before we got up.

"Does he have a mine around here?" we asked Tom.

"Darned if I know," said Tom. "I don't butt in on things like that, either. If he had told me, I wouldn't tell you. So forget it."

We never did find out what Ole was doing. Stout feller. Fifty miles in a day. Gee!

The kind people of Sawtooth Valley did their best to keep us happy at Christmas and New Year. On Christmas Day we dined, the whole tribe of us, at the home of Mr. and Mrs. Dave Williams. For New Year's Day we were guests at the Preston Shaw ranch, a place that had been host to Senator Borah and has recently been purchased by Ernie Day of Boise. Two things were particularly impressive about the visit to Shaws. One was the charm of Marjorie Shaw, a robust daughter of the household. She beat us all at hand wrestling. She further proved her muscle by lifting a side of beef from an icehouse hook and handing it to one of us, knocking him off the ladder.

The second notable item was the length of our visit. We went for dinner and stayed three days — the weather was so bad we couldn't get back to Tom's.

Along in January we were again asked to the Dave Williams ranch, this time to look after the dairy cows while Dave was away. We were there about a week, eating high on the hog. When Dave returned he was a little disturbed by the condition of his cows. "Did you milk them?" he asked. "Sure," I answered. "One or two every day." He didn't ask us to help again.

About a week before Christmas we went in a neighbor's truck to Stanley for the school "doings" — recitations, pageant, and treats, followed by a community dance. During the dance there was a copper boiler of punch on the stove. Somebody laced it pretty heavily with Stanley medicine. While I was dancing with the schoolmarm she disengaged herself to investigate activity around the stove. "You ought to be ashamed of yourselves," she said, brandishing the dipper. "Drinking from a common cup isn't sanitary."

After the dance we piled into the truck to return home. We didn't get far; drifts had closed the road. We walked back to Stanley and spent the night in the old Stanley Inn, built years before by Mrs. H. L. Benner. We had candles for light. There was no heat except a few calories that climbed from a stove in the lobby, lighted for the emergency. But the beds were good and the price charming — free, thanks to influence of Dave Williams, Claude Gillespie, and Clyde Gillespie, twin brothers whose confidence we had gained. One brother was postmaster and merchant in Stanley. The other was foreman of the Rocky Mountain Club.

We plowed back to Tom's place next day to the music of sleigh bells — making spirits bright, laughing all the way.

Jim Kelley and I drew the short straws to see who had to leave this winter wonderland, because there wasn't enough food for five. We hiked to Stanley, spent a free night in a donated cabin, and started for Challis on a February morning so cold the snow squeaked. Bill Centauras, the stage driver, let us get aboard his horse-drawn sleigh about the time we reached Big Casino Creek. It was so cold we got out and walked. At Robinson Bar, where we learned it was fourteen below zero, the manager gave us dinner, beds, and breakfast. Again free. He didn't bother to ask us to pay; he knew we were broke.

The following day we once more started hiking to Challis. Centauras soon caught up with us and once more let us get aboard without charge. At the Oster ranch we changed to an auto for the last lap. At Challis we tapped friends for the price of a room, meals, and tickets to Blackfoot.

Petersen and Kerr stayed in the mountains several more weeks.

The experience made a lasting impression on all of us. The Sawtooths didn't seem to be affected in the least; they went right on doing their stuff as though we hadn't been there.

During a number of summers after that memorable winter, I went with Tom to many places in the Sawtooths such as Hell Roaring Lake, Finger of Fate, Imogene Lake, and Yellow Belly Lake. He showed me where he and his brother had put a log over a dangerous gap on a route to the top of a peak scaled by mountaineers. He showed me how to catch golden trout and where to find mountain goat. He led the way to pools on Warm Springs Creek where two-pound trout were common. He loved the Sawtooths, and his respect was contagious.

Not all the reading material in Tom's cabin was on the shelves; a lot of it was on the walls. They were papered with old editions of magazines such as the *Saturday Evening Post*. I followed a serial story by Mary Roberts Rinehart around the bedroom chapter after chapter, sometimes having to stand on a chair. It was frustrating to find the last installment missing. Tom had ripped it off to wrap fish.

When Mary Williamson and I went to the Sawtooths on our

honeymoon, Tom was not in residence. He knew we were coming and had ducked out. The old boy did not cotton to matrimony. He wasn't about to see a fellow man suffer, so he lit out for his mine and stayed there while we were in the valley.

In spite of his absence I found the fishing good. Mary, no fisherman, went riding on Rocky Mountain Club horses with Bill Hamilton, dude wrangler, and Sally Clark (later Mrs. Ed Springer), director of recreation. Hamilton was a rodeo cowboy from May. He was known as "Chopped-Together" Hamilton because of his pet expression for the pack outfits of a rival string. He said they were sort of chopped together.

Hamilton also gained notoriety for his first conversation with Ernest Hemingway. The writer's hunting party went to Challis to be packed out by Hamilton. A mutual friend did the honors.

"Hemingway?" said Hamilton. "Seems I have heard the name. What do you do, Ernie?"

"He's an author," a member of the party hastily announced.

"Well, well, an author," said Hamilton. "Written any westerns lately, Ernie?"

Hemingway laughed. He and Hamilton became good friends.

Most of the residents of Stanley (Pop. 47) appreciate the scenery. Some don't. It was a shock to hear, on a recent trip, the comments of a cook in a Stanley cafe.

"I guess it's okay," she said. "There are some good things about living here. But those doggone mountains. I can't stand the mountains."

It takes all kinds to make a world.

Stanley enjoys and encourages its reputation as a picturesque remnant of the Old West. It clings to buckskin culture and hearty simplicity. But it also has respect for eternal qualities. One of the major projects of the community in 1976 was construction of an interdenominational church, a log building with a view of the Sawtooths.

Chapter 31

A MONUMENT FOR MAJOR HYNDMAN

FOR MANY YEARS Mount Hyndman was believed to be the highest point in Idaho. At 12,078 feet it is a giant, but recent surveys show several taller peaks. Borah, Leatherman, and Hawley in the Lost River Range and Bell in the Lemhi Range are the big four. Hyndman is fifth in feet but still first in the hearts of many people who have long admired the pinnacle and learned something about the career of the man for whom it is named.

Major William Hyndman was a Civil War soldier, western lawyer, and mining man. He was in on the beginning of the Wood River boom. Before that he practiced law at Bonanza City, where he contributed notably to the legal underpinnings, cut a swath as a civic leader, and found time for fishing and hunting that opened a number of lakes and streams to his contemporaries. For several years prior to arrival at Bonanza he was a lawyer at Corinne, Utah, a community that had high hopes of becoming the hub of intermountain commerce but died almost before the blueprint was dry.

Major Hyndman was best known in the hurly-burly of his time as superintendent and legal advisor of the Philadelphia Smelter and Mining Company at Ketchum, one of the big operators of Wood River. He was also a prime mover in several other mining enterprises. In 1888 he was superintendent of the Silver King at Sawtooth City, one of the last properties to surrender in the collapse of the Upper Salmon. He kept producing and shipping ore until his mine burned in August 1892.

During earlier years on Yankee Fork he incorporated several mines near Bonanza and Custer. In spite of his knowledge of law and his optimism for the future of mining, it is not likely that his name would be perpetuated by a peak if he had not taken vacations. He turned a neat phrase in court. He also tossed a fine fly and was a good hand with a deer rifle.

It is probable that Major Hyndman was the first lawyer in Bonanza. By 1879 he was a partner in the firm of Hoffman and Hyndman. A commercial card in the *Yankee Fork Herald* says the office was on Main Street. It was a place of culture. The paper noted that the barristers had "lately received their very handsome and complete law library. There are over 300 books, including the sixteen volumes of Appleton's *American cyclopedia*, latest edition."

Hyndman was in town during the fatal shooting of Richard King by William Dillon but apparently had no part in the trial at Salmon City. He was very much on deck during the same term of court, however. The *Herald* commented: "Major Hyndman of the law firm of Hoffman and Hyndman made a fine record at the recent term. His associate was called to Salt Lake on account of illness in his family shortly after court met, which left Major Hyndman with a number of important cases on his hands with nobody to assist him. By industry and perseverance, together with his fine legal ability, he succeeded in gaining nearly every case and established for himself a lasting reputation among our people."

A few weeks later the major, William McKinney, and Milton Morning went on a fishing and hunting expedition to the head of the West Fork of Yankee Fork. "They have no bear stories to relate," the paper reported, "but they found a lake at the extreme head of the river about fourteen miles from town where trout abound by the million. Fish were plenty with the party, but fowl scarce."

The lake became known as Hyndman Lake because of that expedition. It still has that name. The millions of trout were quickly thinned. Today it is reported only so-so, hardly worth the hike.

Mr. and Mrs. Robert E. Strahorn visited Major Hyndman at Bonanza in the mid-1870s. Mrs. Strahorn tells about it in her book, *Fifteen Thousand Miles by Stage*. Here are a few excerpts:

"We were indebted to the gallant Major Hyndman, the leading attorney of Bonanza, and to his associate, Hon. E. M. Wilson

Photo by Ernie Day

Mount Hyndman, with William Hyndman inset

[partner at that time] for a day of rare experience in mountain climbing and exploring. . . . It consisted of a trip to the Montana mine on Mount Estes. . . . The air was full of song from our own throats and from those of happy birds that filled the wooded hills. We seemed almost in the depths of heaven itself, with the deep blue vault arched so near us that it appeared to be within our grasp. Never can there be a bluer sky than that which glorifies the Idaho mountains."

Major Hyndman was a friend of Nathan Smith, discoverer of Loon Creek in 1869. The lawyer visited Orogrande to establish the legal boundaries of the mining district. The camp eventually grew to more than five hundred men. As the diggings played out, Chinese followed white miners. They got little but survived, until frugality proved their undoing. Sheepeater Indians had made a habit of replenishing their scant supplies at the white men's mines. When the Chinese moved in there was scarcely enough for them, let alone the Sheepeaters. According to a story Smith told the *Yankee Fork Herald*, the Indians occupied the place by force on a winter night in 1879.

While the Chinese were playing cards in a bunkhouse, Indians massacred the lot. (Another version blames white miners who wanted to get rid of both Chinese and Indians.) Troops came from Boise to punish Tambiago and his Sheepeaters as soon as weather permitted. Soldiers were in and around Orogrande and Bonanza all summer. Major Hyndman followed the campaign with all the enthusiasm of an old firehorse but took no active part in the hostilities.

By Thanksgiving the war was over. The pathetic remnant of the Indian band was in the stockade at Vancouver. Twilight was also settling in for Bonanza City. Hundreds of people pulled out for a more friendly climate. In spite of all the brave words the *Herald* had shouted about ideal weather, healthiest temperature in the West, and so forth, snow fell eye-deep to a Swede, and the sun-tanned mercury sank out of sight. The editor himself took off for Chicago. Hyndman's law associate departed. Hyndman headed for the states, too, but returned after running into nasty weather that let him get no farther than Challis. It was about as easy to go back as it was to go on to Blackfoot.

The sleigh on which he started for Bonanza bogged down before it reached the station near McKay Creek. A rescue party from Bonanza reached Hyndman after he had abandoned the sled and mounted a horse. It took three days to travel thirty miles. Hyndman got back to his office two days before Christmas, just in time for a social blowout at the Dodge Hotel and Ed Butter's Bonanza Billiard Hall.

The next summer he and a good many other Yankee Forkers moved to Sawtooth City, fifty-five miles up the Salmon in Beaver Gulch. Major Hyndman went on to help lay out the townsite of Galena at the head of Wood River. From there it was only a short jump to Ketchum, the brand-new roaring bull of the gulches.

With a cluster of mines coming into flower, Hyndman took a hand in building a road from Ketchum to Challis — seventy-five miles by the Trail Creek shortcut — for the purpose of hauling ore from Ketchum's Elkhorn Mine to the Ramshorn at Clayton for smelting. In the course of working as an associate of H. C. Lewis, the road's chief proponent, Major Hyndman knocked around in the mountains north and east of Ketchum. He prospected at the head of Lost River and took a fishing fling at Copper Basin. The tallest peak in the vicinity, with a spire that looks like the Matterhorn, was one of his favorites. It was named in his honor before his death.

During the time he was living on Wood River, the mining business claimed more of his attention than the law. George A. McLeod's history of Alturas and Blaine counties lists Hyndman among attorneys at court terms from 1884 to 1886 but does not specify the cases. He was in Ketchum when George Pierson shot John ("Johnny-Behind-the-Rocks") Hall at Vienna over the affections of Banjo Nell. He may also have been present when Pierson was hanged in Quigley Gulch near Hailey on August 1, 1884.

Major Hyndman was a resident of the valley when Vic Clary robbed a stage between Galena and Ketchum and was shot dead on East Fork trying to escape a posse. He saw a time when as many as three hundred teamsters a day toiled on the railbed to Ketchum. He was in town when Bill Kennedy, dealer in the Nevada Retreat, shot John Sullivan, a brawling gambler, three times through the hand without breaking a bone. He mourned the death in Salt Lake City of Will Norton, discoverer and owner of the noted Charles Dickens Mine at Custer, from which flowed much of the financial strength of Bonanza at the time Hyndman was among its leading citizens.

Major Hyndman died in the fall of 1896 at Ketchum, after a short illness. He was 54. A few days before he died he had ridden to Atlanta and Sawtooth City. He was buried in his old home town in Pennsylvania. The headstone of his memorial is 2,500 miles west, a natural monument of towering rock, scaled by scores and admired by multitudes.

Climbing Mount Hyndman is described as easy by the mountaineering fraternity. They say it isn't much more than a hike. There is little rockwork unless the climber wants to tackle steep faces just for the adventure. Hundreds of men, women, and children have been to the top. Who was first is not recorded. It may have been an Indian or a beaver trapper nearly 150 years ago.

The first climb by women is known. Although men had been to the top on routine outings not worth mentioning, a trip July 4, 1896, by a party of eight, including two sisters, got notoriety. May and Ida Ivie accompanied a brother and five other men on the holiday outing. All were from East Fork, a mining town north of Hailey. The account was written for the *Ketchum Keystone* by Ida.

They went up the North Fork in wagons, camped a couple of nights, and started the ascent about 9 o'clock on Independence Day. They lunched at timberline. "Then we scaled almost vertical rock, being very careful," the lady wrote. There were dissenting views then and since on how vertical the rock was. Nevertheless, it was an accomplishment for young ladies.

"The view from the top is never to be forgotten," Miss Ivie said. "There is complete isolation. Silence is profound. We looked forth upon the majesty of mountains and plains. We feasted on scenery and game, including bear and goat."

The group put up a flag, left the summit at 5 o'clock, and got back to camp by 8 o'clock.

The experience was more rewarding than that of Jack Anderson, one of many to climb Mount Borah since it was first officially scaled in the 1930s by the survey party of Lyman Marden. Anderson, a University of Idaho distance runner, exercised his legs on Mount Borah one summer. When he got to the top he sat down to eat a sandwich and discovered he was on an anthill.

Several routes have been used for scaling Mount Hyndman. There is the one taken by the Ivie party of 1896, still the easiest. There is another by way of Devil's Bedstead, an 11,000-foot neighbor of Hyndman. The route from Wild Horse is considered the most difficult.

Chapter 32

NAME THAT MOUNTAIN

IDENTIFYING PEAKS in the Sawtooth range is not a simple job. They look different from various points. They are not in a straight line; they rise in irregular ridges. From some distances they seem to be shoulder to shoulder. From others they are far apart.

Naming them accurately from a specific spot is like naming the bristles on a hairbrush — they are as numerous and as much alike in some respects. The bill of particulars is complicated by the fact that several mountains have one or more names officially or locally. Although maps say thus-and-so, tradition sticks to pet names.

As good a place as any to start a geographical roster is from Stanley Lake, working roughly south from bayonet to bayonet. "Roughly" is a word used advisedly, because the peaks are by no means peas in a pod. They are helter-skelter like a scrambling quarterback.

The mountain dominating Stanley Lake is designated on most maps as McGown Peak. Controversy breaks out right there. To many people the peak is Gunsight because of its slotted summit. There are other Gunsights in various parts of the wilderness. The spelling of McGown brings up another question. If the peak is named for Arthur McGown, Sr., first postmaster at Stanley, McGown is right. On the other hand, it may honor George McGowan, an early county commissioner who mined and ranched on Valley Creek. To make matters more chaotic, the triangulation point on Gunsight-McGown-McGowan is called Thompson. The real Thompson Peak (for John Thompson, rancher-miner) is the glaciated mass prominent in the skyline southwest of Stanley. It is 10,776 feet high, tallest in the range. It seems even bigger and broader because Iron Mountain, almost the same height, is close behind. (The Sawtooths are so relatively raw that surveys in progress show new data year by year.)

Continuing south there are Horstman Peak, height unspecified and probably named for Dick Horstman, an early manager of Redfish Lake Lodge; Mount Heyburn, 10,229 feet, the most conspicuous rampart above Redfish Lake, named for Senator W. B. Heyburn; Braxon Peak, 10,353 feet; Grand Mogul, 9,733 feet; and Decker Peak, about 9,000 feet, named for a pioneer whose name is also perpetuated by Decker Flat. Farther west in the thicket of spires are Elk Mountain, Baron Peak, Packrat Peak, and Monte Veritas (perhaps the same as Grandjean Peak). Pinchot Peak honors Gifford Pinchot, first chief executive of the U. S. Forest Service.

Farther south, in the battlements behind Hell Roaring, Imogene, Yellow Belly, Pettit, and Toxaway lakes, stand the Finger of Fate, Reward, Temple, Arrowhead, Cramer and Sevy peaks, the latter recently named for the late John L. ("Jay") Sevy, a Forest Service supervisor.

Others, still farther south and west, include McDonald Peak, El Capitan (a sheer monolith near Alice Lake recently named because it resembles a tower in Yosemite), and Snowyside, 10,651 feet, proclaimed by some photographers as the most beautiful in the entire range.

In the wilderness area west of the ramparts visible from Sawtooth Valley there are scores of mountains and lakes. They bristle around Spangle Lakes, Queen's River, and headwaters of the South Fork of Payette River. Most have names, either homemade or official; some are not named. There are plenty to honor generations of mountain fans.

Castle Peak in the White Clouds is king of the district. At 11,820 feet it is taller than any genuine Sawtooth. Some people who have spent years in various parts of the area consider Castle Peak the most magnificent of the lot. The point cannot be decided, because beauty is a matter of opinion.

Lofty neighbors of Castle Peak include Patterson, 10,882 feet; Washington, 10,527; and Blackman, 10,307.

The three main peaks of the Boulder range are taller than any

Sawtooth. Galena is 11,153 feet, Easley 11,108, and Boulder 10,981. Glassford, part of the Boulder range but so far north and east that it is separated from the trio commonly seen from the highway between Galena and Ketchum, is actually higher than the others at 11,500 feet. It is named for Thomas Glassford, a conductor on the Shoshone-Ketchum branch of the Oregon Short Line. Easley honors J. V. Easley, a miner of the 1880s. Boulder looks like a big one. Furthermore, the road to a mine on its flank was full of boulders.

(For the geographically fastidious, it is proper to note that Ryan Peak, 11,900 feet; Kent Peak, 11,700 feet; and Sheep Mountain or Redwing, 10,910 feet, are all in the general vicinity of Glassford and are giants. But they are not Sawtooths and are out of the Boulder range.)

In the Pioneer range the tallest are Hyndman, 12,078 feet; Standhope, 11,700; and Devil's Bedstead, 11,000. At the head of Wildhorse Creek the Little Matterhorn stabs the windswept sky. Rhinoceros Rock casts its shadow on Modicum Flat, where smoke from campfires curls above aspen and willow.

Warbonnet Peak and Warbonnet Lake, in the Baron Lakes country about ten miles west of Redfish, may have some connection with the legend of Redfish Lake related by Charles Walgamott in *Six Decades Back*, published by Caxton Printers in 1936. Walgamott was a Bellevue merchant for several years and was father of the first child born in Hailey.

Walgamott says the story was told him by Indian Mary at Rock Creek in the 1870s. It relates the adventures of Tok-tee, "the beautiful one," and Shaunty-Muck, "plenty meat." They were lovers. She was sold by her father to a gambling buck to pay a horse-racing debt. As soon as she was carried off she was transformed into an old, ugly woman. Shaunty-Muck killed the gambler, and the lovers fled to the Craters of the Moon. The Great Spirit told them to live in the mountains. An attack by Blackfoot Indians hurried their decision. While hiding in a cave Tok-tee saw the morning sun on the Sawtooths and exclaimed "A-Dah-Ho." They made their way to the peaks, where she regained her youthful beauty. They found plenty of fish and game. In due time they established a tribe known as the Indians of the Clouds. Tok-tee was queen. Criminals and outcasts who joined them were taught to be good Indians.

The tribe learned to dig lead for bullets and gold for ornaments. That was bad. They started shooting one another for the gold. The founding couple survived a long time, however, and tried to run a peaceful, progressive colony. Shaunty-Muck died first. Tok-tee carried on alone several years. She succumbed, perhaps to a broken heart, when a ruffian called Bloody Hand killed a white prospector. Bloody Hand became chief. Under his leadership the Indians of the Clouds quickly lost their character and their homes. The tribe scattered and disappeared.

Tok-tee is credited by the legend with naming Redfish Lake, the White Clouds, and other features of the Sawtooths. Although Warbonnet Peak is not in the story, it may have played a part in her reign. The legend says Tok-tee and Shaunty-Muck were buried on the shore of Redfish. The graves were not marked for fear of desecration by Bloody Hand. But a mountain in the distance may have been designated as a warbonnet to remind future generations that the good Indians of the Clouds had been the first inhabitants of the heavenly heights.

Slide Gulches and Slide Hills are numerous. There is a Slide Hill on the East Fork of Wood River where an avalanche killed fifteen miners in 1917. Another Slide Hill is pointed out between Bonanza and Custer where a wall of snow in the 1880s took several lives and crushed a number of buildings, including part of the school. There are sites of similar tragedies on trails between Atlanta and Ketchum, between Atlanta and Rocky Bar, and in Deadman's Canyon on the South Fork of the Payette, between Cape Horn and Bonanza City, and on Vanity and Morgan Creek summits, to list but a few.

Shadow Hill near Graham is known for a less serious event. The treasurer of a mining company, a gent of about three hundred pounds, got lost on a winter walk. He returned safely while a search party was still in the hills. Members of the party said they knew they were on his trail because they found a frozen shadow where he had rested against a tree. The shadow weighed 150 pounds.

Names of many places in and near the Sawtooths are better known and less controversial than names of peaks.

Hailey is named for John Hailey, stage operator and territorial delegate to Congress who established the townsite. Ketchum, originally Leadville, honors David Ketchum, a former resident of Idaho City who was among the first to mine on Wood River. Muldoon was christened for an Irish prizefighter internationally famous during the era. Obsidian got its name from flinty mineral used by Indians for weapons and other tools. Fisher Creek, near Obsidian, was probably named for August Fisher, a pioneer mail carrier.

Photo by Ernie Day

Little Redfish Lake (foreground), Big Redfish (above) and Mount Heyburn (upper right)

Galena City recognizes the predominant ore of the neighborhood. Sawtooth City — original and transplanted — was named for the mountain range. Naming the range was easy, of course. It resembles the teeth of a gigantic saw.

Vienna is of uncertain origin. It may have been named by Austrian miners. After it had been a town for some years a new twist was put on the name. Unhappy miners who weren't being paid said, "Vienna gonna work no more." Whatever the origin, the name is one of the fanciest in the region. At one time there was an effort to give the place Indian flavor by calling it Redwing. The plan failed.

A place called Alberta sprang up on the plain between Hailey and Shoshone in the early 1900s. The name was changed to Richfield by the irrigation company that created it. The first child born there was Alberta Strunk.

Bellevue was the Gate City — a travel hub. Bellevue was one of the first towns in Idaho to have plans for streetcars, and it was one of three chartered cities. The streetcars did not materialize. "Biddyville" was never the name of Bellevue, except in jest.

Stanley was named for John Stanley, leader of the mining party that first found gold in the area in 1863. The strike was several miles up Valley Creek from the present town.

Sunbeam got its name from a mining company operating at the mouth of Yankee Fork, named by Union miners during the Civil War. Bonanza City on Yankee Fork reflected the optimism of its founders. Custer, a couple of miles up the river, remembered General George A. Custer, victim of a massacre in America's centennial year. Custer is also the name of the county.

Alturas Lake, like Alturas County, means "high." Pettit Lake is named for W. H. Pettit, early manager of the Monarch Mine at Atlanta. Carey derives from James Carey, first postmaster in 1884.

Dollarhide Summit between Ketchum and the South Fork of the Boise was named for A. H. Dollarhide, owner of mines in the Smoky district. Timmerman Hill south of Bellevue is named for John L. Timmerman, a Wood River resident of the early 1880s. Stanton's Crossing was the site of the S. E. Stanton ranch.

Leduc was named for Peter Leduc, first postmaster. The name was changed to Picabo in 1900. Picabo was named by a railway superintendent's daughter who reported the word was Indian for "left out."

Gannett, about eight miles south of Bellevue, was named for Lewis Gannett, owner of the site.

The town of Naples on the main railway line was changed to Shoshone in 1883. Toponis, a neighboring hamlet, became Gooding.

Graham, a ghost town west of the Sawtooth wilderness, was named for Colonel Matthew Graham, owner of many mines in Idaho. His company was one of several English syndicates that invested heavily in the Sawtooth area. He died in London in 1898.

In 1902 a reporter from Colorado who signed himself "Fitz-Mac" accompanied C. C. Tautpaus, a transportation mogul, on portions of a trip to explore a route from Challis to Thunder Mountain. Although not among those who crossed the most difficult stretch, Fitz-Mac reported that Tautpaus and Sid Roberts got lost on Loon Creek and were nearly killed by snowslides. They did not find or lose a mine, but the area where they camped several weeks was known as Lost Freighter. Tautpaus and company returned safely. He later lived at Idaho Falls, where a park is named in his honor.

An article Fitz-Mac wrote for the *Challis-Messenger* expresses a feeling of many Sawtooth admirers:

"I don't want to ever die unless I can be an angel and come back twice a year to Stanley Basin in June and October to see the clustered spires of the Sawtooth range reaching up among the stars."

Chapter 33

GHOSTS OF GALENA

WHEN WINTER COMES, the frost-bitten ghosts of Galena are not far behind. They kick up their heels on the headwaters of Wood River, sparkling in frost and snow. Galena is an old mining camp, one of the first in the valley.

It was there before Ketchum and Hailey. At its peak it had about seven hundred people. Today it is a friendly stopping spot for travelers going over the summit to Stanley Basin in summer and for fans of winter sports who explore virgin slopes beyond the sophisticated drifts of Sun Valley. The increasing popularity of snowmobiling in the upper country marks a return to the place where a lot of winter adventure began.

The snowshoeing ghosts of Galena probably had their finest hour in the winter of 1889-1890, shortly before Idaho became a state and when Galena was about nine years old. A newspaper of that era bears witness to the astonishing accomplishment. A short paragraph relates that a man on snowshoes raced down a hill, 5,000 feet, in sixteen seconds.

He was going so fast he held his breath from start to finish. Who and where were not specified. A little later, however, a Galena resident admitted that the event took place in Gladiator Canyon. If the snow had not been sticky, he said, time would have been better. It was a pretty good clip. It figures out to more than two hundred miles an hour, give or take a few furlongs. For snowshoes of the clumsy plank type, that is going some. If the gentleman had been on a modern pair of skis he would probably have gone into orbit. The speed was in a class with that of pros on Baldy when Friedl Pfifer schussed the slalom. He zoomed the course at breakneck speed after a competition.

There were suspicions in 1889 and in later years that the blur of bluish white light at the finish of the ride down Gladiator Canyon was reported by witnesses whose view was obscured by tongues in their cheeks. Nevertheless, Galena made clear that it was hep to snow sport and would play second fiddle to none, never mind the technical distinctions between snowshoes and skis.

Documented winter feats occurred some years later when Galena had all but disappeared. Pearl Eva Barber, a long-time resident, says in her book, *Galloping Ghosts of Galena,* that Ann Sullivan Doering, age twenty, skied from Vienna to Hailey in 1916. She covered more than fifty miles in five days. Much of the time she fought a blizzard.

Galena suffered damage from snowslides in the big winter of 1890, described in the *Wood River Times* as the worst storm since settlement. The reason it was not hit harder, apparently, was that there was not much left to smash. Prospectors doing two hundred miles an hour down the mountain had few neighbors or buildings.

Hailey, Ketchum, and Bullion were not so lucky. A slide late in January dammed Wood River for eight hours. Avalanches killed several miners. Trains between Shoshone and Ketchum were blocked for days. (Similar conditions existed during many more winters. Traffic stoppers on the line were par for the branch.) Livestock and game starved on the flats. A slide near Hailey on Della Mountain was two hundred yards wide, smothering the trail under seventy-five feet of snow.

When rain came in February, things turned mighty sloppy. Roofs collapsed, including that of the ladies' bathhouse at Hailey Hot Springs. Fortunately there were plenty of towels. Chinese trying to keep warm in their corner of town built such a roaring blaze they burned a block of shanties.

There was no communication with the backcountry. Nobody knew whether isolated people had survived. Among those for whom fears were expressed was the Bulgarian Monk of the Church of Jerusalem, a nomadic missionary. He had spent the summer and fall along Wood River preaching from a soapbox and living, for all anybody knew, on locusts and honey.

He was tall and dark with piercing eyes and hypnotic prophecy. He wore rubber boots, a black cloak and a red fez. He said he spoke thirty-two languages and had been a guide for Mark Twain in the Holy Land. His retinue consisted of two horses and a dog.

Although he found slim pickings in the mining camps for his forecasts of damnation, he was a figure commanding awe and amazement. More feared than revered as he swooped about like a phantom of the opera, he was nevertheless regarded as a harmless old coot.

Concern spread during the storm. Where was the Bulgarian Monk? Didn't he go down to Bellevue? He was not at Bellevue. How about Shoshone? Not there, either. Maybe he was under an avalanche. Too bad about the old monk.

When contact was restored with Galena, word came that the missing man had been there. He had camped on Titus Creek. He rigged snowshoes for his horses, built a pair of long ones for himself, and started over Galena Summit for mining camps on the Salmon.

Rumors that it might have been the Bulgarian Monk who had gone down Gladiator Canyon in a bluish haze with the fez as a headlight were dissipated in the spring when the eccentric missionary showed up at Bayhorse. He was quite healthy. He said he did not like snow or snowshoes. At no time going down the other side of Galena Summit did he go faster than one hundred miles an hour. He swore to it in thirty-two languages.

In the comparative warmth of the Salmon canyon the monk set up his oracular sanctum among a fresh audience of sinners. He shook a bony finger at disbelievers in Bayhorse several seasons until he turned up missing again. Bits of his clothing were found one day along the river. The verdict was drowning, although the body was not found. The community was thrown into a tizzy a year later when boys walking from Bonanza City to Sunbeam reported they were accosted by a frightening figure in a long black cloak. Responding to his beckoning gesture they took several nervous steps toward the specter. It vanished. The mystery of the monk persists along with other strange tales of the vicinity, including the disappearance of Isaac Swim — a miner who dropped out of sight while returning to a claim of fabulous ore in the Bonanza district. Swim, like the Bulgarian Monk, is said to have drowned as previously related. His mine is sought annually by people armed with scraps of paper, maps, legends, and hope. There is occasional talk that the spook the boys saw on the Bonanza trail was Swim. Only the monk and Swim know, and they aren't making public appearances.

Galena has had two histories. It first was a boomtown in mining times. That Galena lasted only a few years. The bloom was off almost before the main buildings were hammered together, and the town fell back into the landscape, disturbed only by powder blasts at several active mines and roused by rumors of treasure about to be tapped. The tide moved farther down Wood River to Ketchum, Hailey, Bellevue, and a host of smaller camps. The second Galena came to life with improvement of the road into Stanley Basin. It was passable but not exactly whizzable in the second decade of the twentieth century. Nervous dudes and natives in sputtering autos paused at the foot of Galena Summit to take stock of oil, gas, water, tire patch, and food. The trip was not to be taken lightly. Topping the 8,700-foot summit was the crowning glory of an adventure. Engines boiled, brakes smoked, clutches growled. Kids and womenfolk usually got out and walked around the bad turns, of which there were many. The grade was steep, with scary hairpins. The road was narrow. Passing was a problem requiring mechanical skill and a stiff upper lip.

Even the home folks, such as ranchers on both sides of the hill and sheepmen who had to keep track of herders and flocks, took the precaution of checking their transportation before they ventured over the hump. They poked a little fun at dudes for their anxiety, but they, too, showed proper respect for the summit.

The auto road, a development of a wagon route built by freighters and stagers when Vienna, Sawtooth City, et al., were going great guns, was fit for summer traffic only. Snow plugged it in the winter. It opened in May or June and closed in the fall. Mail and supplies were carried during the winters by men on snowshoes or with dog teams. In January 1916, Zeph Cherry, who packed mail once a week to Hailey, reported ten feet of snow at Vienna and 107 inches on Galena Summit. Both Cherry and the hickory sled he used on a portion of the journey were strong and enduring. "Perhaps no man is more familiar with the Sawtooths than he," said the *Wood River Daily Times*. When spring came it was his practice to spread dirt on the road near the summit to speed melting and provide traction.

Date of the first auto trip over the summit is a matter of debate; it may have been as early as 1913. However the first trip of the

1916 season is documented. It was May 11, and the car was an Overland. All travelers were from Malad, with Edward Hill as the driver. The car went by way of Blackfoot, Arco, Mackay, Challis, Yankee Fork, and Stanley. Total distance was more than six hundred miles. Hill reported boggy road from the summit to Russian John. He had four punctures between Ketchum and Hailey. In the vicinity of Pierson, on the Stanley side, he took to the Salmon River bottom for better traction around and over snowslides. He camped one night at Borah Springs near the summit.

Galena was a bright spot because it had a store and a service station — after a fashion. Flats were fixed and gas was sold. There were beds for travelers. One of the early proprietors at the time of transition from horse to auto — mostly horse — was Dave Williams, later a mail carrier and still later a rancher in Stanley Basin. The early auto era at Galena is more closely identified, however, with Mr. and Mrs. Charles Barber. Pearl Eva Barber, the energetic wife, preserved much of the history, lore, and legend in *Galloping Ghosts*, which was published in 1962 about a month before she died. Through its pages, generations who did not know Galena have sampled her lively humor and dramatic narrative.

Pearl Barber was the leading citizen of Galena so long it seems she must have been there when it began. She pumped gas, sold groceries, fixed flats, patched up wounded fishermen, and lent a listening ear to hunters relating their mighty deeds. She measured snow and recorded temperatures when nobody else was in the neighborhood. To many a frozen traveler plodding over the mountain on snowshoes, the cheery light of Mrs. Barber's window was a comforting beacon.

When she and her husband went to Galena on a fishing trip in 1923 they had no more intention of staying there than they had of drilling a tunnel through the mountain. But they bought the store for $500, paying $50 down. That started a chapter in neighborly business that lasted nearly forty years and spanned the transformation of a primitive outpost to a more or less sophisticated suburb of Sun Valley and back again.

At the outset, she relates in her book, they bought the wrong kind of groceries. They went in for pickles, lunch meats, and truck like that, thinking their trade would be mostly with fishermen. It was a bum guess. Sheepherders and miners were the regular customers. They wanted beans, milk, coffee, and smoking tobacco. Adjustments were made at a heavy loss on stock that didn't move from the shelves.

It was inevitable that Mrs. Barber would have adventures — and she did. As a rule she had good luck with her customers. They were a trustworthy lot. But there were bad apples. For instance, the man who took advantage of her kindly nature. His car was stuck in a drift. He told her a hard-luck story — said he was down to his last buck. Mrs. Barber fed him, loaned him dry clothes, and put him up for the night.

The visit dragged on for several days. The guy kept puttering around with his beat-up car. One afternoon Mrs. Barber went to Ketchum to have her hair done. When she got back the place had been robbed. The stranger had broken into the till and stolen about $50. What was worse, he stole her car. Officers located him in Oklahoma several months later. He had a long record of criminal offenses.

A frequent visitor at the Barber place was Frank ("Juggy") Niece, a Stanley service station operator who hauled his gas in barrels. He took two days for the trip, loading up at Hailey and staying the night at Galena. He said he wanted to pull the hill while it was cool. The charge for supper, room, and breakfast was a buck and a half. The truck driver's room that he occupied was out of the ordinary. Porcupines had a fondness for it; one had to be shot under the bed.

Sheepherders lingered at Galena. In years when grass was plentiful and grazing restrictions less exacting than they are today, they used to park their outfits near the store for weeks at a time. In exchange for delicacies provided by the station they gave Mrs. Baker sourdough bread. Very good bread it was, too, as most of the range-baked stuff is.

Gypsies used to be a menace. They came in droves, Mrs. Barber relates. Galena was the last stop before they plunged into the unknown, and they made the most of it. Their shoplifting was something fierce. Mrs. Barber fooled one gypsy lady. The visitor priced half the items in the store, trying to divert Mrs. Barber's attention while she located the cashbox. Mrs. Barber pretended the drawer was under a certain counter. At the first opportunity the gypsy made a dive for the box. She came up with a double handful of bottle caps. Mrs. Barber felt so sorry for her she gave her a can of coffee.

Charles Barber, who had operated the store with his wife for twenty years, died in 1944. Pearl continued the business until a short time before her fatal illness, when she sold out and retired to Easley, a hop and a jump down the road.

Hollywood got chummy with Galena in the years after Sun Valley took root in 1937. Parts of several movies were shot in the vicinity. Mrs. Barber suggests in her book that movie stars and directors were as plentiful as ground squirrels. The films included *For Whom the Bell Tolls, It Happened One Night, How to Marry a Millionaire,* and *Bus Stop.* The latter two were shot mostly at North Fork, a few miles below Galena.

One of the female stars — "prima donna type," says Mrs. Barber — wandered into the store and asked for a poached egg. The Galena store did not provide such dishes. It was with some difficulty that Mrs. Barber persuaded the actress to go somewhere else. A road crew waiting in the back room was delighted. "If you had given in to that dame," a spokesman said, "we'd have thrown you in the river." For several years the favorite expression of the crew was "One poached egg on toast, if you please."

A disaster occurred during one film. A logging team was supposed to collide with a cutter. Not quite collide, that is — just close enough to make it look real. Well, the stunt man did it up brown. The two vehicles went kerbam. People and animals writhed in the snow. One horse had to be shot. Women fainted. Cameras ground, however. The wreck was one of the outstanding scenes of the film.

"As I look back over the past I wouldn't trade a minute of it," Mrs. Barber says in her final chapter. "It was often hard work and there were many rough times, but these are outweighed by rich rewards and vivid memories. My only hope is that after the excitement of the past the present won't seem too tame and safe."

Chapter 34

U.S. FOREST SERVICE

THE ROLE OF the U.S. Forest Service evolved from creation of the Sawtooth Forest Reserve in 1905. The original area of about two million acres was increased to more than three million in 1906, comprising much of the present area of Challis, Sawtooth, Salmon, and Boise national forests.

Sawtooth National Forest was established in 1907 and soon split into East and West divisions with headquarters at Hailey and Boise. In 1908 Emile Grandjean became first supervisor of the West Division at Boise. C. N. Woods was supervisor of the East Division.

Executive orders of Theodore Roosevelt (who created the reserve) and of Woodrow Wilson carved the old domain into several forests. Sawtooth Forest West became the Boise National Forest. Sawtooth Forest East became the Sawtooth National Forest. The Challis National Forest was created from portions of the Sawtooth East, Salmon River, and Lemhi national forests. Names, dates, and boundaries are as complicated as an orphan's family tree. Essential details are provided in the publication, *Sawtooth Mountain Area Study – History* prepared jointly by the Forest Service and National Park Service in 1965.

Biographical sketches of early supervisors and rangers are given in that booklet. First was F. A. Fenn, supervisor of the Sawtooth Forest Reserve. Then came Grandjean, second supervisor of the reserve and first supervisor of Sawtooth National Forest West. The switch from "forest reserve" to "national forest" was, to a great extent, a matter of nomenclature.

Grandjean was a third-generation forester from Denmark. His father and grandfather had worked in Danish royal forests. He came to western America as a trapper, passed the civil service examination, and was appointed to the Forest Service. Men who worked with him say he was an excellent botanist, a good timber management man, and well versed in wildlife management. Walter Berry, a former ranger at Idaho City, remembers him as a fine man with a funny accent. He often wore a black bow tie in the office and on the trail, and he spent a good deal of time identifying plants.

Jim Chapman of Lowman spent time in the hills with Grandjean. He particularly recalls a meal he cooked for the supervisor. Chapman made sourdough biscuits. Grandjean hefted one, tapped it on his plate, and asked:

"Vhass is dis?"

Grandjean was bitterly criticized by mining interests and some timber users for carrying out forest policies. He took early retirement in 1923 and worked for a short time as a game warden for the Idaho Fish and Game Department. He was stationed at a cabin near the junction of Grandjean Creek and the South Fork of the Payette River. The place is now known as Grandjean. The retired supervisor then moved to Caldwell, where he died in August 1942.

Walter Campbell succeeded Grandjean as supervisor in 1923 but served only a few months. Campbell's successor was Ernest C. Shephard, who served until his death in the early 1930s. His ashes were scattered over the upper reaches of the South Fork of Payette River. A marker near the mouth of Canyon Creek has the inscription: "Here he lies where he longed to be." He is also honored by Shephard Peak, near Graham.

Guy B. Mains followed Shephard. Born in Wisconsin and a teacher for several years, Mains worked for the Barber Lumber Company in Boise before entering the Forest Service in 1907. He became supervisor of the Payette National Forest in 1908, after serving as a ranger at Mackay, where he married the Custer County superintendent of schools.

Mains was supervisor of the Boise National Forest until retirement in 1940. He wore a Van Dyke beard that gave him a distinguished appearance in the style of King George V. He said he didn't shave because his skin was tender. Mains also had a white eye, the result of a kindling-chopping accident. The combination of stiff whiskers and baleful eye was enough to subdue many critics of forest policies who poured out their complaints in his office.

After retirement, Mains was deputy treasurer for Boise City for several years. He died in 1958. Plans have been started by the Poacher's Club, a group of conservationists to which he belonged, to name a ridge above Bull Trout Lake in his memory.

Photo by Ernie Day

Sheep in Sawtooth Valley near Smiley Creek

At the Hailey end of the Sawtooth National Forest, C. N. Woods was the first supervisor. He served from 1908 until 1914, when he was transferred to Ogden as district inspector and eventually regional forester. He retired about 1944 and died in 1964.

M. S. Benedict was supervisor of the Sawtooth for about twenty years, beginning in 1914, with an interruption for military service. During his administration many miles of telephone lines were strung, bridges constructed, and trails brushed out to distant corners. It was also at that time that motorcycles were introduced as acceptable transportation for a few rangers, much to the dismay of the old guard who relied on horses.

Benedict was responsible for Massacre Flat, a stretch of highway near Easley where he put up Burma-Shave-type signs saying "Kill Fire," "Put Out Sparks," "Douse Coals," "Butcher Blazes," and the like.

Photography was his hobby. He took scores of winter and summer scenes, some of them prizewinners. He is credited with starting the use of slides in public information programs.

Benedict was later transferred to the Targhee at St. Anthony, where he served several years. He died in 1962. Benedict Lakes and Benedict Creek on the Payette drainage — not far from Grandjean Peak — are named in his honor.

Supervisors of the Boise National Forest since Guy Mains have been: Frank Moore, 1940-1944; Tom VanMeter, 1944-1946; Jim Farrell, 1946-1951; William G. Guernsey, 1951-1954; K. D. Flock, 1954-1958; Howard E. Ahlskog, 1958-1971; and E. C. Maw, 1971 to present.

Supervisors of the Sawtooth National Forest from the beginning have been: S. A. Fenn, 1906-1907; Emile Grandjean, 1907-1908; C. N. Woods, 1908-1914; M. S. Benedict, 1914-1917; G. H. McPheters, 1917-1920; M. S. Benedict, 1920-1934; F. S. Moore, 1934-1940; Charles Daugherty, 1940-1944; F. S. Moore, 1944-1949; Charles Daugherty, 1950-1957; John L. ("Jay") Sevy, 1957-1963; Max Reese, 1963-1969; and Ed Fournier, 1969 to present. The Sawtooth and Minidoka forests were consolidated in 1953 and headquarters moved from Hailey to Twin Falls.

Sevy Peak, near The Arrowhead and Finger of Fate, honors Jay Sevy, who died in 1963 while he was supervisor.

Success of the Forest Service in Sawtooth Valley is credited in large measure to William H. Horton, ranger on the Pole Creek District from 1908 to 1929. Sometimes known as the "Brooklyn Cowboy" because he was born in Brooklyn and came west as a small boy, Horton was one of the first men in Idaho to pass the civil service exam for forest employment. He served first at the Muldoon guard station, then Russian John. In 1908 he became guard at Pole Creek and was soon promoted to ranger.

He married Elizabeth Jane Billingsley, daughter of Mr. and Mrs. Archie Billingsley, on whose ranch near Carey he had worked as a youth. The Horton's daughter Alta now owns the Wampum Trading Post in Sawtooth Valley with her husband, Boyd Ellis. Mrs. Ellis grew up in the area, often accompanying her dad on rides into the mountains. Among her young friends were the children of sheepmen, including Juanita Uranga, daughter of Anton Uranga who ran bands in the Vienna district. Juanita is now Mrs. Harold ("Buck") Jones of Boise.

Horton had a multitude of tasks. He marked boundaries for various sheep outfits. He built fence. He marked logs for lumbermen and cabin builders. He trapped bear. He helped plant fish in lakes and aided wardens in enforcement of game laws. He rode sheep trails over Galena to keep bands from tangling. He advised resident ranchers about putting up hay. He gave first aid to the injured and informed sportsmen where and how to fish. He visited miners in remote canyons, keeping them in touch with the world.

The Pole Creek Station, his headquarters until he retired in 1929, has been abandoned in favor of other facilities closer to the main highway. After retirement Horton moved to California. He died there in 1936.

In addition to the legacy of competent service, Horton's career is recognized by Horton Peak, 9,896 feet, several miles north of Pole Creek. Alta Creek, a tributary of Germania Creek, is named for his daughter.

One of Horton's daily chores — common to all foresters — was writing a diary. Excerpts that capture some of the flavor of his activity follow:

W. H. Horton
Asst. Ranger, Dist. No. 3
June 1 to August 31, 1912
Ketchum, June 1.
   Went to Ketchum for my saddle horses, grub, and spikes to finish F. [fence] and pasture on Silver Creek.
R.J. Station, Sunday, June 2.
   Came up from Ketchum with horses, grub, and spikes for pasture.
Galena, June 3.
   Came up from R.J. Station with McPheters, Brown, Turner, and Mr. Woods and worked on drift fence up the Galena hill.
R.J. Station, June 4.
   Finished up drift fence and moved camp to R.J. station and built fence across station yard with McPheters, Brown, Turner, and Mr. Woods.
Pole Creek, June 5.
   Came over from R.J. H. McPheters put his team on the lead of mine and pulled me over the summit. Had to shovel some snow on the grade. Found everything at the cabin OK.
Pole Creek, June 6.
   Went down Salmon river and tried to get some men to work on separating corral. Everyone busy or going out. Had the promise of one man.

Pole Creek, June 7.
Rode over to where I was going to build a corral. Snow is all off but pretty muddy. Some snow where the timber is cut. Picked out a better place for corral. Cut down three trees that had fallen on the telephone wire. Cleaned up dooryard. Wrote letter to supervisor.

R.J. Station, June 8.
Cleaned out the house and scrubbed it out. Worked on my files. Checked up property I had here at the station.

Pole Creek, Sunday, June 9.
Worked on my files and made out expense voucher.

Pole Creek, June 10.
Took team and posts and put up posts along forest boundary on line running west above Clark's to 4th of July Creek north. Put boundary notices on trail and painted all posts white.

Pole Creek, June 11.
Put up trail notices from Lost Creek to the jog going west, south of Pole Creek. Put up posts on Pole Creek. Painted corner posts white.

Pole Creek, June 12.
Took tools and man up to the flat this side of Camp Creek and put him to work digging post holes for separating corral. Went up in the timber about half-mile east, where we had the timber cut for separating corral, and hauled out the posts for both corrals — 120 posts in all.

Pole Creek, June 13.
Rode up to the summit. Found two bands of Newman's sheep on the trail. Raining and snowing all day. Helped dig post holes in afternoon.

Pole Creek, June 14.
Snowed all day. Rode down Pole Creek and down the trail. Newman's outfit mixed up. Let them trail up to Gooding's old corral and cut out. Worked on my files in the afternoon.

Pole Creek, June 15.
Rode along trail to Champion Creek and up to Galena summit. Met two bands of Marker's sheep coming down summit. All new men. Told them how the trail ran down to separating corral. Set a few posts.

Pole Creek, Sunday, June 16.
Rode down Pole Creek to sheep bridge. Found one of Marker's bands off the trail. Put him on. Put up some new trail notices. Rode up to top of summit and back to separating corral. Helped finish setting posts. Posts all set up for both separating corrals.

Pole Creek, June 17.
Rode down to Champion Creek. Eight bands of sheep on trails. Posted mail. Rode up to summit. Found four bands of Ferguson's sheep and two bands mixed. Mr. and Mrs. Locke came in.

Pole Creek, June 18.
Rode up to foot of summit. Found two bands of Keefer's and four bands of Ferguson's sheep on the trail and two bands of Ferguson's off the trail. Put them back. Rode down to Smiley Creek. Found six bands of Cleaveland's sheep on trail. Three bands over on Ormsby's allotment. Put them on the trail.

Rode down to Champion Creek. Found two bands of Marker's at the crossing. Two bands of Cleaveland's mixed. Found him across Pole Creek.

Pole Creek, June 19.

Rode up to summit. Found four bands of Keefer's sheep on trail. Two mixed. Two bands of Ferguson's off trail on Gooding's. Put them back on. Sheep all hanging up on open strip and mixing. Feed poor. Rode over to Washington Creek and marked some bridge timbers for Dave Williams. Went down to Gooding's corral where Ferguson was separating.

Fisher Creek, June 20.

Rode down the trail to Lake Creek. Sheep all the way down to bridge. Two bands of Cleaveland's went on the reserve. Went and saw Shaw about the Alturas hay and his allotment. Found the Reitmeyer corner and put up a stake and flag so Mr. Locke could find it.

Pole Creek, June 21.

Came up the trail. Found bands of Keefer's sheep across the line. Put them back. Found his mixed band in Gooding's corral separating. Went up to cabin and changed horses. Rode to foot of summit and down trail to Pole Creek. Found two bands of Mackse's on trail.

Pole Creek, June 22.

Went along east boundary line from Pole Creek to Lost Creek and put up a stake between every one-half mile stake and put up boundary trail notice and painted stakes all white. Got Mr. Locke to run line on jog so I could set the stakes on the east mile jog. Mr. Woods came up from Big Smokey.

Pole Creek, Sunday, June 23.

Rode up to Galena Summit with Mr. Woods. Came down the trail. Found two bands of Keefer's on trail. Saw Marker's camptender hunting a bunch of sheep they had lost. Saw Newman and Watkins going to Cape Horn.

Pole Creek, June 24.

Rode to foot of summit and down the trail to 4th of July Creek. Found one of Marker's and one of Keefer's bands off the trail on Taylor Creek. Posted some mail at P.O.

Pole Creek, June 25.

Rode to foot of summit and found Halstrode's two bands mixed with Marker's, Keefer's and LeMoyne's. Took them to the Gooding corral and separated three bunches of Keefer's, LeMoyne's, and Marker's. Will separate Halstrode's to-morrow. Bacon's two bands are mixed on the summit.

Pole Creek, June 26.

Rode over to Smiley Creek and counted two bands of LeMoyne's sheep. Rode up to Vienna and found two bands of Skillern's sheep on the trail. Counted one band. Rode up to the summit and found two bands of Bacon's and Uranga's on the trail.

Pole Creek, June 27.

Rode over to Galena to see if Skillern's sheep that came up Wood River had been counted. Found band of Bacon's off the trail and put him back on. Some band mixed with Ormsby over the summit. Saw Herb McPheters and got some mail.

Pole Creek, June 28.
> Rode down to Archer's and counted his horses. Rode to Williams Creek. Two bands of Bacon's sheep on trail. Rode up to Clark's. Counted his cattle and horses. Saw Blackman and he gave me the count on his horses.

Pole Creek, June 29.
> Rode over to Alturas Lake. Saw Mrs. Law. She wanted permit to run a pasture up to the lake. Wanted to know where the corners of her ranch were. Showed her three corners. Rode up to summit. Found three bands of Bacon's sheep on the trail.

Pole Creek, Sunday, June 30.
> No work performed.

Pole Creek, July 1.
> Snowed all forenoon. Made out grazing reports and fire use. Howard cut some posts for closed area and hauled them out below station.

Pole Creek, July 2.
> Made out grazing reports in forenoon and rode down to the post office in afternoon and up the trail. No sheep on the trail.

Pole Creek, July 3.
> Rode over to Galena in the forenoon and posted the mail. Rode to Ormsby's in the afternoon. Five bands on the reserve.

Pole Creek, July 4.
> No work performed. Gooding came in with two bands of sheep. Left one on Pole Creek.

Pole Creek, July 5.
> Rode down the trail to Gold Creek. Found three bands of Bettis's sheep on the trail. Sent Howard to Russian John for fire boxes and tools. Got mail from R.J. Put up closed area notices on Champion Creek.

Redfish Lake, July 6.
> Put two fire boxes together. Took one down to Redfish Lake with Guard Howard. Cached it on hill east of lake and forty steps south from wagon road from tree marked X with arrow. Put up fire notices around lake.

Pole Creek, July 7.
> Came up from Redfish Lake where I put fire boxes and notices. Met Clyde Bacon and his foreman going to Stanley Basin. Mendiola came in with his sheep and went on his allotment.

Alturas Lake, July 8.
> Helped Howard put fire boxes together. Took a box over to Alturas Lake in afternoon. Cached it up towards head of lake. Stayed all night at lake.

Pole Creek, July 9.
> Came over from lake. Saw Mrs. Law. She spoke to me about a permit for a pasture. Rode down to Clark's and shod two horses. Saw Mr. Locke. Put on a horseshoe for him. Saw Bacon's bucks on the trail going to Stanley.

Pole Creek, July 10.
> Rode up to the summit. Found one band of Bennett's sheep on trail. Rode down trail to 4th of July Creek. Two bands of Cleaveland's sheep on trail. Got the mail at P.O.

Pole Creek, July 11.

Took two fire boxes over to Germania Creek. Cached one on the head of Pole Creek and one just south of Jake's cabin. Saw Dan Hackworth and George Blackman on Germania Creek.

Pole Creek, July 12.

Rode up 4th of July Creek to Bennett's corral and counted one band of his sheep. Went to Achens and gave him a free use permit. Saw Preston Shaw and told him to tell his father I wanted to know how much of the Alturas hay he wanted as others wanted it. Met Mr. Locke on road home.

Pole Creek, July 13.

Rode up to summit to meet Folsom's outfit but they were not there. Rode down the trail to Beaver Creek. Saw LeMoyne's two bands going on their allotments. Made out report. Mr. Smith, Mr. Puzee, and Mr. Simms outfit all at the station. Put Turner to help Howard haul poles for corral. Went over to corral and showed them where to put the timber.

Pole Creek, July 14.

Sunday. No work performed.

Pole Creek, July 15.

Fixed up a box of fire tools for Guard Howard and took him to Decker Flat Station. Sent ranger Turner to Mr. Locke's camp to work with him.

Pole Creek, July 16.

Went to Vienna Mine to see them about closing an area for their horses. Went all over the ground. Found they had 49 patented claims. Did not choose an area. Phoned to supervisor about it. Told me to choose an area for them.

Pole Creek, July 17.

Rode down the trail to Salmon bridge. Found Voder's sheep on the trail. Went to P.O. Got mail. Saw Mr. Locke and Guard Howard. Told Mr. Locke about getting in his expense account.

Pole Creek, July 18.

Rode up to the summit. Saw Mudd's outfit on the trail. Showed his camptender over part of the allotment. Mr. Pozier's outfit pulled out for Vienna. Rode down trail in afternoon to 4th of July Creek. Saw Brailsford's sheep on trail. Wm. Hapke was at station when I got there to check up my outfit.

Pole Creek, July 19.

Went throught my files with Mr. Hapke. Got through at 3 p.m. Rode up to the head of Pole Creek with Mudd.

Pole Creek, July 20.

Rode down the trail to 4th of July Creek. Four bands of Cleaveland's sheep on the trail. Rode to the Alturas Lake. Saw Mr. Pozier's outfit.

Pole Creek, July 21.

Counted Mudd's sheep. 1669. Sent in 1650. Went up to the bear trap. Caught she-bear.

Ibex Creek, July 22.

Took pack horse and packed fire box and tools over to Ibex Creek. Put box together and cached it on right hand side of trail about quarter mile up the creek behind big rock. Marked fir tree with X and arrow pointing to cache. Is due east 50 feet from the marked tree.

East Fork, July 23.

Rode down to Bowery Creek and up Bowery Creek but did not see any of Laidlaw's or Asker's sheep. Range getting pretty dry. Saw two bands of Cruzen's sheep on West Pass Creek. Camped on East Fork. Flies bad.

Germania Creek, July 24.

Came up Germania Creek to Camp Creek. Counted two bands of K. Bros. sheep. Showed camptender part of his range. Stayed all night at K. Bros. camp.

Pole Creek, July 25.

Came up Germania Creek. Rode up to Doak's Creek to Mr. Tolman's to see him about closed area for his horses but he was not there. Rode over to Washington Creek. Saw Oscar Perl from East Fork looking for a bunch of lost cattle. Saw Mr. Blackman. Lots of down timber on Germania Creek trail.

Pole Creek, July 26.

Rode down the trail to Salmon bridge. Saw two men who wanted to take up land on Pole Creek flat. Told them to come up to station and I would show them the land they wanted. (Caught big bear in trap. Dick Smith killed no. 3.)

Pole Creek, July 27.

Went up to Ormsby's camp on Vienna Creek to see Uranga about building a separating corral. Rode up to the Vienna mines and saw Dave Williams about a piece of hayland he wanted to lease. Some of the ore haulers left their camp-fire burning and it got out. Ormsby's men put it out.

Pole Creek, July 28.

Sunday. Sims and Poziers outfit all here. No work performed. Made out June 11 and special-use permits.

Pole Creek, July 29.

Rode all over Folsom's range with his camptender. Had notices on trees between Skillern Bros. and Folsom's but someone had torn them off. Reported it.

Pole Creek, July 30.

Rode down 4th of July Creek and over by Alturas Lake up to LeMoyne's camp. Had a little rain. Feed looking good. A few campers on lake.

Pole Creek, July 31.

Rained off and on all day. Rode down to Clark's and back. Met Mr. Locke. Phoned in my time for July.

Clark's Ranch, August 1.

Rode down the trail to Decker Flat. Saw Howard. Told him to make out his time and I would phone it in. Still raining. Saw Bennett's sheep on trail going out.

Pole Creek, August 2.

Howard came up to station and I telephoned in his time. Rode up Smiley Creek. Saw two bands of Ferguson's and Bill Newman's sheep on the trail going in to ship. Saw Antone Uranga working on his corral. Rained like the dickens.

Pole Creek, August 3.

Hauled up a load of wood and shod horse in forenoon. Rode up to the summit and up on Mear's range. Uranga has one band on his allotment. Camptender said they were going to put on one more. Rained for about two hours.

Pole Creek, August 4.

Sunday. No work performed.

William Horton, first ranger at Pole Creek

Pole Creek, August 5.

Rode down to Decker Flat and over the trail Howard is cutting out to Redfish Lake. Found a good easy way. Not over four miles from flat and not much down timber. Shot deer I found with both hind legs broken. Someone had shot and left it to die. The state scab inspector stayed with me all night.

Pole Creek, August 6.

Rode up to the top of Galena summit to see if Lobush was coming in. Did not see any sheep. Rode down to Pettit Lake. Saw one band of LeMoyne's sheep. Passed Legrane's ranch. He has not come in yet.

Pole Creek, August 7.

Rode to foot of summit. Found Lobush on the trail. Rode to Vienna. Saw Antone Uranga building corral. Rode up Pole Creek to Mudd's camp. Told him about a bunch of sheep he had lost.

Pole Creek, August 8.

Rode down Pole Creek to sheep bridge. Counted Lobush's sheep. Showed him his allotment. Rode down to Decker Flat. Howard was working on the Redfish Lake trail. Stopped at Pierson and got the mail.

Pole Creek, August 9.

Went along telephone line. Found big tree across the line. Chopped it off and it broke the wire. Sent word to McPheters. Took fire box up toward the head of river. Cached it about one mile above corral on left hand side of trail 20 steps east of pine tree marked X, with arrow pointing to cache and four trees blazed around cache.

Pole Creek, August 10.

Rode down to Decker Flat and up on trail where Guard Howard was working. Told him to quit trail work and go to patrolling. Went to Clark's and shod saddle horse. Met Segraves and Lockman. They wanted some house logs marked. Told them I would mark them Monday. Mr. Woods and Davis came over from Hailey. They repaired telephone line.

Pole Creek, August 11.

Sunday. Rode to foot of summit. Saw two bands on trail. Told them to keep on trail going over. Mr. Woods phoned they were off the trail.

Pole Creek, August 12.

Went down to Segrave's ranch and marked up a set of house logs for Frank Lockman and made out two free-use permits. Rode up Vat Creek and looked at some hay Segraves would like to cut. Rode over to Clark's and shod bay horse in front.

Pole Creek, August 13.

Rode over to K. Bros. range. Saw Skillern's outfit. Said their feed was getting short. Saw Mudd's outfit on head of Pole Creek.

Pole Creek, August 14.

Hunted horses till 10 o'clock. They got out of field. Fixed fence till noon. Rode down to 4th of July Creek. Found two bands of Cleaveland's sheep going out to ship. Stopped at P.O. and got mail.

Pole Creek, August 15.

Rode to top of summit and down to Pole Creek. Found three bands of Ferguson's sheep and three bands of Uranga's on trail. Rode up Smiley Creek. Found one band of Bill Newman's coming in from shipping.

Pole Creek, August 16.

Rode down to Mr. Pozier's camp and took Mr. Smith as he did not think he could find their camp. Rode up the trail. Found three bands of Dr. Bettis' and four bands of Jim Laidlaw's sheep on the trail. Made out free-use permits for posts and poles.

Carey, August 17.

Went down home. Annual leave.

Carey, August 18.

Sunday. No work performed.

Carey, August 19.

Annual leave. (Same August 20 and 21.)

Hailey, August 22.

Came up from Hailey to office. Looked over my sheep counts.

Ketchum, August 23.

Came up from Hailey office. Got some data on June 11 homesteads on my district from the office. Got horse shod in Ketchum.

Pole Creek, August 24.

Came up from Ketchum. Rode up along the trail. Found two bands of LeMoyne's and two of Ormsby's on trail going out to ship. Rode down to Pole Creek and up to station. Found Guard Howard there.

Pole Creek, August 25, Sunday.

Rode up to where I had my bear trap set. Caught the biggest bear of the season. Phoned to Roy Ivie to come up and take his picture. No work performed.

Pole Creek, August 26.

Went up the creek with Roy Ivie. Took the bear's picture. Rode down the trail to Champion Creek. Eight bands trailing out to ship. Rained in the afternoon.

Pole Creek, August 27.

Rode down the trail to Williams Creek. Rode up Champion Creek looking for Mendiola's outfit. Found them. Have two bands of his 15 count. Twelve bands of sheep on trail going out. Made out two June 11 applications. Saw nine men looking for land on the open strip. Guard Turner came in for a pick to work on trail.

Pole Creek, August 28.

Rode down the trail to Fish Creek. Found a fire back of Samuel's ranch, some trail herd had left. Got Bascoe and put it out. Burned about one-half acre of sagebrush on open strip. Got mail at Clark's. Twelve bands of sheep on trail going out.

Pole Creek, August 29.

Rode up to the Galena summit. Met Mr. Pozier going out to Hailey. Eight bands of sheep on trail going out to ship. Rode down to 4th of July Creek. Sheep all along trail going out to ship.

Pole Creek, August 30.

Rode up to Vienna. Found four bands of sheep on trail going to South Boise. Rode over to Clark's and up the trail. Four bands of Marker's and two of Ferguson's on trail going out.

Pole Creek, August 31.

Rode over to Camp Creek on the K. Bros. range. Stayed all night. Rained and snowed. Feed pretty well all fed-out on their range.

Chapter 35

PUSH FOR A PARK

RESIDENTS OF THE Wood River area began thinking national park almost as soon as they could spell tourist. Excited by glowing reports from Yellowstone — created in 1872 and enjoying a boom with the arrival of autos — boosters for a Sawtooth National Park got in their licks before there were roads to bring many visitors.

Legislation was drafted, although apparently not introduced, as early as 1911. Confident people referred to "our national park" and "Sawtooth Park" as a reality before World War I. Spokesmen for the wonderland took it for granted that the mountains would be set aside as a national playground of the first class within a short time. They jumped the gun. There is no Sawtooth National Park yet, although the differences between a full-fledged park and the Sawtooth National Recreation Area and Wilderness created by Congress in 1972 are technical. The points are visible to concerned interests on both sides of the controversial matter, but they make little difference to the rank and file.

Women took the lead in urging a park. The movement was the outcome of a meeting of women's clubs at Mountain Home in 1912. Eight sections of Idaho were suggested as areas of national interest. The Redfish Lake district received the most votes, and Idaho women went on the stump for it.

Commenting in 1915, the *Wood River Times* said it was an excellent choice because "the bill has been before Congress for two sessions." Quoting *See Idaho First and Idaho Clubwoman* — a combined periodical — the *Times* said Sawtooth National Park "will aid development of Idaho, advance prosperity, and further the well-being of its people." The *Times* also said: "A few hundred people visit the region annually. Thousands will come if the country is exploited, the region developed, and stock excluded. It is a golden fact that Idaho needs to appreciate her scenery. The few people who are objecting to the setting aside of the Redfish area as a park do not realize that the area is a national forest and will not cost Idaho anything."

A woman writing for *The Idaho Statesman* January 2, 1916 said a bill was then before Congress creating a Sawtooth National Park of 145,000 acres. "Someone has said," she wrote, "that scenery cannot be compared. It has personality. The Grand Canyon awes you. Rainier overwhelms. Yellowstone fascinates. But the Sawtooth region welcomes you. It is new and charming. It is lovable."

The park bill she referred to was introduced by Senator William E. Borah and Representative Addison T. Smith. It was endorsed by the Interior Department and Geological Survey. However there were impediments. Geographer R. B. Marshall said Ketchum lacked tourist accommodations. He said the Galena grade was too steep and dangerous for general traffic. He complained that for three miles on each side of the 8,700-foot summit, pines had to be cut and dragged for brakes.

Local advocates said the drawbacks were minor and would be corrected. They further claimed that all residents along the road from Ketchum to Stanley favored the park. An article in the *Hailey Times* said: "There is practically no commercial mining in the park and little merchantable timber." It was contended that most of the best pine had been cut for cabins, mine timbers, and fuel.

Although the perils of Galena Summit were discounted by park boomers, the matter of a route or routes to the Sawtooths raised an ugly wrangle. The Sawtooth Park Highway — optimistically named — was under construction in 1914-1915. It went from Twin Falls to Hailey via Shoshone, Richfield, Picabo, and Bellevue. Only a portion was finished by the end of 1915. The highway ended at Hailey, leaving a long stretch to the park. Taking note of that fact, businessmen of the Boise area proposed a road by way of Atlanta. They said a "government trail" traveled a country of "grim wilderness and elysian beauty" and added that "road experts claim that, by following a grade laid out, a road without difficult grades may be built." Perhaps. But it would have been a monumental under-taking around or through miles of solid rock.

Challis offered to settle the dispute between Hailey and Boise by having a nice road up Salmon River from Challis to Stanley. That was just the ticket, Challis people said. It would save a lot of money and give people a better crack at scenic wonders adjacent to the Sawtooths.

As early as 1913, Hailey men encouraged the Idaho Highway Commission to build a road across southern Idaho linking Yellows-tone Park with the Sawtooths. J. R. Fox of Hailey wrote Theodore Turner of Pocatello, commission chairman, that the original Oregon Trail ran across Blaine County by way of Carey, Silver Creek, and Stanton's Crossing to Camas Prairie and thence to Boise. He said that route would be better for a highway than a road proposed farther south.

Turner and others traveled from Pocatello to rendezvous with several officials at Arco to explore the route. Turner's party got lost in the desert. Roads were bad after a rain, and phones were down. The group occupied much of its time shooting twenty-six sage grouse and finally reached Hailey late at night. Turner, Miles Can-non of Weiser, Professor C. N. Little of the University of Idaho, and F. P. King, state engineer, were dined and wined at the Alturas Hotel. State Senator Irvin E. Rockwell was toastmaster. The com-mission promised to push a route from Shoshone Falls to Sawtooth National Park — the premature name adhered to regularly by the *Hailey Times*. Then the commissioners returned to their hometowns by rail; roads were too bad.

Senator Borah and Senator James H. Brady visited the Saw-tooths in July 1915 as guests of the Hailey Chamber of Commerce. The Brady tour came first. Senator Brady spent July 11 in the mountains as a passenger in the new buick of J. L. Fowler. Teams were hired at Stanley by Mrs. H. L. Benner to take him on a wagon trip to Redfish Lake. He returned to Stanley for dinner at the Ben-ner Mountain Inn and back to Hailey by auto. The trip from Stan-ley to Hailey took only four hours — a little shorter than the jour-ney up.

Senator Brady was quoted as saying he would do all he could for the park. He said he was enraptured by the panorama of peaks, lakes, and forest primeval. Then he went on to Yellowstone Na-tional Park, which was opened to auto travel for the first time in the summer of 1915.

Senator Borah arrived in Hailey July 21. He had an entourage of three cars, in contrast to two for Senator Brady. He rode in L. L. Sullivan's Cadillac. The others were Fowler's Buick and Carl Neusil's Stanley Steamer. The party included I. E. Rockwell, L. L. Sullivan and his son Eugene, Editor Picotte, and E. P. Armstrong, president of the commercial club.

On the way they met R. T. Tustin, mine manager, who had been involved in a car wreck between Galena and Vienna. Injuries were minor, and the damage was quickly repaired. Borah and company rolled on to Stanley, stopping briefly at Borah Springs, between Galena Summit and Pole Creek. At Stanley the senator's party, like Brady's group, dined at the Benner Mountain Inn and returned to Hailey in the evening.

Senator Borah was cautious in his remarks about a national park. Editor Picotte said he did not comment on probable congressional action.

"Whether man ever frames the record to read 'National Park,' God has made it and placed it there," Borah said.

Senators Borah and Brady were following the footsteps of Senator Weldon B. Heyburn who visited Hailey in the fall of 1908. He did not make tracks in the park, exactly, because there was no auto road to the Sawtooths at that time. But he was in Hailey, where he was described as "the warhorse of Idaho politics" and was exposed to talk about the inspiring peaks. Senator Heyburn died October 17, 1912, in his second term. One of the most impressive peaks in the Sawtooths was named in his honor in 1913. The battlement above Redfish Lake, 10,229 feet high, had been known as Tower Peak. The honor for Senator Heyburn was suggested by Dr. Harvey W. Wiley of Boise, a national food expert whose efforts on behalf of pure food and drugs had been aided by the senator. He was a consumer champion, a sort of Ralph Nader of his time. (Incidentally, Dr. Wiley carried on a feud with railroads because he said he had contracted a cold in a Pullman car.) At the time Mount Heyburn was named for her late husband, Mrs. Heyburn said the senator had probably never seen the peak but had admired the snow-clad range as he rode from Pocatello to Boise by train.

Some old-timers still call the mountain Cathedral Peak, disdaining both Tower and Heyburn.

Addison T. Smith of Twin Falls, an assistant to Senator Brady, was elected to congress in 1913. He joined Senator Borah in one of the first pieces of legislation to create a Sawtooth park. Several other representatives and senators introduced similar bills from time to time. They differed as to size of the park and its regulations.

All had two things in common: They praised scenic values, and they went down the drain. There were many hurdles between introduction and passage. One way or another nearly all the bills, if not the entire lot, withered on the vine without being put up for final roll call. Along the road there were hearings, motions to amend, field surveys, department reports, and other maneuvers. Sessions of Congress ended without final action. When park bills were trotted out again, the same process was repeated. Sawtooth National Park was often conceived but never born.

Agricultural, mining, and timber groups did not find Sawtooth Park a lovable thing. State and national wool growers associations were particularly critical. Their opposition was a hangover from the time President Theodore Roosevelt created Sawtooth Forest Reserve in May 1905. The reserve of nearly two million acres included much of what later became Sawtooth, Challis, Salmon, and Boise national forests. Livestock people took a dim view of that. They continued their fight whenever there was a proposal to fiddle with management of the land, whether by the Forest Service or the Park Service. Frank Gooding, a former governor of Idaho (1905-1908), was president of the National Wool Growers in 1911, replacing his brother, Fred, a Montana sheepman. Frank Gooding is said to have brought the first bands of sheep to Sawtooth Valley in 1887. Over a period of many years there were so many sheep on the range the outfits had trouble finding grass. Ketchum was the leading shipping point for sheep and lambs in the United States. Business was good, but there was concern for the natural resource on which livestock depended. That situation was responsible, in part, for establishment of the forest reserve, one purpose of which was to conserve grass and watersheds. Grazing fees were put into effect and increased from time to time, controlling the number of sheep to meet carrying capacity.

Senator Heyburn was critical of the Forest Service. He disagreed with Gifford Pinchot, head of the agency, on many points. As a man from northern Idaho, where mining was and is the leading industry, he was cool to action that would curtail mining while aiding timber and scenery.

A noisy flea in the lovable ointment buzzed in another part of the forest, that is to say, in the Idaho City area. The Boise Basin was geared to mining by tradition and practice, and it came to a boil when mining rights were threatened. Miners feared homesteading could develop on timber claims which had been filed on only partially and which might contain minerals. Language of

Senator Heyburn's photo courtesy Idaho Historical Society

Mount Heyburn, with Senator Weldon B. Heyburn inset

forest regulations cast a shadow on some property staked, or almost staked, as mine ground. The controversy had arisen soon after the forest reserve was created. Idaho City poured torrents of criticism on foresters and all their works. The mining fraternity said dummy claims were being filed by squatters on mining land with the intent of turning them over to a logging company. One of the chief targets of scathing attacks by the *Idaho World* was Supervisor Grandjean. The springboard for an avalanche of verbal boulders was the John Ort case. Ort had land above Lowman on the Payette River. His acreage was not surveyed. The supervisor allegedly told him he could not sell timber but could burn it and then claim a quarter section for agricultural purposes.

"Isn't that a timber preservation principle that would shock an idiot?" the paper asked. "Such incendiary idiocy is beyond belief. If Grandjean is obeying the rules of the Forest Service, the proper place for promulgation of those rules is an asylum for the feebleminded. If he is running counter to those rules, he should be removed immediately."

After a study by Albert Bergh, grazing supervisor on the Sawtooth, the Forest Service replied that laws and regulations were complicated. Timber claims, it said, were useful for individuals and the general economy.

In reply to that, Editor C. E. Jones of the *World* wrote President Roosevelt protesting timber claims. An assistant land commissioner replied that change was unlikely, that timber claims would stand, that surveys were being made, and so forth.

Charges were made that the Barber Lumber Company, predecessor of Boise-Payette and Boise Cascade, was encouraging individuals to file on public land, paying the price of the land plus a bonus, and taking the land for itself. Several officers of the company (including William E. Borah, its attorney) were indicted by a federal grand jury for timber fraud. Borah had just been elected to the U.S. Senate by the Idaho legislature. The trial jury deliberated fourteen minutes in reaching a verdict of not guilty. In June 1908, following the trial of the previous September, President Roosevelt removed the district attorney and marshal. Senator Borah nominated their successors.

The *Idaho World* was not convinced, however. In July 1908 it said: "The sooner the Barber Lumber Company is put out of business the better it will be for the Basin. But it looks as if it has come to stay." It had. Not only did logging overtake and pass mining as the leading business in the area, but the Forest Service generated one of its most important payrolls.

The controversies undoubtedly had a bearing on legislation for a Sawtooth National Park. Miners, stockmen, and timbermen learned to get along with the Forest Service even though they did not love it. They resisted further erosion of resource use which they feared would come with a national park — a brand new ball game. Therefore it is understandable that Senator Borah's passion for a park was barely visible. He helped introduce a bill but didn't put himself out. That may be one reason no peak in the Sawtooths bears his name. His mountain is in another range, the Lost River of Custer County. It has two outstanding credits: It is the highest mountain in Idaho at 12,665 feet, and it is the crowning promontory of the only ridge in the Rocky Mountain system that runs contrary to the geological pattern. That fact, some observers have noted, is appropriate for Senator Borah.

For many years the dream of Idaho clubwomen was nurtured by several bills for a Sawtooth Park or its facsimile. All went down the drain for one reason or another. Ill-fated park bills were launched in 1913, 1916, 1935, 1960, and 1966. In 1937 there was a partial victory when the Sawtooth Primitive Area was established to set aside about 200,000 acres of upper country. The area was very rugged, visited by few, and not appreciably changed in use after primitive status was granted.

A joint study of Sawtooth status was requested in 1964 by the Forest Service, Park Service, and the Bureau of Outdoor Recreation. A report of this study in 1965 concluded that the Sawtooth Mountains should be managed as either a national recreation area or a park. Legislation for a recreation area was introduced in 1966. The area nominated was 350,000 acres. The bill was dropped. Another, for 750,000 acres, was proposed in 1969. That, too, was left hanging, in deference to legislation introduced in the Senate in March 1971 by Senators Frank Church and Len Jordan and a bill introduced in the House about the same time by Representatives Orval Hansen and James McClure. House hearings in Washington, D.C., were conducted in June 1971. Senate hearings were held in April 1972, also in Washington. Much of the input was similar to that which had been unfolded at previous hearings about the Sawtooths. The formal proceedings included Senate hearings at Sun Valley in 1966, Senate hearings in 1967 in Washington, House hearings in 1969 in Washington, and House hearings at Sun Valley in 1970. There was much to be heard, some of it as repetitive as an owl hoot. Basically, the arguments pro and con remained constant; only the voices and phraseology changed. Park and/or recreation area supporters proclaimed scenic grandeur, blessings of matchless solitude, and nourishment of the human spirit in primeval environment. Persons more interested in economic resources took up the cudgel for minerals, timber, livestock, and other private development.

The legislation on which the hearings of 1971 and 1972 were conducted established the Sawtooth National Recreation Area of 754,000 acres and the Sawtooth Wilderness of 216,000 acres. The wilderness area replaced the Sawtooth Primitive Area and provided a new set of regulations.

Scores of persons and organizations gave written and oral opinions to the Subcommittees on National Parks and Recreation of the Committees on Interior and Insular Affairs — House and Senate. Their statements fill a couple of 250-page documents.

Drama of the hearings was heated up considerably by a mining flap in the White Clouds. In 1968 the American Smelting and Mining Company filed a molybdenum mining claim at the base of Castle Peak. Test holes were dug, roads pioneered, and a camp established. Environmentalists fumed. A majority of citizens appeared to believe in the protection of White Cloud grandeur, although not subscribing to the environmental creed as the Ten Commandments of land use. They also opposed the mine, first because it was a wart in a beautiful place, and second because molybdenum was not critically needed. Governor Don Samuelson supported the mine. Ernie Day, chairman of the Idaho Park Board and a long-time staunch advocate of conservation, took issue with the governor and resigned. Cecil Andrus, Democratic candidate opposing Republican Samuelson, fought the mine. The issue was prominent in the election of 1970. Andrus was elected. Political analysts said Samuelson stubbed his toe on the White Clouds. Andrus reappointed Day to the park board in 1976. Andrus became secretary of the Interior in 1977.

Echoes of the White Cloud battle were still ringing when legislation for the Sawtooth National Recreation Area was put on the operating table for public examination. Supporters, opponents, and in-betweeners had their say. All angles were thoroughly aired by experts and by ordinary citizens, one of whom expressed his contempt for outsiders who sat on fence rails writing poetry about the scenery while trying to regulate the lives of genuine inhabitants.

The bulk of testimony, however, favored the recreation area.

Ernie Day agreed it was a step in the right direction but argued for a national park. "Only national park status," he said, "will have the required muscle to protect the base of Castle Peak and Upper Little Boulder drainage from a vast open-pit mining operation for a metal in surplus supply. . . . A park complex similar to the Yellowstone-Teton administration is called for here. The valley lakes could be made to accommodate the macadamized majority of recreationists, and wilderness classification could protect, yet make available, the delicate Alpine upper reaches. Projected over a number of years, these are a more valuable asset than a one-shot, one-use, open-pit mine or a clear-cut. Idaho deserves a national park within its boundaries. The nation as a whole deserves to have these spectacular Sawtooth, White Cloud, Boulder, and Pioneer mountains preserved and protected as fully as possible. And even more important, this outstanding area deserves on its own merits to have the highest degree of permanent protection for its unique grandeur."

J. H. Breckenridge of Twin Falls, a stockman owning property in Sawtooth Valley and president of National Wool Growers and Idaho Wool Growers, reintroduced proposed amendments to the SNRA act that he had requested at earlier hearings. Their primary thrust was that condemnation rights should not be extended to the acquisition of private property for recreation and administrative facilities because there was plenty of public land within the area to meet those needs.

Senators Jordan and Church agreed that he had a good point.

Said Senator Jordan: "You are always a good witness, and no one could accuse you of a Breckenridge filibuster because you are succinct and precise. I can appreciate the apprehension you feel, as probably the largest landowner in the valley, when you read that valley land, private and public, is going to be administered under regulations promulgated by the Forest Service. This is a new venture, and I dare say your observations and the safeguards you suggested in this statement will be looked at very carefully."

Said Senator Church: "He has tried very hard to cooperate with us in trying to achieve a bill that would serve the public need and at the same time be fair to the private sector. He has been most helpful. He has presented his arguments very hard, which we expect him to, but his arguments have never been unreasonable."

Fear of condemnation was also expressed by Thomas G. Nelson of Twin Falls, representing the Stanley Basin Cabin Owners Association. "We wish to make it clear," he said, "that we are in favor of the general objectives of the bill. . . . We are not attempting to make it impossible for the Forest Service to clean up some existing problems or control future development. We do feel that the bills contain certain provisions which give the Forest Service powers not needed to fulfill the purposes of the proposed legislation and which present to the Forest Service weapons to use in eliminating private homesites, in direct contravention of the underlying theory of preserving existing uses."

A statement from Governor Andrus was read into the record by Jack Hemingway of Sun Valley, a member of the Idaho Fish and Game Commission. The governor proposed a Sawtooth National Recreation Area for the lowland valley areas. He urged creation of a national park to assure protection of the high mountain areas. "The development of a national park management plan for the high country," he said, "along with the adoption of a Sawtooth Valley National Recreation Area would provide adequate protection for the entire area in an orderly and fair manner."

Vernon Ravenscroft of Tuttle, president of the Idaho Public Land Resource Council, Inc., said the organization endorsed, in principle, the recreation area bill. He noted, however, that a couple of public opinion polls indicated fifty percent in favor of multiple use for public land in one instance and, in another, thirty-four percent in favor of a national recreation area, with forty-four percent saying leave the area as it is and twelve percent in favor of a national park. Residents of Blaine, Camas, Lincoln, and Gooding counties — nearest the Sawtooths — responding to one poll, he said, did not favor either a park or a national recreation area. Less than 3 percent wanted a park, less than 10 percent a national recreation area.

Stewart M. Brandborg, executive director of the Wilderness Society, Washington, D.C., asked that the Sawtooths be made a national park. So did Lloyd Tupling, a former Boise resident now of Washington, D.C., who represented the Sierra Club.

On the other hand, the committees received many letters opposing national parks in general and a park in the Sawtooths in particular. Some were also against the recreation area. But, on balance, a large number of testifiers seemed ready to accept a recreation area as a compromise with park proposals rather than come out with nothing at all.

After studying the input and digesting as much of it as was digestible, sponsors of the legislation made amendments that took care of some of the essential points. With those additions and sub-

Photo by Ernie Day

Galena Summit, a gateway to the Sawtooth Wilderness

tractions, the Sawtooth National Recreation Area and Wilderness became a reality by vote of the Congress August 22, 1972, as Public Law 92-400.

Then began the task of translating language into action. The job of setting up the recreation area presented problems, some still to be solved. Administration was assigned to the Forest Service, which took the assignment as a new departure. Running a park — okay, make it "recreation area" — was not its long suit. The fact that the layout was to be governed by the Forest Service caused brain-bending among foresters and confusion to the public, which is accustomed to having a parklike area run by the Park Service, an agency of the Department of the Interior. The Forest Service is under the Department of Agriculture. The two departments hold hands publicly, but there is keen rivalry, as there is in any large family with division of responsibility and rewards.

Vern Hamre, regional forester at Ogden, compiled an environmental statement as the transition proceeded. The first draft was filed with the Council on Environmental Quality in April 1974. Many interested organizations and individuals were asked to comment. As was the case at hearings on the legislation, dozens made their ideas known. The final draft was filed May 27, 1975. It contains numerous bits of advice calculated to guide the Forest Service in setting up rules and regulations.

The League of Women Voters expressed concern for "fragile environment" in view of projected quadrupled use in a couple of decades. Environmental West Research and Planning, Inc., suggested a bicycle path along old U.S. 93. The Geothermal Energy Institute asked further study of the energy potential. The Idaho Fish and Game Department asked more protection for resources on which game and fish depend. The Magic Valley Association of Governments asked more consideration for harvesting of timber. The Greater Sawtooth Preservation Council urged that livestock grazing be phased out. The Idaho Mining Association opposed restrictions on mining.

The environmental statement is a compendium of data and suggestions, rather than a bill of particulars for management. Rules and regulations are promulgated from time to time under the law.

Of the 754,000 acres in the recreation area, 726,000 acres are national forest. There are 25,000 acres of private land and 2,000 acres of state land. Private landowners who use their land in compliance with regulations are assured continuation of all private rights. Livestock use is accepted as part of the authentic ranching atmosphere adding to visitor enjoyment.

Public use of SNRA is heavy. The report for 1974 shows 286,000 camping days, 83,000 fishing days, 44,000 hunting days, 57,000 hiking days, 12,700 trail-biking days, and 2,000 mountaineering days. The report also shows harvest of 1,200,000 board feet of timber, 127 summer homes, 11,400 animal-unit-months of grazing, 300 miles of roads, 900 miles of trails, 494 camping units, and 45 picnic grounds with a capacity of 2,700 people.

The Sawtooth National Recreation Area has thirty-six full-time employees in the Hailey-Ketchum area and ten in Sawtooth Valley.

Gray Reynolds is administrative officer. The main office was constructed on the North Fork of Wood River about ten miles above Ketchum. The site caused grumbling by some citizens of the area but was justified by the Forest Service as a suitable gateway.

The environmental statement says no new mining claims can be filed in SNRA. Subject to valid existing rights, all federal land has been withdrawn from location, entry, and patent. The report further states: "The legislation provides for utilization of minerals, provided this will not substantially impair the purposes for which SNRA was established. The secretary of agriculture is directed, after consultation with the secretary of the interior, to prepare and issue rules and regulations to insure protection of surface values. Before these regulations become effective or any subsequent modifications are considered, adequate time will be provided for public review and discussion."

A general management plan at a cost of $8,800,000 for twenty years was tentatively adopted. Three alternate plans were considered: One would cost $16,200,000. The second would cost $9,500,000 (substantially the same as the plan chosen). The third would cost $3,500,000 and would be a minimum, keep-it-open-but-don't-grow budget. The main difference between maximum and moderate plans is road construction, estimated at $5,000,000. Each plan provides for $440,000 headquarters construction and $284,000 maintenance.

Eleven main problems are listed for the ten-year planning period. They are: 1. Recreational use to be accommodated. There are some objections to a projected 6 percent annual increase. 2. What is substantial impairment of natural resources? 3. Grazing. 4. Off-road vehicle noise pollution. 5. Timber removal. 6. Protection of wildlife — game and nongame species. 7. Water quality. 8. North Fork headquarters site. Why there? 9. New wilderness study areas. 10. Snowmobiles. 11. Ranking of resource values. Why are some given priority over others?

With regard to snowmobiles, the statement advocates an educational program to promote self-restraint. "If conflicts cannot be resolved cooperatively," it says, "then additional controls and closures will be necessary. The Sawtooth Wilderness is closed to all motorized vehicles, including snowmobiles."

Management of the recreation area will be influenced by continuing study directed by the U.S. Environmental Protection Agency, which is concerned with water, vegetation, wildlife, fisheries, recreation, history and archeological resources, minerals, and roads.

Development of the recreation area, already enhancing public enjoyment in three years of operation, is still in a state of flux. Needs, methods, and means of serving people are considered constantly. One of the problems cited by an area administrator is increased use. The area has such appeal and the new status and facilities attract so many people that it may be difficult to maintain the pristine environment. The peaks, however, remain serene and supreme.

Chapter 36

SOUTH FORK OF THE PAYETTE RIVER

THE SOUTH FORK of the Payette River is so close to the Sawtooths it is practically part of them. In fact, headwaters are within the Sawtooth Wilderness.

One of the favorite vantage points for people approaching the Sawtooths on the Lowman-Stanley road is a turnout near the Grandjean junction. From that point one can see the range at an angle different from the view at Stanley. A major crag on the right, as seen from that spot, is locally known as Grandjean Peak although it is not so designated on maps. The name honors Emile Grandjean, first supervisor of the Sawtooth National Forest, whose career is outlined in Chapter 34.

Bob Sessions had a summer home until recently on Bear Creek, near Grandjean. He is the author, with Hank Senger and Nick Villeneuve, of *Sawtooth Saga*, a book about amazing beasts such as the wampus cat, whiffer-snifter, whangdoodle, and high-behind. The illustrations by Villeneuve suggest that the Sawtooths are inhabited by creatures that could whip an abominable snowman without getting up a sweat.

Events along the South Fork have been significant in mountain history, ancient and modern. An early trail from Idaho City to Bonanza went by way of Banner and down Archie Creek to Jordan Bridge, seven miles above Lowman. The trail then went up the South Fork several miles, where it left the canyon and climbed to Cape Horn. It was at Jordan Bridge that George Pierson, an escaped murderer, left tracks that resulted in his capture and execution at Hailey in 1884.

There is a flat two miles below Jordan Bridge near Kirkham Hot Springs that was once the home of Emma Edwards Green, designer of the Idaho state seal. One creek on the property is called Green, the other Emma. The acreage, owned by Jim Chapman, has several summer cottages. Across from Chapman Flat is Whangdoodle Creek with a switchback trail through an old burn to a plateau with rewarding views of the watershed.

There are summer homes all along the South Fork, from Banks to Grandjean. Many are used the year around, as are cottages along several routes to the Sawtooths. Population in the popular boondocks is booming.

For several seasons about thirty years ago, the upper reaches of the South Fork were noted for abundance of cougar. Government and private hunters killed scores. Such hunters as Pat Reed, Rob Donnelly, and "Babe" Bingham Hansen were credited with removing a total of about a hundred, mostly with dogs and pistols, some with bow and arrow.

The community of Lowman, started by Nathaniel Lowman about 1907, blossomed as a recreational area late in the 1930s, with construction of a highway from Idaho City over More's Creek and Beaver Creek summits. Prior to that time there was access only by way of Banks and Gallagher Flats or a formidable Forest Service road from Idaho City.

Until a highway was built from Lowman to Stanley up Canyon Creek in the early 1970s, Lowman was the jump-off spot for a route to Stanley by way of Clear Creek and Bear Valley. That road is seldom used today; most people heading for the Sawtooths from that side find the Canyon Creek Highway much better. It is also shorter.

Clear Creek was the site of a manhunt of national note in 1952. Thomas Edward Young and Margaret Reta Young, sought for robberies and other crimes and ranking high on the most-wanted list of the FBI, drove into Idaho from Montana, made a wrong turn at Stanley, and wound up near Lowman. Apparently deciding they were so far back in the brush nobody would catch them, they camped on Clear Creek. It turned out to be a mistake. Nobody is more conspicuous than a stranger in the forest. They added to their error by their high-handed attitude with natives. They were unfriendly. They banged away with an arsenal of weapons. The racket drew unfavorable attention.

The final straw in their undoing was a note of appreciation Reta Young wrote to a radio station. She said thanks for a musical program. She signed a name that was not the name the couple had been using at Lowman. Her ironic postscript quoted: "What does it profit a man to gain the whole world if he loses his own soul?"

Federal, state, and county officers converged on the camp. They blocked roads, then cornered and arrested the couple without resistance. Thomas Young got 25 years, Reta Young got 20. On the way out to trial they admitted miscalculating the sticks. They said they should have gone to a city like Chicago. Nobody would have given a hoot about them there.

One evening at a cafe near Lowman a regular customer drinking beer was reminded of meal debts amounting to $60. He offered a payment of 50 cents. The incensed woman behind the counter pulled a pistol and fired. She missed the debtor but plugged her cigaret machine.

During the summer of 1975 two residents of the South Fork bet each other they could cross a log that spanned the river rapids at Kirkham. They made their try late at night. The first guy stepped it both ways. His companion took the lantern, fell off the log, and drowned.

Obnoxious types get the cold shoulder along the South Fork. They do barge in now and then with their rackety bikes and repulsive conduct, but residents have ways of keeping them in bounds.

For instance:

Several yahoos brawled in a cafe. The boss chucked them out. They roared up the highway toward Stanley, speeding by the home of a deputy sheriff who gave chase, overhauled them, and wrote a ticket. They tried to manhandle the deputy. That was poor judgment. Within the time it takes to throw a couple punches and put on a hammerlock, the toughies were in custody. The magistrate at Idaho City dampened their enthusiasm for disturbing the peace.

A clutch of long-haired characters skinny-dipped in a fishing hole near a place frequented by loggers and truckers. Gumming up the fishing was tolerated reluctantly. But when a child reported that the skinny-dippers were taunting her, there was direct action. Husky workmen roared out of the beer parlor. They tossed skinny-dippers in all directions, mostly into the river. It was like the Pittsburgh Steelers on a kickoff. Everybody creamed somebody. Repentent bathers climbed into what clothing they could find and beat a humble retreat. The incident illustrated the point that there is freedom to enjoy the beauties of nature but no patience with desecration, no matter what the Supreme Court says about individual liberty.

It used to be that high schoolers converged on the Lowman area for "sneaks" redolent with beer and grass. Officers and private citizens put the lid on that. Groups of youngsters and adults have learned that they are welcome to enjoy outings, but they have to be reasonable. Lowman does not have anarchy on its totem pole.

Motorbikers trespass on forbidden ground at their peril. A veteran mountain man with passionate hatred for the vehicles found two near a high lake in a restricted area. The riders were absent. He waited several hours. When they had not returned at dark he shot out a couple of spark plugs and left a note with his name and address in case they wanted to do something about it. He never heard from them.

The Lowman area is rich in huckleberries. The purple-fingered clan harvests gallons, although there is an unwritten law among the home folks that any season — particularly the current one — is poor because of early frost, late frost, logging, highway construction, or bears. There hasn't been an average season in half a century.

It's the same with fishing. The water is too high, too low, too cold, too murky, or too clear. Sometimes those discouraging conditions do prevail, singly or in bunches. It is notable, however, that the typical Lowman sourdough who recites these miseries slips out by himself and lands a limit. All native trout. One of the miracles of angling in that area, as in many other Idaho waters, is that nobody catches a planted fish. The Lowman code forbids it.

Persons interested in details about pioneers of the South Fork are directed to *All Along the River* by Nellie Ireton Mills. She lived on lower stretches near Montour and compiled a book of biographical sketches of men and women who pioneered the stream from bottom to top. A son, Ike Mills, was district forest ranger at Lowman for many years.

Chapter 37

CANYON CREEK

IN THE EARLY 1970s a highway was built up Canyon Creek, connecting Lowman and Stanley by a fancy boulevard that is much shorter and a good deal less twisty than the old Clear Creek route. The new road would be incredible to robust gents who blazed the trail a hundred year ago.

The old trail tobogganed down Warm Springs Creek, a steep drainage between Canyon Creek and Clear Creek. Miners going from Loon Creek to Idaho City or vice versa didn't waste much time looking for an easy route. They plunged into the brush and made tracks. They didn't give a hoot for the terrain or such spooky spots as Dead Man's Canyon.

Who first used the trail is anybody's guess. Indians, probably. Pioneers banging around in the mountains in the 1860s (toiling as the spirit moved them from Florence to Loon Creek to Yankee Fork to Stanley and finally into Boise Basin by the back door) followed its dependable course. Part of the road today is on about the same terrain; some sections of the trail are remote from the honk of horns and the flotsam of picnic baskets.

Old maps show the route used by pack strings and foot sloggers. Rain or shine, blizzard or balmy breeze, traffic moved. Starting at Idaho City, the trail went up More's Creek, over the summit, and down to Beaver Creek. Then it turned right to the old Mose Kempner place and north to Banner. From there it dropped down to the

Payette drainage, crossing the South Fork at the mouth of Archie Creek at what is now called Jordan Bridge.

What about Lowman? There wasn't any Lowman. That junction was not on the map until years later. It was after the turn of the century that Nathaniel Lowman homesteaded on the flat where Clear Creek enters the Payette. The early trail missed the site by about six miles upstream.

After crossing the river at Archie Creek the trail stayed on the north side of the river about fifteen miles to the mouth of Warm Springs Creek. At that canyon it turned left and climbed the high divide, topping out west of what is now known as Bull Trout Lake but unnamed in early days. From Bull Trout to Cape Horn it was a short jump. At Cape Horn the trail split several ways. The main drag went to Loon Creek, way back in the wilderness. Another took off for Yankee Fork. A short distance southwest of Cape Horn a trail went to Deadwood. Some of the early maps show no trail from Cape Horn to Stanley Basin; others do. The inference is that in the beginning people heading for Idaho City from Stanley went over the mountains to Atlanta and thence to the North Fork of Boise River and to Boise Basin. It sounds a little involved. It was — and still is. The geography is abundant. It does not lend itself to simplicity.

Dead Man's Canyon earned its name honestly. An August 1878 issue of *The Idaho World* (Idaho City) says it was named for an incident several years earlier in which two men lost their lives. They were carrying the mail from Idaho City to Loon Creek and were swept away in a snowslide. Names are not recorded.

Another man was killed near the canyon in 1879. He was William Klinau, a carpenter on his way out from Yankee Fork. His horse fell on him. Other travelers gave aid, but he died next morning.

In 1878 the vicinity was dangerous for other reasons than snowslides and falling horses. Indians prowled. Marauding bands split from the main war party that went with Buffalo Horn into Owyhee County. They made things interesting for miners.

Two Cornishmen in a party bound for Yankee Fork turned up missing. The last man to see them passed them on the Bull Trout side of Cape Horn. He said they had two horses. One horse carried a large brass clock, still ticking. One man had a rifle, the other was unarmed. They did not reach Bonanza, Stanley, or Loon Creek. Nobody saw them again. The clock was not found either.

The Loon Creek trail was a military route in 1879. Captain

Photo by Ernie Day

Pack string above Atlanta

Reuben Bernard's troops went that way to subdue the Sheepeaters. Maps and diaries show they pulled out of Boise May 30 and reached Cape Horn June 3 — four days and 140 miles in country as steep as a cow's face. Troops scouted around Cape Horn, investigated Orogrande on Loon Creek, took a look at Meyer's Cove, and went back to Cape Horn in July. Then the company went to Warm Lake by way of Bear Valley. The Indians were finally rounded up far away on Big Creek. The troops saw a lot of country and wore the trail to a dusty path from Cape Horn to Idaho City.

For several years before the Indian wars the Loon Creek trail — Dead Man's Canyon and all — was the route of a mountain express company taking passengers and freight to the mines. The base was Idaho City. Pack strings took off once a week or whenever there were enough customers. Few of the optimists struck it rich. One who did was "Gentle Annie," an Idaho City cook. Tom Donaldson relates in his book, *Idaho of Yesterday*, that Gentle Annie, weighing about 220, took to the hills with her pots and pans at the first chirp of gold. She rode a horse and led two mules. At a narrow spot on the trail she met a pack string of the mountain express. The string crowded her, and she fell and broke a leg. She sued the company and collected substantial damages.

Lum Sam, a Chinese of Loon Creek, frequently jogged to Idaho City. On snowshoes it took him five days; in summer it was a four-day breeze. On one trip in 1873 he reported twenty-eight white men and thirty Chinese wintering at Orogrande. There was not a sick man in camp, and they had plenty to eat. He also reported thirty feet of snow in Dead Man's Canyon and a bear at the hot springs on the Payette. (Probably Kirkham, a short distance below Archie Creek. The springs were frequently visited by Banner miners.) Lum Sam visited three or four days in Idaho City and went back to Loon Creek with a sack of mail. He figured that because of the sixty-pound load it might take him six days.

A wagon road from Idaho City to Banner was opened in 1873. That much of the distance was therefore easy by the time of the Indian excitement several years later. But the longest and toughest stretch remained a trail for many years.

Loon Creek mines, the main reason for the trail, were discovered in 1869 by Nathan Smith, who had mined earlier at Florence. He saw a loon at the mouth of the creek where he made his strike. That gave the place its name. As many as 1,000 men were in the camp at its peak. Orogrande was the hub. Bonanza City on Yankee Fork, another boom camp on a branch of the trail, was first visited by Joel Richardson in 1867. Captain V. D. Varney and Sylvester Jordan breathed second wind into the district in 1870. By the late 1870s most of the traffic to Yankee Fork went by way of Challis. A wagon road was built from Yankee Fork to Challis for transportation of ore and supplies.

The Canyon Creek route from Lowman to Stanley has no relation to Loon Creek or Yankee Fork. However, the highway link is also a link with the historic past of communities associated with the Sawtooths.

Canyon Creek is a fairly recent name. On old maps it was Fogus Creek. Colonel D. H. Fogus was a mining magnate of Owyhee and Boise counties. As a contemporary of Matt Graham and Marion More he developed many profitable claims.

The Canyon Creek route cuts the distance between Lowman and Stanley to fifty-seven miles. The old route over Clear Creek was sixty-eight miles. It is still open at times and is maintained for local logging trucks. The prospect of running the Lowman-Stanley road farther up the Payette, past Grandjean and on to Stanley Lake, was explored by engineers. They determined it would take considerable rockwork. The route selected and built turns off a little short of Grandjean, which was practically unexplored when the Cape Horn trail was under heaviest use.

Chapter 38

SUN VALLEY

SUN VALLEY came on the scene in 1936. The scene hasn't been the same since. The Union Pacific Railroad turned snow into an asset and transformed Ketchum from a lamb-shipping hamlet to a winter and summer resort of international renown. Union Pacific got even, and then some, with the snow that had plagued its trains from the time a branch line from Shoshone to Ketchum was completed in 1883. The railroad determined that playing in the snow could be made fun for thousands and a profitable venture for business. Skiing with a capital "S" was brought to the Sawtooths.

Sliding down hills on boards had long been a sport — generally for kids but occasionally indulged by adults. As early as 1881 Robert McTaggart was advertising plain coasting shoes, eight-feet long, for $5. Heavy, extra long, were $7. He called them snow-shoes, but they were boards rather than the standard webs used by mountain people.

Skiing was the subject of laughter at the beginning. The following story in the *Hailey Times*, winter of 1885, is typical:

"Do you see that man climbing the hill on two boards?" "Yes. The boards are called snowshoes. They are twelve feet long." "Where is the man going?" "He is going up the hill to run down. It will take him two hours and thirty minutes to get to the top of the hill. It will take him one minute and seventeen seconds to come down. If the man runs against a tree or a rock, he will be all broken up." "What is the object?" "The object is pleasure. Man is a strange thing."

Other newspaper articles of the same era tell of broken bones, chills, and spills suffered by citizens. Until Sun Valley put the sport on a popular plane it was kid stuff.

Averell Harriman, chairman of the Union Pacific board, chose Sun Valley as the site of a pleasure dome on the recommendation of Count Felix Schaffgotsch, an Austrian. Harriman was no stranger to the area; he had visited the Sawtooth country previously. A news item in April 1914 said:

"Wm. Averell Harriman and five other distinguished and substantial-looking gentlemen are in Hailey. Harriman is a son of the late E. H. Harriman, head of the U.P. He reported he will drive a tunnel under Galena and extend the railroad to Stanley, Salmon, etc. to get the jump on the Burlington and Chicago and Northwestern."

The venture did not materialize. However, Harriman's enterprise more than twenty years later generated considerable traffic for the railroad and put Idaho on the resort map for big and little wigs.

The site chosen was the old Brass ranch, a mile up Trail Creek from Ketchum. The place was not only a working ranch but a spot frequented by fishermen and hunters. (If all the people who say they camped there in the days before Sun Valley could be assembled in one bunch, the crowd would equal the population of Omaha.) Natives gasped in disbelief as buildings were put up. Side-slapping ladies and gents strolled out to see developments, expressing particular amusement at a pile of bathtubs as large as Picket-Pin Hill, all destined for the Lodge and its satellite accommodations. Luxurious trappings were a far cry from traditional bed and board in Ketchum. The thing was fantastic. It couldn't happen here.

Sun Valley took hold and grew. It strung ski lifts on Baldy, Dollar, and Rudd mountains. It created a golf course, rodeo grounds, trapshooting ranges, a theatre, tennis courts, swimming pools, and skating rinks. It attracted the cream of the social, financial, political, literary, and entertainment world. During World War II it was a rest and recreation area for the U.S. Navy. In recent years ownership passed from the Union Pacific to the Janss Corporation. More condominiums, golf courses, and the like have been constructed at Sun Valley and neighboring Elkhorn. To old-timers the transformation is incredible. It is more than evolution; it's a brand new world. The age of blankets and beans has given way to king-size beds and *pâté de foi gras*. For better or worse, an aura of affluence has come to Wood River.

Ernest Hemingway was a resident of Sun Valley and Ketchum from 1939 until his death in 1961. He enjoyed hunting ducks, pheasants, and big game in the area. He wrote much of *For Whom the Bell Tolls* there. As the most famous writer of the period, he was on ground distinguished as the birthplace of Ezra Pound, the poet. (It can be noted, parenthetically, that during the week in 1914 when Averell Harriman was proposing a railway tunnel under Galena, Pound was married in London to Dorothy Shakespeare.)

The Hemingway period at Sun Valley is related with gusto by the late Lloyd Arnold in *High on the Wild with Hemingway* published by Caxton Printers in 1968. Arnold was chief photographer at Sun Valley and one of Hemingway's cronies on hunting trips. The fact that the crew harvested much game is the basis for the title. Hemingway admired good guns and was an excellent shot, Arnold says. He was keen for waterfowl, upland birds, deer, elk, and antelope but didn't care much for trout fishing. Idaho trout, even those of Silver Creek, were too small compared with the gigantic creatures he caught in the sea.

Hemingway's presence brought a parade of movie stars to Sun Valley. Among them were Gary Cooper and Ingrid Bergman, who played leading roles in *For Whom the Bell Tolls*, and Spencer Tracy, who starred in Hemingway's *Old Man and the Sea*. Hollywood luminaries who made the Sun Valley scene also included Clark Gable, who hunted with Hemingway, Claudette Colbert, Marilyn Monroe, Ann Southern, Robert Taylor, Barbara Stanwyck, Norma Shearer, Sonja Henie, and Bing Crosby. Directors, script writers, and biographers of national prominence mingled with political figures and barons of industry on the slopes of Baldy and exchanged stories over mugs of hot, spiced wine at the Round House.

The atmosphere of Sun Valley was influenced to a great extent by Pat Rogers, general manager. Along with Eugene Van Guilder, public relations man for the Steve Hannagan agency, Bob Miles, sports director; Taylor Williams, guide; and photographer Arnold, Rogers blended activities and services into a spa that welcomed the well-heeled and the medium-heeled from Idaho and Bar Harbor.

Van Guilder, a westerner who looked like Gary Cooper, was one of the prime movers in luring Hemingway to Idaho. He was

Photo by Ernie Day

Authentic old freight wagons in recent Ketchum parade

killed in 1939 in a duck-hunting accident. Hemingway wrote the eulogy. A portion of that tribute became the epitaph on Hemingway's memorial. Hemingway was buried in the Ketchum Cemetery. The memorial stands on Trail Creek. The wording, selected by Mrs. Hemingway from Hemingway's farewell to Van Guilder, reads:

> *Best of all he loved the fall*
> *The leaves yellow on the cottonwoods*
> *Leaves floating in the trout streams*
> *And above the hills the high blue windless skies*
> *– Now he will be a part of them forever.*

Sun Valley has had many events in addition to ski holidays. Early in its history it staged one of the finest rodeos ever put on anywhere. World champion cowboys competed. The roster was a who's who of the saddle. Stands were reasonably well-filled with spectators, but the seating capacity was not large enough to make the event a financial success. The grounds were abandoned and the site turned over to other purposes.

Shotgun and pistol marksmen have won regional championships on Sun Valley ranges. Flycasters of renown have tossed feathery tidbits on its ponds. Olympic skaters have twirled on its ice. Bishops have preached and politicians orated in its opera house. Delegates to conventions of everything from obstetricians to undertakers have sipped its nectar. It is a point of departure for horseback trips through the Sawtooths and the launching pad for flights to fishing and hunting at Devil's Bedstead. It is the starting gate for snowmobile races to Sawtooth Valley and the hub of cross-country skiing. One of the attractions in most of these exercises for name-droppers is that the guy on the next horse may be a senator from Illinois or the girl behind the dark glasses a television celebrity. One can drink a beer at a Sun Valley bar with a good prospect of rubbing shoulders with somebody who sold Hemingway a typewriter or taught Ted Kennedy the stem turn.

The cluster of shacks at the edge of the road where pioneers used to keep warm between sheep drives or prospecting trips has become a melting pot of society in mink and blue denim. It's a cosmopolitan doorway to the Sawtooth National Recreation Area and Wilderness. There is abundant recreation at Sun Valley but precious little wilderness unless you get lost in a chromium-plated washroom.

At the outset Sun Valley was regarded by many Idaho citizens as cold to home customers. Whether or not that reputation was justified, things took a warmer turn after an incident in the lobby, alleged to be true but perhaps magnified.

A man in a sheepskin and wool pants seated himself by the fireplace where he watched comings and goings while stropping a knife on his boot. The clerk presently asked if he was comfortable. He said things were tolerable. Then the assistant manager stepped up. He inquired what room the man had. He was not registered. The assistant manager sent the bellhop to proceed further.

"Staying here, sir?"

"No."

"Having dinner?"

"No."

"Do you have any money?"

The man folded his knife, slipped it into his pocket, and hauled out a fat wallet.

"A little," he said. "How much do you want for the place? Better make a deal now. It's the last time I'll sit in one of your chairs."

The gentleman was an Idaho sheepman of ample means.

Pat Rogers took steps to see that such things didn't happen again. For several seasons, however, there was a feeling that local yokels did not meet fastidious standards of the pleasure palace. That attitude was corrected early by the Union Pacific, and the policy of cordiality to high and low has since been maintained.

Chapter 39

FLOATING DOWN THE RIVER

SALMON RIVER is legally classified as a navigable stream, along with thousands of others that will float a six-inch log. Traffic on the upper Salmon is light, except for increasing numbers of rubber rafts that take sightseers and fishermen along stretches from Redfish Lake Creek to Clayton for expeditions that sometimes plunge into the wilderness as far as two hundred yards from the highway — and down the Middle Fork, which is genuinely primitive but so popular that travel is on a quota basis.

From Salmon City to Riggins and on to the Snake River, flotillas of small craft buzz up and down, making poor prophets of people like Henry Guleke who gave the stream its label, "River of No Return." When he launched his first flat-bottom boats about 1893 the scows traveled downstream only; they didn't go back. Modern pleasure craft with powerful engines climb the current as readily as they descend with it. They return again and again.

Captain Guleke built his barges at Salmon. They were twenty-four to forty feet long and eight to fourteen feet wide. The big ones carried eight tons. The river supplied all the power. Sweeps in bow and stern kept the barges on course. Guleke and his veteran lieutenant, Monroe Hancock, made scores of trips to Riggins and Lewiston, a total distance of 301 water miles. Sometimes he floated as far as Celilo on the Columbia. By 1918 it was reported he had made 400 trips without loss of life and with little damage to cargo.

The scows were generally loaded with mining machinery and supplies. On the way they picked up hides, wool, vegetables, and fruit from ranches and gardens in warm oases between stretches of impassable canyon. A correspondent for *The Idaho Statesman* said in 1918, "Guleke knows the rapids like a preacher knows his Bible."

Guleke's navy served North Fork, Indianola, Shoup, Big Creek, Owl Creek, Calson Creek, Butt's Bar, Disappointment Creek, Crawford, Thomas Ranch, Prescott Ranch, Hot Springs, Myer's Landing, Churchill's Ranch at Little Mallard, More's Ranch at the Old Thunder Mountain ferry, Painter's Ranch near Dixie, Ludwig's, South Fork, Bemis Ranch, Shepard and Klinkeimer's Ranch at Crooked River, French Creek Ranch on the old state road, Howard's Ranch, Fred Riggins' Ranch, Riggins Post Office, Lucile, Freedom, and White Bird. The trip took about a week. Guleke usually abandoned the bigger boats at the port of delivery and sold the lumber. Occasionally he took his smaller barges apart and hauled major portions back to Salmon by wagon over a long road through Montana. In the main, though, he found it more sensible to start from scratch and build new boats.

Guleke said the most treacherous rapids were the Big Mallard and the Growler, six miles farther downstream. Two boats upset in the Growler about 1908. Machinery and instruments worth $3,000 were lost, but nobody drowned.

One trip about 1914 got a great deal of notoriety at Salmon and Riggins. Guleke had a request for house cats from a prospector in the canyon who needed them to kill mice. Surmising that other loners in the sticks would appreciate cats as much as the man who asked for them, he loaded about twenty. It was a mistake. On the second day the cats got out of their cages and scratched passengers, clawed cargo, and generally raised merry hell. Some fell overboard.

The hermit who wanted cats would take only two. Guleke parked several more at various ranches. But as he floated on, word got ahead of him by the mysterious hunch telegraph. Miners and ranchers met him at the docks with orders not to unload cats. He finally left about a dozen near Riggins, where a ranch woman agreed to care for them. He later got nasty letters from Riggins about the shipment; the community was already well fixed for cats and didn't appreciate the additions.

Guleke piloted railway survey trips down the Salmon when the track to Lewiston was proposed. Engineers said the route was possible but would cost a great deal, so the idea was abandoned. For a short time the railway to Lewiston was planned as a link to the Idaho Midland Railroad proposed in 1900 as a line from Boise to Butte via Atlanta, Sawtooth City, Challis, and Salmon. It was to have 464 miles in Idaho, most of them in challenging rock. Capital stock was $15,000,000, of which about one-half million was on tap. Work started from Boise and got as far as More's Creek, nearly twenty miles out of town. Even so, it went farther than the proposed road down the Salmon to Lewiston.

For several years immediately after World War I there was a push for improved navigation down the Salmon. Advocates urged blasting of major falls to accommodate commercial traffic. Guleke was in favor, but it didn't make much difference to him whether there were rapids or not. By that time, Salmon had been served several years by the Gilmore and Pittsburgh Railroad from Armstead, Montana, so there was no crisis in transportation. Plans to improve the river came and went, as did proposals to irrigate western Idaho by tipping Redfish Lake. The Sawtooths and the Salmon go right on, serenely indifferent.

Flat-bottom boats are still going down the river from Salmon, but they are outnumbered by fancy power jobs, the like of which Guleke never dreamed.

Chapter 40

FISHING AND OTHER SPORTS

HOW WAS the fishing? By today's standards it was fantastic. Seventy years or so ago hefty trout were so commonplace they were hardly worth mentioning. Anything less than a hundred on a day's outing was humdrum.

The easy fishing that helped sustain trappers of the early 1800s continued through periods of mining and ranching. For example, in 1915 Roy Bell, state mine inspector, said he would like to take a few Wood River trout to Boise. His train left in an hour. A friend caught ten, ranging from one and one-half pounds to six pounds, and presented them to him at the station. The Hailey paper commented that anybody could catch "a mess" in ten minutes.

Three men of the same era complained of bad luck at Stanton's Crossing and Magic. They wasted a weekend on only fifty pounds. The average was a couple of barrels.

And Silver Creek! Whoppers were so numerous and easy to catch that teamsters of the Kilpatrick Construction Company, building the railbed to Ketchum in the early 1880s, protested their fish diet. They wanted mutton and beef.

Fishing in the upper country was so simple that it was taken for granted, like cold winters and muddy trails. Salmon River and its tributaries were full of trout and salmon. Alpine lakes were stuffed, too, although they were not fished much because anyone who wanted fish could harvest a batch on the flat without climbing all over creation.

Tons of redfish were hauled out of Redfish Lake and tributaries. Miners of the 1880s smoked, salted, and canned wagonloads. Some were sold for a few cents a pound at Hailey and Ketchum. Most went into winter larders at Vienna and Sawtooth City. Redfish were speared or snagged. For many years it was believed they wouldn't strike lures because they were blind, except during spawning season when nature thoughtfully let them see what they were doing — and then they were so busy courting they were not interested in bait.

Slaughter of redfish was deplored from the beginning. Conservationists fought the practice vigorously. Their efforts eventually gave protection to the fish, but it was too late; the population was down to a shadow. Relatively few of the colorful species remain.

A large share of blame for reduction of redfish and salmon in upper portions of Sawtooth Valley was placed in fairly recent times on Sunbeam Dam, a barrier in Salmon River near the mouth of Yankee Fork, twelve miles below Stanley.

Sunbeam was named for a mine on Jordan Creek. Before that it was known as Junction Bar of Ebenezer Cunningham. The dam was built about 1910 by the Sunbeam Mining Company to provide power for mines on Yankee Fork. Before and after the dam was built, the junction claim had many owners. It changed hands like a chip in a poker game. One of the early proprietors offered it for sale at the turn of the century. Colonel W. H. Dewey put in a bid. It was turned down, and he launched Thunder Mountain instead.

By 1915 the dam and power plant were on the rocks in more ways than one. The property was sold by the sheriff for delinquent taxes. The buyer (at $8,500, half of which went to the county) was the Custer Slide Mining Company, owner of the Lucky Boy and Custer Slide mines.

From the day it was put in the river the dam was a pain in the neck for fishermen. It blocked migration of salmon and other species. A bypass was constructed at the insistence of the Idaho Fish and Game Department. That didn't work either. Angry natives threatened to blow the dam. They refrained until the deed was done legally in 1934, after the dam was no longer needed by mines. The new channel gave passage to fish. The job also left a tunnel through which fishermen had one way, among several, to reach a popular spot for catching salmon. For many years the Sunbeam rock was a choice point for the stiff-line brigade. On summer days during spawning runs as many as twenty anglers would perch on the rock at a time. Tackle tangles were horrendous. Miles of line and bushels of spinners contributed to the jumble. The store at Sunbeam displayed a salvaged mass of bits and pieces as big as an eagle's nest.

Dredging on Yankee Fork near Bonanza was another blow to fishing and to people who hated to see the channel churned. The dredge began working in 1938, under the management of Silas

Mason Company of New York. The first phase lasted until 1942. After an idle period of several years it worked again from 1945 to 1950. Baumhoff and Simplot were the final proprietors. The dredge, stripped of most of its portable apparatus, is now a museum. Heaps of stones mark its march up the river from Preacher's Cove to Jordan Creek.

Salmon fishing was good at Sunbeam and other famous holes from Decker Flat in Sawtooth Valley to the Flume, near Challis, for many years. Whether or not there is a dam at Sunbeam hasn't mattered much lately. Salmon runs appear to have suffered a mortal blow from dams on the Columbia and lower Snake.

Until the mid-thirties, the most common way to take salmon in the Sawtooths was spearing. People slogged along shallow streams, such as Valley, Marsh, and Bear Valley creeks, prodding fish from resting areas beneath overhanging banks and stabbing them with barbed iron. This method is no longer permitted.

Salmon of fifty and sixty pounds used to be common. Current fish are much smaller.

As early as World War I — give or take a few years — stocking of high lakes was undertaken by the Idaho Fish and Game Department and the U.S. Forest Service. S. B. ("Barry") Locke, a biologist assigned by the Ogden regional office, directed the planting of several species of trout in Alpine waters. Pack strings lugged milk cans of fry. Sportsmen's organizations cooperated in the program, heeding the warning of the Fish and Game Department that swarms of people flocking to the paradise were depleting the resource. Trout released in several lakes included California golden, a variety with brilliant colors and vigorous fighting spirit. Locke also brought in a few Kaibab squirrel from southern Utah. The creatures did not thrive. Some of the planted fish didn't do well, either. In certain lakes, however, they were the foundation for current supplies.

Planting fish by plane was tried in the 1940s by the Fish and Game Department. Aircraft with special tanks flew low over remote lakes in the Sawtooths, discharging tiny trout. Reports from men who fished the lakes several seasons later showed marginal success. Many of the fry survived, but because of food shortage, temperature, or other factors they did not grow much.

Lost River and its tributaries, all within the Sawtooth orbit, still provide lying-and-bragging trout. The meandering streams are favorite haunts of such flycasters as Herman Hilfiker, Jere Long, Max Yost, Carol Youngstrom, "Buck" Jones, Howard Roylance, and

C. H. Enking, all of whom join me in solemn charade that the treasure is secret, although it is known to, and frequented by, platoons. Choice stretches yield excellent rainbow, but it is frustrating to find tubers floating in the finest pools, playing their guitars.

Lucky fishermen who beat the mob to the creek can find perching room in Muldoon Canyon and the old Cow Camp, not to mention other retreats which shall not be identified in the fading hope that Modicum Flat and Black Rock are veiled in mystery.

Fishermen who admire the territory and sneak into it at every opportunity are not selfish. They gladly invite the multitude, cautioning that the roads are tough, wood scarce, camping spots few, and weather likely to be terrible. The area is full of bulls, bees, bears, bats, and bogholes. Aside from such blemishes it has redeeming features. Mosquitoes are no bigger than buzzards. Fishermen seldom see more than half a dozen snakes to the mile, and nobody has been mauled by a cougar for several years. Snow is rarely more than six inches deep on Labor Day. Men mired in quicksand at Thousand Springs usually struggle out in several hours. Otherwise it is tolerable. Let's see. When does the season open? Maybe the big one is still in the Black Rock hole.

That trout is a cross between a submarine and a Sawtooth sunset. The color on his side would make a bicentennial flag. The mouth, seen by several amazed fishermen, could swallow a football. The big one makes one strike a day. It lunges for the lure, flips a mighty tail, and descends to its office. No matter what tidbits are dangled, it does not rise again. It is indifferent to flies, worms eggs, mice, grasshoppers, weenies, cookies, and pickles.

Want to know where Black Rock is? Take the old road to Antelope from Wild Horse. There's a deserted house across the river. Don't turn there. Keep going to a clump of sagebrush. Flush a flock of sagehen. Mark the spot where they light. The Black Rock is about a hundred yards up the creek. Got it? Good luck.

Game animals in the Sawtooths used to be thick as fleas on a hound dog. Variety was wide. There were mule deer, elk, mountain goat, mountain sheep, antelope, and ibex. Most of the species are still to be found. It takes longer in modern times to bag an animal. As is true of fishing, the quick and easy hunt is something for the memory album.

Wild beasts found in the Sawtooths by other generations and regarded as predators included grizzly bear, brown bear, cougar, wolves, and coyotes. They could be killed anywhere at any time. Today all kinds of bear are game animals. So are cougar. Wolves

Photo by Ernie Day

Fishing at Lower Cramer Lake

are gone. Only the coyote goes its cunning way, subject to destruction if it intrudes but enjoying certain freedoms from poison and casual gunning. Early in this century coyote hunters killed thousands each year in the Sawtooths and adjoining districts. One hunter eliminated 250 in a single month. Bounty used to be paid out but has long since been discontinued by the Fish and Game Department. At one time the bounty on a cougar was $75. That, too, has been dropped. It costs a nonresident more than $75 these days to kill a cougar.

According to Lucille Hathaway Hall's *Memories of Old Alturas County* there were several hundred bear around the valley near Tikura. She said: "Our riders killed several, and sheepmen accounted for a great many." She said that on one occasion a grizzly yanked a Basque out of his bedroll. He ran to a camp three miles away — in a sweater which he put on over his feet and bottom to be more presentable. Bears were bad, Mrs. Hall conceded, but crickets and green frogs were worse. Frogs were so thick the trails were slick.

Several adventures with bears are related in another chapter of this book, the main one being about Idaho Jack, the Sawtooth terror.

An animal that caused double takes padded along Salmon River near Lower Stanley in the late 1930s. It was an African lion, purchased from a circus by a rancher. It was inside a fence, but that fact was not readily apparent to astonished travelers. The Sawtooths are so endowed with amazing treasures, they reasoned, it just might have lions, tigers, and elephants.

In the list of game species you may have noticed ibex. No fooling. The animal used to be recognized and hunted — bag limit, tag, and everything. If there actually were any in Idaho at that period there are none today. Doubt is expressed that "ibex" was a misnomer for goat or pronghorn antelope. The question is hotly argued by oldsters who insist they shot ibex in the Sawtooths. Mounted horns and hooves identified as ibex are to be found in mountain cabins. They are not goat or antelope; whether they were bagged in the White Clouds or Asia is a matter of speculation. Nevertheless, ibex were officially recognized by legislative act. They were later removed by updating the code, which at one time also provided limits and seasons for buffalo. During the early 1800s buffalo did roam portions of Lost River and perhaps some valleys along the Salmon. No wild ones have been reported for a hundred years.

Brushy canyons are the habitat of ruffed grouse and their kin.

Foolhens are often found along Sawtooth trails, clucking and tip-toeing so close they can be hit with a stick. Peaks and flats also have a wide variety of nongame birds such as robins, bluebirds, ravens, eagles, buzzards, magpies, flickers, jays, and juncos. Occasionally there are ducks, but they are not numerous and do not linger long because of cold weather. Silver Creek is an exception; it has lots of ducks and geese.

Sage grouse strut on Sawtooth plains such as the Muldoon area, Lost River, and Camas Prairie. The big flocks are down to a nub-bin.

Fifty years or so ago there were many pine squirrels — big, dark, scampering clowns chattering through the forest. Encroach-ment of civilization has reduced them to a corporal's guard. How-ever, chipmunks and ground squirrels are more than holding their own. The little rascals race all over campgrounds, begging hand-outs as though they had never heard of inflation. Conies are fre-quently seen in high shale, whistling beside their haystacks.

Hunting of game animals and birds is not what it used to be. Four men went after grouse on the East Fork of Wood River in the summer of 1897. They reported to the *Hailey Times* they shot fifty before lunch and intended to quit, but the "fool birds kept rising," so they downed a total of eighty-six. A little later the same year LaVerne Sullivan and Lyttleton Price, Jr., drove a wagon over Trail Creek to Lost River for deer and whatever else they might en-counter. At the head of Wildhorse Creek they ran into three grizzly bears. The she-bear was across the creek from her cubs. Sullivan was between. The cubs set up a fuss, and the old girl charged out of the brush. Sullivan shot her at about fifteen yards. They killed the cubs, too, and brought the hides to Hailey where they were identified as silvertips. Grizzly were rare in those parts, but word of the identifier was not to be disputed. He was I. N. Sullivan, chief justice of the Idaho Supreme Court.

Sawtooth people had, and still have, a great deal of recreation other than hunting and fishing. There are square dances, commu-nity socials, benefit dinners, dramatic productions, card games, school doings, holiday festivals, and as much visiting as travel be-tween homes permits.

Facilities and deportment were not those of Fifth Avenue, but they were adequate. They were delightful attributes of the envi-ronment. Flim-flam and false sophistication found no champions. Young and old were honest in their pastimes. At a Christmas party in a Stanley store a youngster on a new tricycle rammed a branch of the decorated tree, nearly decapitating himself. He didn't cry. He picked himself up and said, "That's one hell of a place to put a Christmas tree."

One of the favorite sports of long winters was the telephone game. All phones were on one line; you cranked shorts and longs to call so-and-so. When the phone rang, everybody lifted his receiver, no matter what the signal. The person placing the call might as well have been broadcasting. Privacy was a myth. The game was to identify the most breathers cutting in on a given call.

Sometimes on nongame occasions the audience was an impediment to conversation. There was so much breathing on the line that it was a regular windstorm. One character had an effective way of shutting off eavesdroppers. When he heard the click of a certain lifted receiver he shouted into the mouthpiece: "Did you know the old bat is having a baby?"

Amid giggles and gasps along the line there came the angry snort: "I am not."

"Pardon me," he said. "I must have the wrong number."

Baseball was big stuff at Custer and Challis. Stanley had less time and space. Games in 1902 between Challis on one side and Bonanza City and Custer on the other produced remarkable scores. Bonanza-Custer won the first at Bonanza, 45 to 29. The *Challis Messenger* commented that "Challis tried to win by running Custer to death in early innings." Bonanza-Custer lost the return game at Challis, 30 to 25. The game was played in the unusual combination of snow and dust. The rubber game was the most incredible of all. Date and place are not given by persons who say they remember it. The score was two and one-half to two. The winning hit split the ball. The cover died in the infield, and the rest went into the river. The umpire ruled it was half a run.

Marksmen of the Sawtooths put on many rifle and shotgun contests. Howard Davis, former postmaster at Sunbeam, was a prime mover. He won trapshooting championships in several states, made guns, and is recognized as a master of ballistic skills. His home is now Idaho Falls.

Clayton invited Sunbeam to a turkey shoot on a Sunday afternoon in the 1930s. Davis rounded up a bunch of riflemen, including a few good shots from the dredge at Bonanza and the Lucky Boy Mine. They arrived in Clayton in time for the competition scheduled for 2 o'clock and were told the match had begun at 11.

"Only a few turkeys were left," Davis said. "We won them all. Then we invited Clayton to a return match the next Sunday. Not a man from Clayton showed up. We were going to tell them the match had been fired on Saturday! Not really. They could have had their chance. But we weren't worried; they wouldn't have won a feather."

Davis lived many years at Sunbeam. In addition to his work as postmaster he managed a store, guided fishermen, landed some of the biggest salmon caught in the river and whipped up hearty meals for guests at his diggings.

Tennis came early to Hailey, thanks to Peter Lorillard Kent, member of a family prominent at Tuxedo Park, New York — Tuxedo tobacco, Kent cigarets, and so on. Peter L. Kent was a Wood River citizen. He had mines in the area. He enlisted in World War I, serving overseas in the ambulance corps. On his return he built a tennis court in the heart of Hailey's business district for the enjoyment of gentlemen in white trousers and ladies in long dresses. For many years he conducted invitational tournaments that drew top players.

Although he had lost much of his athletic zing by the 1930s, Kent made a hobby of managing tournaments. He arranged seedings and umpired all matches from the Kent throne, a fancy perch with an armchair, sunshade, pitchers of lemonade, salt tablets, and towels. The most distinctive feature was an apparatus obtained from a pool hall. Kent pushed colored counters along a beam — white for games, gold for sets. It was swanky. There was one drawback, noted but not complained of by players. Kent's eyesight was poor. He couldn't see base lines. He could hardly see the other end of the net.

He mounted his throne, put on his floppy cloth hat, introduced the contestants, and waved his baton like an orchestra leader directing a symphony. His scoring was whimsical. He announced whatever he thought it might be, leaping from "fifteen-love" to "game" without filling in the gaps. He was particularly fond of "deuce." If he wanted a couple of players to perform longer than their comparative skills justified, he "deuced" games and occasionally gave the underdog a gold ball for a set in which he had won only a couple of games. On one occasion he called the score "forty-love" when the players were still warming up.

The gladiators understood Kent's excursions into wonderland. They respected and admired him — and knew they would be banished if they protested. They kept their own score. At the end of a match they set their private records straight, even surrendering trophies that Kent presented to players he mistakenly decreed had adequate gold balls on his string.

Kent's career as a patron of tennis was cut short by a blackmailer. He received letters demanding money and threatening his life. Officers said they were probably from some crackpot who wouldn't follow through. However, they worried Kent and he departed.

James McDonald, another wealthy resident of Wood River, was also in military service during World War I. Contacts he made in England led to a practical joke with embarrassing trimmings. About 1920 McDonald invited several British friends and relatives to Idaho. He met them at Shoshone and loaded them into his limousine. He stuffed them with tales of highway robbery in the Wild West. At a scary place between the Ice Caves and Timmerman Hill several masked men, coached by McDonald, jumped the car. They relieved the visitors and McDonald of watches and money. As soon as the highwaymen galloped into the sunset, the party drove on to McDonald's home.

Several hours later the robbers went to the house to confess the joke and return the loot. Unfortunately, an Englishman saw their arrival from a bedroom window, recognized one of the bandits, and opened fire. Nobody was wounded, but it was some time before McDonald could put a lid on the excitement. Throughout the visit he had a hard time convincing his friends he was only spoofing. The pro tem bandits took a dim view, too, pointing out that they might have been killed.

McDonald had a summer home on Pettit Lake. A peak in the neighborhood is Mount McDonald. There is also McDonald Lake, near Yellow Belly. It was at McDonald's summer home that Glenn Balch, a Boise author, began writing his dog and horse books that have earned him national readership.

Chapter 41

WHISKY BOB

"Whisky" Bob's last trip with the mail has been told so many times by the mountain folk of the Sawtooths that the facts are cloaked with fable and it is no longer safe to say that thus-and-so is truth straight from the shoulder. The story is an epic of Sawtooth Valley, unfolded with charm and strength from time to time by old-timers gathered on a stormy night for celebration of Christmas, New Year's or the arrival of a new heir to a proud neighbor. Particularly do the stalwart spinners of rugged tales enjoy their art when a stranger from the city is within their gates and within their confidence.

It may be that Whisky Bob never carried the mail. Perish the thought! Certainly there must have been a Whisky Bob. It's obvious there must have been mail, even in those rawhide days before motion pictures taught cowboys how to wear their chaps and rope a calf. With or without a grain of salt, Whisky Bob carried the mail. His route was out of Ketchum, past Russian John's place, over Galena Summit, off the edge of the ridge, and across Scrapper Flat to Obsidian.

In all the valley there wasn't a man on snowshoes like Whisky Bob. In wet snow and against a wind he could make fifteen miles a day. Give him a crust no thicker than a watch crystal and he fairly flew at twenty-five, sometimes thirty miles at a stretch. A tireless plodder he was, sturdy as the granite face of old Cathedral Peak. He packed fifty pounds of mail on a round trip every week, three days in and three out, with a day between to hike fifteen miles from Obsidian to Stanley to play poker with the boys.

To efficiency experts it would seem a sin that Bob did not drive a dog team — or by today's standards putter along in a snowmobile — but it is not well to suggest such things to men who knew Whisky Bob before and after his last trip. They are likely to take a long, sad look at you, spit on the stove, and start a game of solitaire. When old-timers of the Sawtooth start playing solitaire when company is in the cabin it is a sign the stranger is about as popular as a magpie in a marten trap. Spitting on the stove is not such a sure sign of disapproval; it happens right along.

Now, if you are prepared to listen without butting in and asking about this and that and trying to make everything come out as logical as the color of Ruth McRae's eyes, we'll get into the story.

That's as good a place to begin as any. Ruth McRae had big brown eyes to go with her soft dark hair, which was usually done up in the latest Salmon City style when she came to school each morning to teach a dozen little Stanley cowpunchers and miners the secrets of multiplication, George Washington, and grammar. She had passed the years of glowing youth; still she was not old and was quite aware of her charm at occasional dances in the schoolhouse. That's not quite right, either. She was aware of her sweetness twenty-four hours a day but didn't bother to preen herself up special and cast coy glances until the young bloods rode in for an evening of square dances called by old "Dad" Thompson.

For two years the sweet schoolmarm had been at Stanley. For two years half a dozen or more wranglers, trappers, and bushyhaired mountaineers had shaved carefully on Saturday nights, anointed themselves with aromatic concoctions, and put on their best sleeve holders. They would have done more, if they could, for lovely Miss McRae.

There was talk of affection as they danced with her — stumbling words wedged between reports of the bay mare that died on the Shaw ranch, a wolf on Huckleberry Creek, and the condition of the road to Ketchum. The schoolmarm liked best to hear of the road to Ketchum, because she went that way frequently in the fall and spring to visit her aunt. She hated to see Whisky Bob come in on snowshoes, because that meant she was shut up with her blackboard, her pupils, and her retinue of men. Not until April or May could she get a glimpse of the outside world. Schoolmarms didn't ride snowshoes sixty miles; that was left to brawny guys like Whisky Bob and Fred Patterson and Dick Lightheart.

Perhaps that's why she admired those three more than the rest. Certainly there was not a thought of matrimony in her normal-school heart for big Bob. He was old enough to be her father. She was merely attracted by his smile, his hard blue eyes, his wide mustache, and the way he lifted his hat to scratch the back of his head. He brought her choice cuts of venison, frozen whitefish, and once a cross-fox he had shot on the summit. She fed old Bob on smiles. The friendship flourished like syringa in the balmy spring.

Partly because Fred and Dave were like Whisky Bob and partly because they were the most reasonable companions of the entire lot, Miss McRae allowed them the pleasure of a good deal of her company. All others were definitely out after the first six months. Yet they came to the dances and box socials glowing with hope and envy.

By no means did she encourage Dave or Fred. Had there ever entered the head of either of the rivals any notion of pressing matters further than a friendly squeeze, her two large police dogs would have discouraged them. Into passive deadlock went the lovers. Between two fires the lady kept cool. And Whisky Bob packed the mail.

A week before Thanksgiving a trend of events started that ended the dual romance and nearly ended several other things, including Whisky Bob.

A letter for the schoolmarm came on the stage. The stage was still getting through from Challis at that time because there was very little snow; Bob didn't take over on his webs until it was deep. In the letter was a message that Miss McRae's aunt was seriously ill. The teacher must go out on the next stage — that was in three days. There was no doubt in the minds of Fred and Dave that those days would be the last opportunity in weeks, perhaps forever, to hold the little lady's hand and look into her brown eyes. Her aunt was an old lady and likely to kick off at any time, which would likely mean that Miss McRae would give up her job to keep house for her uncle.

Fred solved the problem nicely as far as he was concerned. He would go with her. He had saved a little money, and there wasn't much to do until spring. He piled his traps in his cabin, packed his suitcase, and offered his services as guardian and protector. Miss McRae took it calmly. No objection. No enthusiasm. It was just as though it would make no difference whether Fred stayed behind or came along.

To Dave Lightheart it was quite another matter. Could he sit idly by with a hayfork in his hand and watch a trapper run off with his girl? He took his courage by the horns, his best tie by the big red end, and went to the boardinghouse of Miss McRae, there to employ his best language of love toward the solemn goal of matrimony.

"I will tell you now that I will not marry you," she responded.

"Don't do that," Dave implored. "Wait until you've seen your aunt and had a chance to think things over. Don't make up your mind until Christmas. You can tell me then, after Fred is back and you are all over your visit."

That was a clever idea because it would cut Fred out of any inside advantage in case he and Miss McRae were thrown together quite a bit on the trip.

Miss McRae patted Dave's hand. She smiled.

"All right, Dave," she said. "I promise not to tell you or Fred I'll marry him until Christmas. Do you like my hair done this new way?"

She dismissed the matter as lightly as that. Next day she rode out to Challis on the buckboard, with Fred beside her.

The first of December it began to snow. It turned out to be the year of the biggest snow the valley had seen since the horses froze on Williams Creek. It was wet, heavy snow that broke branches, pushed boulders down canyons, and made things generally bad for getting around. Hardly anyone stirred from his sourdough crocks except Whisky Bob. He didn't skip a mail trip. He went to Ketchum and back to Obsidian each week.

He didn't get up to Stanley again after the first big storm, but he wrote a letter to Dave from Obsidian, and "Tink" Cottrell packed it in with his first sack of mail. It told of Fred Patterson committing suicide at Ketchum the day he got there. Shot himself with a six-shooter in the hotel. Didn't leave a note or anything. It was very strange.

Weeks went by without a message from the schoolteacher. Whisky Bob was quiet as a clam. He had been to Ketchum three times and had attended Fred's funeral, but when he got back to Obsidian he didn't talk about it. He didn't say anything about Miss McRae.

"I guess she is busy looking after her sick aunt," said Dave

Heavy snow on Steele Mountain

Lightheart with a mouthful of hope. "I believe she will let me know at Christmas what it is all about."

Whisky Bob didn't answer. He was busy scraping a new rawhide lace for his next snowshoe trip to Ketchum.

The weather continued wicked and wild. A soaking rain came on top of three feet of snow. For the mountain country it was weird. More than that, it was dangerous. Snowslides roared right and left. From Stanley the ranchers could see huge puffs of white rising from passes below the peaks.

Whisky Bob, in Ketchum, knew it was a villainous time to cross the summit. Better men than he had been killed in slides that came suddenly and swept everything into the canyon. He wasn't afraid, but he wasn't a fool. It was the better part of valor to wait a few days until a good freeze hardened the surface. But in the Christmas mail there was a letter for Dave Lightheart written in the hand of Miss McRae. It was important to Dave, at least, that he get it as soon as possible; he had been waiting a long time. Too bad about Ruth and Dave and Fred. Nothing to do about it now. Dangerous weather? What the hell! Whisky Bob decided to carry the mail. He lit his pipe, gulped a shot of whisky, put a pint in his pocket, stepped into the toe straps, and headed for Galena in a morning fog.

Christmas eve came at Obsidian. No Whisky Bob. Midnight and still no sign. At dawn Dave got up and snowshoed as fast as he could toward Ketchum.

About fifteen miles out, at a trapper's cabin, he discovered what had happened. The cabin was gone. Evidence of the tragedy could be read in the broken bits of logs scattered in a twenty-foot heap of snow, rocks, and trees at the bottom of the gully. Above the site the slope had been swept clean; the avalanche had left nothing standing. Whisky Bob's snowshoe tracks came over the ridge, heading for the hut. That was the end of the trail. He had spent the night there, and disaster had caught him broadside.

For two hours Dave dug into the snow. All he found was a pick and the broken crossbeam of the cabin.

"I guess it's no use digging more," he said. "Old Bob's a goner."

He hit the beam with the pick. He raised it again for a final gesture.

"Don't." The faint plea came from the heap of ice and earth.

"He's alive," Dave shouted. "Thank God."

Another half hour of digging uncovered Whisky Bob. He was

pitifully crushed. Both legs were broken. One arm shielding his head was mangled. That last act of protection had saved his life, such as was left.

"I heard you say you were going to stop digging," Bob gasped. "I couldn't yell. I could feel you working in the snow. It was awful; I knew I was dying. Then you hit that beam, and it jarred something loose so I could open my mouth. There's a letter in the sack for you, Dave."

Dave didn't bother to look for letters or Christmas cards until Whisky Bob was back in Obsidian and had been put to bed in the Fisher cottage. Next morning they took him to Stanley, where there was a doc who knew how to look after men in Bob's shape. By spring he was getting around on a cane. One little old avalanche couldn't stop him. But it crippled him so he couldn't carry the mail again.

Oh, yes, about that letter for Dave. It was from the schoolmarm with the big brown eyes.

"Dear Dave," it read. "I promised to tell you at Christmas about what you asked me at Thanksgiving. Do not take it hard, Dave. I told Fred as soon as we got here. Maybe that is why he killed himself, but it is difficult to believe.

"Dave, I do not have an aunt anywhere. I am married to a young bookkeeper; we were married a year ago. You would like him. He is Whisky Bob's son. He has a good job now, so I do not have to teach school any longer. Merry Christmas."

Chapter 42

GOOD OLD MOUNTAIN SCHOOLING

(*Author's Note:* This account is based on a legal action. It is a dramatization of the case of the people of Idaho on behalf of John Thompson, Tom H. Williams, and Ed Huffman against R. B. Cothern, C. S. Thompson, and Sadie Merritt, trustees of School District No. 6, Custer County. The action for maintaining a school site was carried to the Idaho Supreme Court in 1921 by the defendants, after judgment against them in district court. It was ultimately decided by the Idaho Supreme Court in 1922. Judge J. McCarthy wrote the opinion upholding the writ of mandate.)

TOM HAD NO sensible excuse for getting himself into a schoolhouse row. The school people had little reason for battling Tom. That made it a mess all around. It was one of the most peculiar cases in Idaho educational history. This can be said in full recognition of the fact that rural school trustees occasionally concoct the weirdest notions known to organized society.

In the first place Tom was a bachelor. By all the unwritten rules of elementary education he should not have had the slightest interest in the progress being made by a score or so of Stanley youngsters in their arithmetic, geography, or parts of speech. Nobody ever accused him of being educated himself. Once at a box social, primed by the spirit of Christmas, he confessed to having passed the fourth grade. Doubt was cast upon this by other claims on different occasions that it was the second, third, or fifth. It made little difference. Tom's youth was not cluttered with spelling books. Learning was not his stronghold.

On the other hand he was no dullard. For common sense and practical reasoning of mountaineer problems he was a genius. He could build a fence hog tight, horse high, and bull strong. He had some of the best stock in Sawtooth Valley. He trapped prime fur, had excellent bucking horses, and made the best sourdough hotcakes for miles around. Until the fall when things began to happen at Oldtown, he had no idea whether his school-tax money went for chalk or Emerson's essays — and he didn't care.

By sheer coincidence he rode to town the evening the ladies of the Bluebird Club started selling chances on a quilt to be raffled for benefit of the literary fund. Tom had enough blankets in his cabin to smother a hibernating bear; he didn't need more. If he had, he would have bought one, and he told the ladies so. They would not take his reply for an answer. Finally he dug out six bits and bought a ticket. Back in his cabin he skewered it on a nail with the grocery bill and forgot it.

Nothing happened for a week. Chances on the quilt sold well. The club decided to set aside twenty percent of the money for repair of the school. Desks were in bad shape; they had been thoroughly whittled by a generation. The blackboard was cracked. One leg of the teacher's desk was held together by apple-box splints. Repairs were seriously needed.

On a Saturday night during a country dance the ladies made their drawing. Tom was there, of course, although he didn't go in for dancing. But he had seventy-five cents invested, and he wouldn't miss the show. A lady stood on a chair, shook the ticket box, and reached within. She fished out Tom's number. He came forward and stood for an embarrassing minute while the president of the Bluebirds draped the quilt over his arm. Tom mumbled words of thanks and astonishment, including "Pleased to meet you," "Thank you ma'am," and "I don't know what to say." As soon as possible, he escaped.

The quilt looked fine on his cot. It was a blaze of patchwork, with a silk flag in the middle, the best coverlet the valley had seen in many a year and far better suited to a honeymoon boudoir than a bachelor's shack.

Next day a neighbor dropped over to Tom's while he was fixing a barn to tell him the women wanted him down at Oldtown to do some repairs on the school building. If there was one thing Tom liked to do more than tell tall stories, it was to carpenter. He went to the village — tools, bedroll, and all. The good women outlined what they thought would be nice, such as a porch over the doorway, a platform for the teacher's desk, some slats over the worst cracks in the blackboard, and a sturdy plank or two on the floor where it was wearing thin. The president of the Bluebirds was a member of the school board. She exercised her authority and gave Tom the job. It meant a good deal more to him than the quilt.

For half a day he messed around the property, drawing lines here, driving a nail there, and measuring boards. At night he spread his blankets on the schoolroom floor, put his shoes on the teacher's desk, and slept.

Unfortunately for the peace and quiet of the community for a year to come, the woman who hired Tom did not constitute a majority of the board. There were two other members, both men, and they felt something had been put over on them by the repair deal. They got together for a formal meeting. The Bluebird lady was invited but found it impossible to attend.

"What I would like to know," said the chairman, "is who is doing the hiring and firing on this school board. Aren't we trustees?"

"Sure are," said the other member. "Nobody asked me about fixing the school or hiring Tom. High-handed. No legality. And another thing — how many tickets did you have on the quilt?"

"About a dozen, I guess. Tom had just one. That's not hardly right, either."

"Been bothering me, too. I had about five bucks in the raffle. Tom doesn't live in Uppertown where the quilt was made. They shouldn't have sold him a chance. The old coot doesn't need a fancy quilt in his boar's nest."

"We can fire him off the job, can't we?" said the chairman. "The two of us are a majority; we'll show somebody who's running this school."

They voted two to nothing to oust Tom. They called on him next morning before he went to work. Their remarks were as sharp as the frosty dawn. They told Tom he wasn't working for the district and would not be paid for what he had already done. Tom didn't say much, but he thought plenty. He was pretty mad. Without gathering his tools or blankets he marched to the home of the Bluebird woman.

"I don't aim to get in a fight over a school," he said, " but there isn't anybody can run me off a carpenter job when I've been hired and started work. You're on the board; you told me to do this job. Those guys can't scare me. I'm a taxpayer and I've got rights. Let 'em come back and put me off."

Without lifting a hand either way, the Bluebird trustee watched him steam back to the school. She was more distressed than Tom. She was in a pickle because of a desire to do good.

Along in the afternoon the two men trustees happened by the school again. Tom was tearing up the floor, and desks were stacked against the wall.

"Say, Tom, we told you to quit and we meant it," said the chairman. "Get off the grounds or we'll have you arrested."

"Go away or I'll chop your foot off," said Tom. "I'm working here. Leave me alone or you'll get me mad."

They retreated but did not let up on Tom. They worked out a new plan of attack. At a hasty meeting they decided the Oldtown school was not fit for the younger generation of the district. It should be condemned, and school should be held in Uppertown until a new building could be put up — not by Tom, by any means.

It took only about a week to get instructions from the county superintendent and the health officer at Challis. Documents with official signatures proclaimed the old log school unfit for pupils. It was too small. Light came in from the wrong direction. There wasn't enough air space per pupil. The roof was too low. It was suddenly a miserable place.

By that time Tom had finished his repairs. He prided himself on a neat job. He had nearly forgotten the trustee trouble when he dropped into Uppertown for a pound of Peerless tobacco. There he saw a truck loading desks and school books into the nearby hotel.

"What's going on here?" he roared.

"They're moving the school from the old site," replied the storekeeper. "The trustees say the old building's not fit for kids to learn anything in."

"By the jumping blue blazes," snorted Tom. "They've got me real mad now."

Tom didn't know much about books and such, but he knew lawyers. He got on the phone to a triple-barreled firm in eastern Idaho. As quickly as the legal processes could move, a writ of mandate was served on the school board members, commanding them to take the equipment back to the old building as fast as they could get it there. Ordinarily the two board members would have been willing to drop the matter for the sake of community peace. They wouldn't have gone to trial. But they were peeved about the quilt raffle and the way Tom had chased them out of the school.

The trustees hired a battery of attorneys. While legal papers filled the air in the inevitable course of the courts, school classes were conducted in two places. Uppertown stuck by the new location. The stand-pat group stood with Tom and sent their youngsters to Oldtown, where the school seemed not the least bit unsanitary or dangerous, in spite of dire predictions by the two trustees and the county health officer.

The district court ruled in favor of Tom. The board of trustees appealed to the Idaho Supreme Court. That authority delivered its opinion in December 1922, agreeing with the district court. It said trustees had no right to move a school. Location, it said, must be determined by a two-thirds vote of district electors. No such ballot had been taken at Stanley, therefore the school was not legally transferred.

On another point, however, Tom lost. The court said an order requiring the trustees to make necessary repairs and accept donations of material and labor was not proper. So Tom had labored for little but personal satisfaction. He took some comfort in the fact that the trustees had to pay the costs of the lawsuit as individuals because they had acted wrongfully.

The entire issue became moot in a short time. The old school burned, and a new site was approved in Uppertown. Tom didn't get to work on it. He pretended indifference to welfare of the young. But every Christmas for many years he bought a peck of hard candy to take home, and the candy somehow showed up at the school party. Just a coincidence, of course.

Chapter 43

BEAR FIGHT IN THE CRATERS

By Tom Williams
Sawtooth Miner and Hunting Guide

ONLY A TENDERFOOT will pick a bear fight with a six-shooter. If I had known that in 1905 when I started trapping in the lava beds of eastern Idaho, which have since become the Craters of the Moon National Monument, I would not have had my narrowest escape.

It was along in late November that I nearly cashed in my chips. I had been trying all fall to catch a grizzly bear that ruled the roost. Luck was bad. All I could catch was fox and coyote no matter how many bear traps I set and how plain I made it that I didn't want coyotes getting gummed up in the works. It seems a coyote will be sure to get in a trap if you don't want him to. They are the meanest animals in the country that way.

Bears hole up for the winter rather early in the craters because it starts getting cold as a January pump handle long before Thanksgiving. I had nearly given up hope of skinning out a grizzly rug when I left my cabin early one morning to take a final look at the traps. I had to cross the road to get to the lavas, and right in the middle of the road what should there be but a large bear track. It had been raining the night before so I knew the sign wasn't over two hours old.

You don't need a heavy slug to shoot a coyote so I hadn't packed my rifle. Well, maybe you do. It all depends. That is my excuse for not having a rifle, even if it is not a good reason. All I carried was a

.45 Colt, which is heavy and makes a roar like an old cannon but is
a big bluffer in a pinch.

When you have a good dog you have about all the weapons you
need for an ordinary trip through the mountains. A dog that is wise
to the hills will know about any foreign stuff long before you get
into trouble with it.

Mickey, my bear dog, was as good as they come. She never
backed down from anything that clawed or roared. She would
rather fight than eat. Several times she came near being eaten herself because she didn't have sense enough to let go. Once we were
running cougar on Lost River and she chased an old one all over
southern Idaho before she caught up with him in a pile of rocks.
There was a sort of opening about as big as a skillet. The lion
squeezed through with Mickey right at his heels biting the fuzz off
at every jump.

I told her that was far enough and that she had no business
going underground for a cat. If they wanted to play that way that
was their trick and they could stay hid. Mickey just shook her head
and said she could handle any cougar that went in a gopher hole
like that. Before I could stop her she went into the cave, too.

In about a minute there was the most awful howling you ever
heard. I figured that was the end of my dog. Out they came, and I'll
be darned if the lion wasn't in the lead trying to get back to the
trees. Mickey was talking for all she was worth. She was cut up
pretty bad but too mad to know it. That's the kind of dog Mickey
was. Whip her weight in wildcats.

So I didn't feel scared about meeting up with a bear as long as
she was on my side. On the other hand, that bear track looked
mighty large.

I told my dog we ought to go back for the real artillery because
we were a cinch to meet that bear. Mickey looked up and sneered.
I don't let my dog call me a sissy, so we went off into the craters.

I could see old Skeleton Butte in the east. The nearer cinders of
what they called Blue Dragon Flow were purple in a cold way.
Nothing was stirring but a few big bats and some rabbits running in
the sagebrush. Mickey and I had the place to ourselves. That is, the
two of us and the bear track did. We knew the bear that made it
was not long out of sight.

By taking a wide circle I hit the trapline at the far end. I wanted
to give the bear plenty of time to mix with one of the traps in the
hollow if she was going to do any business with me at all.

In the first set, just as I had expected, there was a danged

Photo by Ernie Day

Baron Lake and Mount Veritas

coyote with both his front legs caught in my bear trap. I let him
have one behind the ear with a club to put him out of his misery. I
didn't dare shoot the pistol for fear it would scare the bear out of
the valley.

The next trap was sprung. Nothing was left but a fox foot. It was
cut clean off. I felt sorry about that, but a fox should have been
more foxy than to try to steal bait out of a bear trap. Lucky it didn't
catch him on the snoot. Lucky for the fox, that is. As for me it meant
blowing about $50. Foxes were worth something in those days.

I stalled around as long as I could, resetting both traps and mak-

ing a new lug for one in case any more bear came around and
started dancing on the pans. I was really itching to peek over the
ridge where the bear was most likely to be. Mickey kept running
ahead and sniffing. She whined like there was a bear right close. I
couldn't smell, but I had a hunch she was right. I was excited. I
hadn't bagged a real good bear for three years.

Scrunching low, we topped the rim of an old crater. Nothing
was in sight at first, but there was a racket going on behind a ledge.
Somebody was pounding on the lava like a jackhammer. I was
ready to turn loose a blast on a trapline jumper when the biggest
bear I ever saw lurched around a stump and let out a roar that
nearly started Big Butte spouting lava again.

She was a monster grizzly, mad as six hatters. Her jaws were
foaming, and she roared and fought the trap that held her by a front
leg. That trap weighed better than fifty pounds, and she swung it
like a bracelet. She banged it against the lava as though she would
bust the bottom out of the crater or snap that steel into chunks the
size of bird shot.

I crouched down and wondered about my hunch that bears
were too big to handle with a six-shooter. I had heard of people
killing bears with a pistol, but it didn't seem reasonable at the time.
Mister, she was a whopper.

Mickey didn't think so. She wagged her tail and rubbed against
my leg a second or two. She whooped it up straight for the bear.
Either the bear didn't give a hoot about the dog or she didn't see
Mickey, because the first thing I knew Mickey had her by the
breeches.

The bite didn't go deep. Mickey was smart enough in a bear
fight not to hang on long at a time. She knew more about the business than I did, but her brains leaned more to the sport of the thing
than the danger.

Things began to look bad when the old bear biffed Mickey a
good one. That made me mad. I slipped into the crater and picked
up an ax where I had cut some trees for the set. As soon as I got
close enough to take good aim and still be far enough away to run
for it, I fired a couple of shots into the bear.

All they did was make her snort and come for me. Even on
three legs and held back by the trap and clog, she made time too
danged fast. I dodged behind a bush and let her have two more
right in the chest. Might as well have been cream puffs. Then I
emptied the gun right at the bear's head within six feet of me. One
shot took her in the nose. Did that make her mad! She was about as

boiled up as a bear ever gets, but she didn't seem to be slowing down.

I knew I would soon be lying under a bush without a funeral if I didn't find something else to do right now. I saw a small place where the lava had run when the crater was active. A little tree had fallen across the break. With a nickel's worth of luck, that would give me a getaway. I figured the clog trailing the trap would catch under the tree so I would have time to climb out of the hole. I didn't waste any time thinking about it; I made for the hollow.

I had to jump. The bear hit me at the same time. It wasn't a gentle tap. She hit better than I jumped. It wouldn't have taken more than a six-inch poke with that trap to knock me cold. As it was, the old devil reared back on her hip pockets and let drive. I hardly felt it coming. That was all I knew for probably two hours. I was out like a light.

When I came to I found I had turned completely over and lit sitting down with my back to the bear and just out of reach. She was a couple of yards away, standing on her hind legs and straining at the clog. Her mouth was big as a furnace door and twice as red inside. There were slashes across the tree and a pile of lava chips where she had tried to get at me.

I was pretty groggy but not so stupid as to stay there long. I grabbed the ax and busted the grizzly as hard as I could, right between the eyes. I had to throw the ax to do it. She stopped roaring and yelled "Oh," just like a human. Yes, she did. Then she died and fell over the tree. I dropped on top of her and passed out again.

Mickey came up and licked my hand. That brought me around. I got up and went over to a rock pile and sat down and tried to fill my pipe. I shook so much I spilled the tobacco. I knew how close I had come to being the one that was dead. Mickey kept trying to tell me what a fine fight we had been in, but I told her if the Lord would forgive me that time for trying to shoot a grizzly with a pistol He wouldn't have to do it again.

I still sweat ice sometimes when I look at the bear hide on the cabin floor in Sawtooth Valley. She spread over eight feet across the shoulders. I guess I wasn't born to be killed by a bear.

It wasn't until the afternoon after the fight that I discovered she had hit me twice. She must have raked pretty close with her free paw while she swung the trap with the other because my pants were ripped and there wasn't enough left of my shirttail to wipe my skinning knife.

— This story was related to Dick d'Easum by Tom Williams at Stanley in the winter of 1931.

Chapter 44

BLUE

TWO RIVER DUCKS arched their wings and settled down in the pasture slough. Black ouzels gave up their dipping in the rushing Salmon. The pale sun dipped behind old Cathedral. Patches of snow reflected the early spring sunset through Huckleberry Canyon. A bell clanged from the fringe of timber marking the edge of the Tom Williams ranch and the beginning of wilderness. It hung from the neck of Barmaid, bell mare of the pack string as she plodded to the bridge. Behind her came the rest of the horses, fat and lazy. They bulged with the fat of winter and their coats were ragged, for the turn of the season had not yet developed sleek hide.

Barmaid walked down the trail more slowly than usual. Her head hung low and swung from side to side. The flowing mane tossed before her eyes. She did not stop to nibble on weeds, even though the tops of fresh, green sage brushed the white star on her forehead.

Bringing up the rear trotted Tornado, a fiery roan stallion, snorting at badger holes, charging forest signs, and racing at intervals toward shadows on the river. Spring was in his veins. Impending parenthood didn't worry him. The foal Barmaid was to have that night was to be his son, but it did not concern his defiant head. It was spring, and he was boss of the range.

Barmaid's colt was born at dawn, all legs and head it seemed.

From withers to nose he was like his father. A colt like all colts —
immediately hungry.

Tom came down early that morning to pitch a bit of hay to his
stock. Barmaid and her colt lay quietly in the log shelter. The
creaking of the door startled the little bundle of legs and head. He
darted for the opening on wobbling stilts and gained the open air
before Tom could stop him.

"Whoa there, boy. What's the rush? Running like a blue streak
from your old mammy. Hold on, there."

The rancher laughed when the colt stumbled and fell over a
bush. Then a groan from Barmaid turned his attention to the
mother.

The mare did not rise when Tom approached. She gave another
groan when he lifted her head and looked in her eyes. This was the
only sign that she knew he was in the barn.

"Poor old Barmaid," he chatted to one pricked-up ear. "Sick
pony, old girl. No time to be puny, with that colt running around
trying to lick the world. Come out of it. He's a fine little feller."

But Barmaid did not come out of it. For a week she moped
about the pasture. Most of the time she did not leave the barn.
Then one day she walked up the hill trail and entered the forest.
She picked a place to lie down far from the trail, and at sunset she
died.

The colt never knew his mother. After several attempts to get
other mares to adopt him, Tom got a bottle and fed the orphan by
hand. Friendship came slowly. The colt was shy as a coyote, ready
at the least sudden move to streak for the pasture.

"Run, you little bugger," said Tom. "Streak like blue blazes.
You'll come and eat out of this when you get hungry. Run, you
little blue devil."

The combination of the little colt's nervousness and unusual
blue coat led to his christening. Tom was calling him Blue a week
after he was born.

The first stunt Blue pulled was to pick a fight with Mud, the
fish-killing cat and undisputed boss of the ranch. It happened
while Blue was learning to eat from a bucket instead of a rubber
nipple. Blue's dinner was on the back porch. It was fresh with the
clean smell of milk still warm from the cow shed. Blue's nose
poked cautiously into the foam. He jerked back, spread his long
legs, and tried again. As he made his first gulp there was a snarling
at his heels. Teeth sank into his leg. Mud was on the attack, claw-
ing, biting, and growling his war chant. Cats usually do not tackle a

horse, but Mud was no usual cat. He was born and bred in fighting clothes. The back porch, and the front porch, too, were the private domain of Mud, an autocrat who squared off with bulldogs and badgers.

Blue went straight into the air. Up came his muzzle, taking with it the milk bucket. His dinner poured into his eyes and across his back. At the same time his left hind leg shot out. Mud hung on and reached with another paw to claw higher. The bucket came down, bounced against a post, and landed on Mud's head. For the first time in his life he was knocked cold — out like a poisoned gopher.

It was fortunate for Blue that Mud never knew what hit him. When the cat's head cleared and he could see through the streams of milk, he found the colt challenging him. Mud had a vague idea Blue had kicked him. He felt a twinge of pain at the base of his skull.

"That colt isn't any pickings," he thought. "I had him figured for a pushover. Maybe we'd better get along. He packs a mean hoof."

Friendship budded and grew. That was an omen in itself, because Mud had never before made a friend among the ranch stock. The only thing he had previously had any use for was Tom. Now the three of them were the big shots — Mud always first, Tom second because he owned the layout, and Blue, a promising pony.

The first year was hilarious for Blue. He and the cat got into devilment from gatepost to pasture. They pestered the dogs, sprung mink traps, chased fish up the creek, fell through the door of the cellar, broke the barrel around the spring, and worried everything that moved.

Blue was a thorn in the side of the pack string. He was forever getting in the way and raising the dickens just for the joy of living. A few of the younger horses kicked him occasionally, and once Tornado bit a chunk out of his shoulder when Blue let Mud crawl through the end of the manger and scratch Tornado on the nose. Mud got down behind the hay while Blue was taking an early snack. He waited until the old stallion reached down a weary head for a mouthful of alfalfa, then he got in one good scratch and ran. Tornado seemed to know what was going on. He took it out on Blue. The scar remained. There were really two scars — one on Tornado's nose and the other on Blue's shoulder. Father and son did not appreciate each other.

Blue's legs gradually filled out, and his body came down to meet them. By the end of the fourth month, if Mud had tried any tricks around his heels the cat would have been kicked out of at least one of his nine lives. Blue's head was still large and out of proportion. The ears were perched far back, and there was no refinement about the muzzle; it was short and fat. There was mustang in the fiery eyes. A zig-zag streak down the flat forehead suggested the speed his legs could do when necessary. Blue was always a streaker, even in his romps with the cat.

They didn't try to gentle him for a year. Tom put neither blanket nor bit on the pony. The closest approach was in his first winter when Blue strayed down the snowshoe trail to the mailbox, flushed a rabbit, and made a side leap. He landed belly-deep in soft snow and floundered there while Mud danced on the crust purring sarcastic advice. Tom came up with a team and put a halter on Blue. Protesting against the rope, Blue was dragged back to the trail. Then he got on his feet and was led quietly to the barn.

Tom decided Blue was ready to be put to use on his third birthday. He used Tornado and Chubbie, both old rodeo horses, as snubbers and let Blue buck with an empty saddle on his back before trying a rider. Tom felt he was too old to make the ride; besides, he wanted someone to break Blue in better style than he could.

He called on Fred Fleming, a wrangler for a dude ranch and a rodeo star. Fred was a long, lean piece of cowboy with legs that split clear to his ears. For hips he wore practically nothing at all. He couldn't keep his Levi's up with a belt. Long red suspenders stretched down over his green shirt. He wore neither neckerchief nor fancy boots — which then were the marks of a drugstore cowboy.

Fred grabbed the reins as he eased his feet into the stirrups and nodded to the holders. Blue stepped slowly away from Tornado and stopped in the middle of the corral. The nose that had lifted the milk bucket went into the air with a snort. Mustang eyes blazed. Blue looked once at Tom and once at Mud, who was curled on the harness-room roof enjoying the activities.

Fred waved his hat. It was the flag that started an earthquake. As a bucker Blue was a flop, but he had other qualities. After a couple of stiff-legged leaps he shook himself in a half-hearted attempt to dislodge the rider. Fred fed him a spur. That did it. Blue took off in a flash of green and blue across the corral. He jumped the fence and landed in the pasture as though the devil was after him. Fred stayed more or less in the saddle. He lurched when one of Blue's hind feet hit the top rail, but he regained balance in the clear.

The colt headed straight for the river. Once he made a rocking halt that jarred Fred to the toenails. Blue made another leap in the air with his back arched in a knot. The buckaroo bounced high, but he grabbed the horn and hung on as Blue raced for the river. The second stop was at the bank. Down went the head and neck. The best rider in God's green pastures would have done what Fred did. Anything on Blue's back at the moment would have done the same thing. Fred took a dive over the horn and into the river.

He didn't go deep. A rock broke his fall. He lay there groaning, nearly submerged, until the corral gang brought him ashore. Blue stood near the river several minutes until a gentle purr and a friendly rubbing of a leg soothed his anger. Mud had raced to the scene to be in on the kill. He praised Blue for the results but cussed him in cat language for failure to dump Fred without going out of the corral.

The memory of a man on his back and the madness of not being able to throw the load immediately stayed with Blue the rest of his life. He was never ridden again. Nobody considered his services as a saddle horse worth the risk.

Tom's patience brought out the real value of Blue. By coaxing and teasing, using sugar lumps as a reward, Tom managed to flop a packsaddle on his back. Blue became accustomed to the pack and in a few months went on pack trips with hunters riding to the most remote parts of the Sawtooths.

Blue learned not to dodge duty. That was impressed on his mind as firmly as his hate for riders. Mud scratched him one morning just after Tom had loaded his pack with food and a cased shotgun. When the claws stung, Blue danced. A can of syrup got loose. A bag of flour followed.

"Come here, Blue," shouted Tom. At the same time there was a boom from the rear of the pack — what there was left of it. The shotgun had been fired by the jolting. It shouldn't have been loaded, but somehow it was. Most of the shot went into the barn. A few pellets stung Blue in the rump. He made haste to get to Tom before anything else happened — anything to stop that bunch of bees. Tom healed the wounds in a short time.

Blue didn't savvy guns. He thought Tom had some way of whipping him from a distance. The sound of a gun never failed to bring him trotting to the kitchen window. All the rancher had to do was grab his shotgun off the rack and fire a blast. It saved hours of

Packing in an Alpine basin

chasing. However, Blue was not witless, for all the rare respect he
had for gunfire. He was smart as an owl. Just a small pass at him
with a saddle and he was gone for the day, shotgun or no shotgun,
gone beyond shotgun-hearing distance.

In the fall of 1928 Major McCormick came for his usual hunt.
He had enough elk heads, goat whiskers, and bear rugs in his
Alabama lodge to furnish a museum. It wasn't trophies he was looking for, but he never missed a trip with Tom. After the dudes had
thinned out, the major arrived with a couple of trusty guns, a
beaten bamboo rod, and suitcases that a hobo wouldn't swipe. The

major never put on the dog. What he found in the Sawtooths was the spell of open country, the warmth of old friendship, the satisfaction of tramping the mountains and wading down the Salmon in a ragged pair of pants. Of all the men Tom piloted through the ravines, he liked the major best.

"He's the kind of guy," Tom said, "who doesn't expect you to get up every morning and cook him a mess of fancy food and heat his shaving water in a silver dish. He's more like a partner. He does his share of the cooking and woodcutting. Not one of those birds who sit around in the mountains and wonder what the stock market is doing and never do a lick of work more than turning over in bed. Why, me and the major can do more fishing and hunting — well, you know what I mean."

The major was a good shot. He could hit a tomato can at thirty yards with his revolver. He could use a rifle effectively on any bear in range. The major would as soon shoot bear as tell stories around a campfire. As telling stories was one of his long suits, it is certain he liked to hunt bear.

Blue and Mud didn't have a bit of friendship for bear. It was all right with them if hunters cleaned out the entire lot, so they got to be pals of the major. For several seasons Mud went along on the hunts. The cat rode Blue, perched on a gunny sack, as comfortable as a mink in a fish hatchery.

The first time Tom mixed with bear, Mud went up a tree. He slowly worked his way to an observation post on a branch, and by the time the bear was kicking its last, Mud was between Tom's legs talking about what a fine bear they had killed and how glad he was that Tom had helped a little, too. The cat rushed in and scratched a bear ham when the major came up a few minutes later. Mud was trying to show the major how he had brought the big beast down with a couple of licks.

Blue didn't mind packing bear. He stood quietly when bear were loaded. Nothing pleased him more than to thunk the body against a tree or rock close to the trail. Occasionally Mud rode with him and a dead bear.

About the fourth day of the 1928 hunt, while under the rim of Hell Roaring ridge, the major bagged a big buck with a splendid set of antlers. Blue was with the major, pawing dirt at every stop and excited by the trip. Mud had wandered off by himself and had been missing a couple of hours.

When the major saw his buck fall at the edge of a fir thicket across the steep gorge he knew he could never reach it on horseback. But Tom was heading over to start skinning, and the major knew he would need help. He slipped Blue's halter around a sapling and started a roundabout hike for the buck.

Before he had covered half the distance, the sun went down. Under his tree, Blue pawed forest duff and squealed. His excitement grew to terror. A quarter mile away waddled a black bear, sniffing the air and heading straight for the stallion.

The bear had been scared out of the brush by the major's shot and was in an ugly mood. There was no doubt he had scented the horse. The bear advanced. Blue pulled back to the end of his halter. His eyes bulged and his feet danced.

Twenty feet from the tree the bear reared and rushed. Blue's squealing suddenly stopped. Faster than the bear's rush were Blue's two heels. He wheeled in a flash and lunged out with both at once. One crashed into the neck, the other grazed a paw. Claws raked the bone before he could jerk the hoof back.

The bear was knocked back on its haunches by the blow, but there was little damage. He came on again. The second attack caught Blue unprepared. A paw crashed against his side behind the pack saddle. Blood streamed from the raking wounds. Blue hunched to kick again, but the bear was too close.

The bear hit again, this time higher on the back. Blue jumped as he had jumped when he was saddled for the first time. The halter ring snapped, and he was free.

But he wasn't clear of the bear. Cruel blows gashed his side. Escape was the only hope; further fight was useless. Blue thundered into the dark, the bear hot on his heels.

A few yards behind the bear came two balls of green fire attached to the tail of a cat. Mud was on the job.

The animals plunged over the rim. The bear lost footing first and rolled to the bottom. Blue fared a little better; he took a sliding route down the gully. Rocks banged his knees and brush whipped his eyes, but he kept going until he could no longer smell bear. Almost at the bottom he changed gait. A front foot sank into a hole and he went down heavily.

A shotgun roared a short distance away. Blue raised his head and whinnied. He was making an effort to answer Tom's familiar signal to come home. Blue heard three more shots and then a jumble of shouts in the darkness. The major reached him first.

"Steady, boy. No use trying to get up on that bad leg. Nothing to worry about. We got that bear for you. Settle down. Tom will fix you up as soon as we light a fire. Nice work, Blue old boy."

Blue lay back on the pine needles. Tom and the major presently pieced together what had happened.

"I was never so scared in my life," said the major, "as I was when that devil came out of the brush. I've seen and killed a lot of bear, but this was the worst. And me without a gun except your pea-shooter.

"I had walked about half an hour toward the spot where my buck fell, but the cliff was too steep and I started back. Then out of the dark came this bear. I got the shotgun up and pulled the trigger, but it jammed or something. The bear was right on me when that traveling cat of yours skidded up and let out a growl like he was sore because I was butting in on his fight."

"Mud got there, did he?"

"You bet he did. The bear turned to look at him, and that gave me time to flip one of those hammers back and give him the left barrel. That slowed him down. The next shot got him in the eyes. Lucky for me I had more shells. The bear was down but not out. I had to shoot a couple more times. I'm still shaking like a leaf."

Blue groaned. The two hunters went to the horse.

"Good Lord, man. Look at that side. The bear chased him down here."

"Sure, Tom. I was coming this way to see what all the fuss was about when the bear jumped me. They must have come down the canyon together. Plenty of nerve in that horse. Hope he isn't badly hurt."

Careful examination showed a bad sprain and deep wounds.

"Day's rest and some of that horse liniment, and he'll get well," said Tom. "He's too tough to get killed by any bear."

Part of the rancher's prediction came true. Blue survived the punishment, but he was never husky again. He hobbled around the ranch and tamed his romps with Mud to a slow walk each evening.

The spring after the bear fight he was turned loose on the range near Stanley. On opening day of trout season a car chugged along the grade to Seafoam. Blue strolled casually down the middle of the dugway, giving no quarter.

Finally he stepped to one side and looked intently at the front of the auto. Then he raced ahead a short distance, planted his front feet against the bank, and let fly with both hind legs just as he had under Hell Roaring ridge. He broke the headlight and dented the radiator. That done to his satisfaction, he dropped off the hill and squealed.

"I don't say Blue did it or not," chuckled Tom that evening as he split a sourdough biscuit. "It did look sort of funny. Those folks claimed a big blue horse kicked in their headlight. Serves 'em right, packing a sign saying 'Bear Valley or Bust.'"